George Friedman is the founder and chairman of Stratfor, the world's leading private intelligence company. Friedman is the author of four books and numerous articles on international security, warfare, and the intelligence business. A recognized expert on intelligence and global geopolitics, he has featured, along with Stratfor, in such publications as *Time*, *The Wall Street Journal* and *The New York Times Magazine*.

AMERICA'S SECRET WAR

INSIDE THE HIDDEN WORLDWIDE STRUGGLE BETWEEN THE UNITED STATES AND ITS ENEMIES

GEORGE FRIEDMAN

LITTLE, BROWN

A *Little, Brown* Book

First published in 2004 in the United States of America by Doubleday,
a division of Random House, Inc.
First published in Great Britain in 2004 by Little, Brown
Reprinted 2005

A CIP catalogue record for this book is available from the British Library

ISBN 0 316 72862 4

Book design by Tina Thompson

Typeset in Sabon by M Rules
Printed and bound in Great Britain by
Clays Ltd, St Ives plc

Little, Brown
An imprint of
Time Warner Book Group UK
Brettenham House
Lancaster Place
London WC2E 7EN

www.twbg.co.uk

In Memory of
Matthew S. Baker

Contents

Preface

THE WAR THAT BEGAN on September 11, 2001, might be called the Fourth Global War, the U.S.-Jihadist War, the U.S.-Al Qaeda War, or the U.S.-Islamist War. Some would argue that it isn't a war at all but an isolated act of terrorism that has been manufactured into a war. Nothing tells us more about the extraordinarily ambiguous and divisive nature of the war than the fact that three years into it, we do not even have a name for it.

This book is called *America's Secret War* not only because so much of the war is hidden. It is the nature of war that each side must hide as much as can be hidden. The secrecy of this war goes deeper. More than in any other war I have studied, the true reasons for each side's actions are hidden from view. If I look at the war through the lens of public discourse, nothing makes very much sense. Actions seem unconnected to one another, leading nowhere, lacking meaning. In the words of Macbeth, it is "a tale told by an idiot, full of sound and fury, signifying nothing."

That is not how I view the last three years. In retrospect, sometimes we can see that the apparent chaos actually had a clear if deep order to it, an order sometimes not even apparent to the actors who, having said their lines and done their deeds, shuffle off the stage, unaware of the full meaning of what has happened. But it is my belief as well that if one fully understands the motives and reasoning of the players, it is possible to understand events while they are happening, or even before. The key is to understand the actors as they understand themselves and to understand the forces that drive and constrain them even better than they understand them.

In a game of chess, it appears that there are many moves available. There seem to be twenty possible first moves, for example. In fact, there are perhaps six. The better you understand chess, the fewer options you have. You come to realize that most of the apparent moves are disastrous, and the good moves are limited. The better the players, the more predictable and understandable the game is, until that extraordinary moment when a brilliant player invents a new variation on an established theme.

Stratfor was created to study the global chess game through the prism of geopolitics. Geopolitics teaches the importance of place in the world. But it also teaches that while humans make history, they do so from a menu dictated by the reality in which they find themselves. Stratfor's purpose is to study the global chessboard and explain the moves that are being made and predict the moves that must be made by each side. We are aware that there are many who view the world as Macbeth does. We do not. Our understanding may be imperfect, but it is not nonexistent.

There are two basic themes to this book. The first is that the events we have passed through form a coherent pattern and that the political actors who have shaped the world are rational—if not necessarily moral or decent—actors. Americans tend to think of its leaders as fools and knaves and of its enemies as psychotic. This seems to comfort us. This book argues that while America's leaders might be knaves, they are not fools, and that while our enemies might have utterly different moral values that are repugnant to us, they are far from insane. All around us, Stratfor sees excellent chess players, not always recognizing the unintended consequences of their moves, certainly not always making the right move, but, in the broad sweep of events, engaged in actions that are explicable.

The closer you stand to an object, the less sense it makes. The closer you watch this war, the more incoherent it becomes. This book uses Stratfor's geopolitical method to step back from the events and see the order hidden within.

The second basic theme is that this is not a passionate book. To the extent possible, it intends to be cold and clinical. Nothing has become cheaper than passionate discourse. This book deliberately treats Al Qaeda and Osama bin Laden as what they are, skilled and dedicated men with a clear vision of how they want the world to look. It treats George W. Bush the same way. I understand that both views will be vigorously attacked by those who would wish to make each into monsters or idiots. They are neither. They are leaders, playing chess with the lives of others and the fate of the world. Fools and psychotics do not accumulate and hold such power.

This does not mean that I am indifferent to the outcome of the war. I am an American, and my fate is intimately bound to that of my country. Apart from that, I regard the moral principles of my republic as superior to those of other regimes. I understand that Osama bin Laden believes the same of his dream of Caliphate. That makes us enemies. Nevertheless, walking around in a fog of rage will not make me or anyone else more effective. Passion has been praised too much. It leads to loud noises and incoherence.

The title of this book is *America's Secret War.* I am focusing on the idea of "secret war" not only in the sense that there are many secrets being kept from us in this war—who would expect otherwise? Rather, the secret I am referring to is the one that is sitting there right out in the open: the clear intentions, rational behavior, and inevitable errors in judgment and unintended consequences that have created the pattern for the past three years.

Writing a book in the middle of a war is not easy. There is a core problem: Between July 5, 2004, when I write these words, and October 5, 2004, when this book will be published, three long and dangerous months will elapse. Therefore, in something that is not common, an additional chapter of *America's Secret War* will be written to close the gap just before publication date and posted to the Internet. This may have been done before with a book, but I am unaware of it.

I would like to thank Stratfor as an organization and as a collection of colleagues. While I founded it, Stratfor has long since transcended me. It is a collective effort involving many people. The concepts that were developed, the intelligence that was gathered, the principles of analysis contained here were developed by Stratfor. This is a Stratfor book. I thank all of our friends and our readers—particularly our harshest critics among them—for making us better.

There are some colleagues I must thank individually. I would like to thank Don Kuykendall, who supported Stratfor when others thought him mad, and David Hoppmann, who is now trying to bring order out of ferment. This book would not have been written without them. My gratitude and admiration for Jim Hornfischer, my literary agent, is boundless. I want to thank my dear friend Leonard Hochberg for reminding me of the fundamental principles that ought to drive this book. Among others who gave of their time and thought, I would like to thank Rodger Baker, Fred Burton, Kamran Bokhari, Les Janka, Anthony Sullivan, and Peter Zeihan. One could not have enjoyed a more cantankerously divided group. They ranged from Islamic activists to those who hunted them. I also want to thank Jason Kaufman, my editor, who introduced me to the novel idea that nonfiction should be terse and paced. I apologize in advance for failing to be a good student.

Above all others, I want to thank my beloved wife, Meredith, without whom this, like so much else in my life, would never have been realized. And of course our four children, whose unfolding lives were the ever-present backdrop to this book.

Driftwood, Texas
July 5, 2004

AMERICA'S
SECRET WAR

Prologue

ON THE MORNING of September 11, 2001, special operations units of the international jihadist group Al Qaeda struck the United States. In a classic opening attack, they struck simultaneously at the political, military, and financial centers of the United States. The attack on the political centers failed entirely when the aircraft assigned to that mission crashed prematurely in Pennsylvania. The attack on the military center was only partially successful. The aircraft assigned to that target crashed into a section of the Pentagon that had been modernized with fire-resistant materials, which effectively contained the explosion. The planes assigned to attack the U.S. financial center succeeded completely, not only destroying the World Trade Center towers but closing down the financial markets for several days and disrupting the U.S. economy.

The nineteen men who carried out the mission were capable operatives. Their achievement was not taking control of four airliners simultaneously, although that was not a trivial accomplishment. Rather, it was planning, training, and deploying for the operation without ever being detected by American intelligence—or, more precisely, acting in such a way that in spite of inevitable detection, the data never congealed into actionable intelligence. While their military capabilities were enormously inferior to those of the United States—they had to steal an air force—their skills at covert operations were superb.

Al Qaeda had spent years trying to understand how U.S. intelligence worked. On September 9, the Sunday before the attack, Osama bin Laden, by most accounts, placed a phone call to his mother. During the short conversation, Osama told her, in effect, "In two days you're going to hear big news, and you're not going to hear from me for a while." He placed that call on Sunday knowing that it would be intercepted by National Security Agency signal intelligence satellites. He also knew that the intercept-interpret-analyze cycle at the NSA for the region was running at about seventy-two hours. He knew that by the time the phone call was actually listened to and understood, the attack would already have taken place.

This was the real strength of Al Qaeda, a strength that it retains to this day. It understands the craft of intelligence and security and applies it rigorously. But Al Qaeda has another strength. The nineteen men who launched the attack on September 11 were not just prepared to risk their lives. They were prepared to go to their certain deaths and did so exercising discipline and control until the moment they died.

If Al Qaeda consisted of simplistic incompetents, the United States would not be in the global war it is embroiled in today. Fools do not make serious opponents. The challenge posed by Al Qaeda is that they are neither simple nor incompetents. However we judge their beliefs and however we evaluate their morality, the fact is that from a technical standpoint, they proved themselves to be highly competent covert operators.

The United States was taken by complete surprise on the morning of September 11, a surprise even greater than the attack on Pearl Harbor on December 7, 1941. With perfect hindsight, the evidence for an attack was there. Indeed, there had been some consideration given to such a scenario by North American Air Defense Command, which had scheduled a simulation of multiple hijackings crashing into buildings for later in 2002. The problem was that this was one of dozens of scenarios that had been considered, and there was as much intelligence pointing to other attacks in other countries as there was to airlines being crashed into U.S. buildings. Everyone knew Al

Qaeda was out there, but no one knew what they were planning. Many now say they had forecast the attack. They need to be asked how many other things they warned of that never happened.

In 1941, the United States knew a war was coming with Japan. Indeed, a war plan had existed since 1920—Plan Orange—and the Naval War College had gamed out a war with Japan every year for a generation. The United States knew roughly how that war would be fought and knew approximately when it would start. Planning for the war with Al Qaeda had never taken place to the same extent because no one knew whether the enemy was going to attack, where they would attack, how to prevent the attack, or how to respond to the attack. No one treated Al Qaeda as seriously as they had treated Japan, in large part because the United States was good at thinking about threats from nations. It didn't know how to think about threats from non-national groups.

The truth is that even as evening fell on that Tuesday in the United States, no one really understood the magnitude of the war that had begun—or that a war had begun at all. The worst fears of the American public had been stimulated. The civilian airline industry was shut down. The financial markets were shut down. Travel in and out of the United States was shut down. People were on the edge of their seats, expecting the next shoe to drop at any moment. No one really understood the enemy, his thinking, or his plans. It was a war in which the enemy was almost completely unknown.

The reality of the war first struck us on the evening of September 11. The day had been long and brutal, and I was in the unfortunate position of needing to make sense of the day's events. Stratfor, the company my wife and I founded in 1996, was struggling to understand what had happened, feeding analysis to our Web site and clients. As evening fell, we thought we understood what had happened and privately dreaded what would likely result.

My wife and I live in the Texas Hill Country. We went for a walk around 10 P.M. to try to clear our heads from the day's stunning events. Our conversation turned naturally to two of our four children. One was a captain in the Army National Guard, recently returned from Bosnia. Another was a second lieutenant in the Air Force, just beginning his military career. We had always known that our children had chosen professions that would inevitably call on them to go to war, but now that the war was here, abstraction turned into reality. We both felt the dread that only parents of children in wartime can feel. They were going to go where we could not possibly join them. They would be in danger. We would be only analyzing the danger.

In our normal evening walks, the brilliant Texas sky is usually filled with moving, silent lights—civilian planes, commercial and private, landing and taking off from Austin, San Antonio, and Houston. That night, as we looked up at the sky, nothing moved. There were only stars. The empty sky was electrifying. Then, a few minutes into our walk, we heard the sound of an unmuffled jet engine—the unmistakable sound of a fighter plane. An aircraft, lights on, was moving toward the south, very fast. It passed directly overhead. We figured it was an F-16 heading to the frontier. *Frontier* was a word that we had never used before about our borders, a few hundred miles south of us, but it was a word that came naturally that night. We were citizens of a country at war, a country with frontiers that had to be protected. Overhead, a pilot was taking a fast plane in harm's way. The Fourth Global War had begun.

CHAPTER 1

The Origins of the Fourth Global War

LIKE ALL GREAT WARS, the Fourth Global War has its origins in the previous war. World War II grew out of the belly of World War I. The Cold War—the Third Global War—grew out of World War II. The U.S.-Jihadist war grew out of the Cold War. You cannot understand September 11 unless you understand how the Cold War ended, because the two stories are intimately bound together.

It is also important to understand something that Karl von Clausewitz, the great theorist of warfare, said: "War is politics carried out by other means." To understand a war, you have to understand the politics. You also have to understand that the means of war are constantly changing. We are used to wars that consist of millions of men and machines fighting on vast battlefields. The Fourth Global War doesn't look like that at all, which does not in any way mean it isn't a full-fledged war. Clausewitz does not specify the other means of war. They could be massive tank battles; they could also be four hijacked airlines. The nature of war changes constantly except in one respect—it always originates in politics, and politics creates enemies.

On one side, you have the United States, the victor in all three prior global wars and, after the collapse of the Soviet Union, the only true global power. The United States clearly emerged from the Cold War as the only nation in the world that could project its military force anywhere it wanted, whenever it wanted. On September 11, the

U.S. was a country rich beyond belief on any historical scale: peaceful, self-confident, and self-absorbed, neither wanting its power nor imagining that anyone would ever challenge it. It neither sought war nor could resist it.

On the other side, you have the dispersed and defeated remnants of another great empire. An Islamic empire once stretched from the Atlantic to the Pacific. At various times in its history it occupied all of the Iberian Peninsula, north into Russia, and to the gates of Vienna. At its peak, it constituted one of the great civilizations in human history—economically, culturally, and politically. Right after World War I, this civilization reached its lowest point when the Ottoman Empire, the last multinational Islamic empire, collapsed. The rest of the Islamic world had been subjected to what was termed Christian oppression. Pakistan, Malaysia, Indonesia, the vast, non-Arab Muslim world, had all been occupied by Europeans. European decolonialization had left behind inevitable chaos. Between the fall of the Ottomans and the collapse of European imperialism, the Muslim world was in complete disarray.

The debris left in its wake is today's Islamic world, unstable individual states with corrupt governments dominated by rulers who secured their position by accommodating themselves to foreign powers. There were many Muslim men with dreams of resurrected greatness. All failed. But out of the ashes of failure—and the end of the Cold War—emerged a group of men who dreamed of the restoration of the Caliphate, as it was called, from the Atlantic to the Pacific, governed under Islamic law. They were patient men. They had waited for centuries.

The United States, engaged in its desperate struggle with the Soviet Union, gave these men the first sense of hope since Britain and France carved up the Ottoman Empire. The last years of the 1970s were among the grimmest and most unsettling in recent American history. Defeat in Vietnam had given the United States a sense of vulnerability and uncertainty that was rare in its history. The American economy was in shambles, interest rates were over 15 percent, and inflation was over 10 percent, as was unemployment. There was a deep and serious belief that the United States was in decline. Add to this the great oil shortages of the 1970s and the profound fear that the American economy would be shattered by additional oil price rises, and you get a sense of the "malaise" Jimmy Carter described in a famous speech to the nation.

While the United States was struggling with its internal crises, its position in the world took another massive blow: the fall of the Shah of Iran to an Islamist revolution in January 1979. Iran had been a long-term ally of the United States and a stable source of oil for the U.S. and the West, even in the midst of Arab oil embargoes. Indeed, the United States had helped establish and maintain the Shah on the Peacock Throne following an American-managed coup in 1953. The Ayatollah Ruollah Khomeini, sitting in exile in Paris, took advantage of the deep dislike of the Shah's secular regime to foment a revolution that created something that had never existed before—a Western-style republic based on Islamic law. This was an unprecedented hybrid, and it galvanized the Islamic world.

From the American point of view, the establishment of the Islamic Republic of Iran represented another defeat. This was rapidly followed by what was—from a psychological perspective—the low point of American post–World War II history, the seizure of the American Embassy in Teheran in November 1979. The Iranian hostage crisis appeared to be a demonstration of American powerlessness. Apart from tying yellow ribbons on trees, it seemed nothing could be done. Iran neither respected nor feared the United States.

The situation simply grew worse. Jimmy Carter, realizing that the hostage crisis was potentially interminable, ordered a complex military rescue operation. The operation would have been extraordinarily difficult to execute in the best of circumstances but was poorly organized to begin with, owing to structural weaknesses in the U.S. military. The hostage rescue ended in catastrophic failure at Desert One—the rendezvous point for aircraft in a remote desert location from which the attack on Teheran was to be launched. Frustration and anger gripped the American public, much of it focused on Iran, and a great deal of it focused on the Arab world in general—which to most Americans mistakenly included Iran. With the oil embargo of 1973 still fresh in the public's minds, the perception was that the Arab oil states were effectively taking over the world and spitting on the United States. There was a sense of impotent rage.

But there was more. The primary focus of the United States in those days was the Soviet Union. The United States had encircled the Soviets with a system of alliances that ran from the North Cape of Norway to the Bering Straits. Wherever the Soviets looked, they were surrounded by American troops, ships, planes, or those of their allies. The Soviets desperately wanted to break out of this encirclement, and the Americans desperately wanted to contain them. This struggle defined the Cold War.

From the objective American point of view, what was important about the Khomeini regime was not its beliefs, or even its humiliation of the United States. America feared most that the Soviets, either covertly through their communist allies in Iran or overtly through an invasion of Iran, would punch through to the Persian Gulf, breaking their encirclement, gaining access to the Indian Ocean Basin and, not incidentally, taking control of the Saudi oil fields. This would shift the balance of power decisively in their favor. It was one of Washington's greatest nightmares.

In December 1979, this nightmare was about to become real. The Soviets invaded Afghanistan about a month after the Iran hostage crisis began. Invading Afghanistan in winter seemed a risky operation, but the Soviets were known to be careful planners and geopolitical thinkers. U.S. intelligence and military analysts worked desperately to try to identify the meaning of the invasion. The Soviets were intervening at the request of the communist Afghan government that was facing massive unrest. The Soviets knew Afghanistan well and understood the difficulties of invading in the winter, so it had to be assumed that there was a reason for this kind of risk taking beyond maintaining stability.

The United States concluded that this was a calculated risk by the Soviets—that it was part of a grand strategy to break out of their encirclement at the time and place of America's greatest weakness. It was assumed that the Soviet invasion of Afghanistan was intended to create bases for attacking Iran from the north and east. As it later turned out, the Soviets invaded for a host of reasons that were much more modest. There was a tottering pro-Soviet government in Afghanistan, and the Soviets simply did not want it to fall. In addition, there was fear of a growing radical influence along the Soviet border.

There was a strong belief within the Defense Department, its nerves raw after a decade of defeat and economic failure, that the invasion of Afghanistan would set in motion forces that would eventually drive the U.S. out of the Eastern Hemisphere. When U.S. intelligence started reporting that the Soviets were rapidly building airfields in southwestern Afghanistan, the scenario was complete. The only reason for building these bases would be to put Soviet fighter aircraft in range—with refueling—of the Persian Gulf, challenging U.S. air superiority over the Strait of Hormuz and canceling out the only military advantage the U.S. had. As the New Year began, there were serious analysts who felt that 1980 would either be the year a general war broke out between the Soviet Union and the United States or the year in which the Soviet Union began the expulsion of the United States from the Eastern Hemisphere.

The United States rapidly threw together staffs to plan the American counter to a Soviet invasion of Iran. In those days, the U.S. Central Command had not yet been created. There was no entity in the Pentagon directly charged with planning and executing operations in the region, except something called the Rapid Deployment Force. Therefore, no one had studied the matter systematically until after the Soviet invasion of Afghanistan. The results of the study were stunning. The United States could, with effort, get elements of the 82nd Airborne Division into the Zagros Mountains of Iran within a week. Other reinforcements—still very small—would take longer. In other words, except for nuclear war, the United States could do little to stop a Soviet invasion. This realization was probably the lowest point in American military history since the fall of Corregidor in World War II.

Zbigniew Brzezinski, Jimmy Carter's National Security Advisor, was a hard-line anti-Soviet who had seen the Soviets use wars of national liberation against the United States for decades. The Soviets provided weapons, training, and political support for guerrillas who fought American forces to a standstill. These forces took advantage of their knowledge of the countryside, their support among the population, and their willingness to take casualties to drain the strength out of American and allied troops. The Soviet Union weakened the Americans without risking much itself, Vietnam being the classic case.

Brzezinski knew that a substantial action would have to be taken before the Americans' position in the Eastern Hemisphere disintegrated. The Carter administration's public solution was to boycott the Moscow Olympics and impose economic sanctions, including stopping grain sales, something that hurt U.S. farmers as much as the Soviets. But Brzezinski saw a sweet potential counter—one that would create the opportunity to turn the tables on the Soviets. By moving out of their encirclement the Soviets made themselves, for the first time, vulnerable to their own favorite tool: the sponsored war of national liberation. Their troops were now in hostile territory in Afghanistan. They were ripe for a counterpunch—if there was time and if they didn't move too fast.

The United States had tried to wage guerrilla warfare against the Soviets once before. During the late 1940s and early 1950s, the U.S. tried to raise guerrilla forces in Eastern Europe. It ended in disaster when Soviet intelligence penetrated these groups and destroyed them. The U.S. had tried guerrilla warfare in Vietnam with mixed results. The U.S. was not a nation proficient at insurgency or counterinsurgency. Nevertheless, Brzezinski argued that this was the only option available. Just five years after defeat in Vietnam, payback was an irresistible motive, and it made strategic sense. This was an opportunity to make the Soviets bleed.

Carter ordered the Central Intelligence Agency and the special operations units of the military—not yet organized into a single command—to recruit, organize, and supply a guerrilla movement in Afghanistan and to utilize indigenous forces that were already rising to resist the Soviets six months before the invasion. This was to resist the established communist government. Carter signed the first "Intelligence Finding," a document that authorizes covert operations, on Afghanistan. The finding was designed to aid Afghan guerrillas in the "harassment" of Soviet troops in Afghanistan. It was this "Finding" that served as the legal and operational basis for the U.S. intervention in Afghanistan. It was also this "Finding" that would culminate, via a long, circuitous, and unpredictable route, in September 11.

Afghanistan, Money, and Saudi Arabia

During the 1970s, following revelations of assassinations, domestic spying, and other nasty things, Frank Church, a senator from Idaho, had held spectacular hearings demonstrating duplicity and incompetence in the CIA, and passing laws that seriously tied its hands. Since Congress held the purse strings, they could control actions by controlling money. Still in the throes of the Vietnam defeat, Congress had little appetite for defense expenditures, let alone for funding a covert war. Going publicly to Congress to vote funds for a covert war not only wouldn't happen—it would mean it wasn't a covert war. Thus, the first problem to be solved was how to fund the war. Part of the money could come from existing CIA funds, but not all of it.

President Carter and Brzezinski realized that the United States was not the only country frightened by the Soviets and the Iranian situation. Saudi Arabia had a lot more to lose if the Soviets succeeded—or, for that matter, if Shiite Iran did. Having damaged the United States with their 1973 oil embargoes, the Saudis now realized that a weakened United States could leave them at the mercy of forces that would annihilate the House of Saud. They badly needed an American revival, quite as much as the Americans needed one.

What the Americans needed was Saudi money. At that point the

Saudis were the economic powerhouses of the world, with money to burn and no legal constraints on spending it. The U.S. wanted the Saudis to finance the covert war in Afghanistan. But the United States needed something else. Afghanistan was unknown territory to the Americans and never seen as particularly significant. The United States not only didn't have a significant network of intelligence sources among the Afghan tribes, it didn't have many intelligence officers in the CIA with experience in the region. To the extent that anyone had worked that area, it had been the Drug Enforcement Agency and people from the CIA's counternarcotics group who monitored the annual poppy crop that supplied much of the world's heroin. That focus excluded most other intelligence missions in the area, and the U.S. needed far greater resources to mount Brzezinski's plan.

The U.S. had little understanding of the fundamentalist brands of Islam practiced by Afghans. The U.S. knew that the prime motivator for the Afghan resistance was not nationalism—the Afghan nation was an abstraction. It was a land of tribes and clans. The one unifying theme was Islam, which the U.S. had to tap into in order to drive the guerrilla war. Ever since the rise of secular Arab socialism—closely aligned with the Soviet Union—the United States had linked itself to conservative, Islamic monarchies such as Saudi Arabia.

Therefore, turning to the Saudis for help in 1980 was natural for the United States, and looking to Saudi Wahabi religiosity as a strategic asset was a continuation of fixed policy. The U.S. structured the following deal: The Saudis would provide funding and personnel to support a covert effort by the CIA to build an anti-Soviet guerrilla movement in Afghanistan. The goal was to build a quagmire for the Soviets while the U.S. urgently rearmed. The means was an alliance between the United States and Muslim fundamentalists.

There was one additional factor: Pakistan. Pakistan was a long-term American ally, torn between the secularism of its founders and the Islamism of a large segment of its population. It was also terrified of being trapped between a Soviet-occupied Afghanistan and a pro-Soviet India. Pakistan did have long experience in Afghanistan as well as territory contiguous to Afghanistan, where training camps, logistics systems, and bases of operations could be constructed. The North Vietnamese had Cambodia and Laos; the United States had Pakistan.

A three-way alliance was created. The United States would provide training, coordination, and strategic intelligence. The Saudis would provide money and recruitment of mujahideen. The Pakistanis would provide their territory plus their intelligence service, the ISI, to provide the liaison with Afghan forces resisting the Soviet invasion.

Jimmy Carter presided over the creation of this fateful alliance. Earlier in his administration he had spoken of America's "inordinate fear of communism." He was not as interested in destroying the Soviet Union as much as he wanted to find a basis for accommodation with the Soviets and end what had been a decade of decline in American power. Carter certainly did not consider—nor would any reasonable person—that the result of aiding Afghan guerrillas against Soviet occupation would help stimulate the collapse of the Soviet Union and, a generation later, lead to the rise of Al Qaeda.

The Reagan Intensification

Carter was defeated in the 1980 elections, though his basic strategy in Afghanistan was not reversed when President Ronald Reagan took office in January 1981. Indeed, Carter's core decision was affirmed and expanded. Reagan had come into office in part because of the economy, and also because of the Iran hostage crisis. Most important, he had won the elections because he wanted to arrest the deterioration—and the perception of deterioration—in American power. Reagan had every intention not only of halting the slide in American power, but also of confronting and defeating the Soviets. Reagan intended to intensify the defense buildup that Jimmy Carter had begun and to embed Carter's Afghan strategy in a broader anti-Soviet strategy.

In order to do this, Reagan intended to revive the Central Intelligence Agency. Carter had appointed Stansfield Turner, an admiral with limited experience in intelligence who had gutted the Agency's clandestine capabilities in favor of technical intelligence—satellite imagery, intercepted phone calls, and the like. Turner was deeply disliked within the CIA for his views on "humint" (human intelligence) and for his mission to clean up the Agency. He had served Carter well in the first part of his administration, when Carter's mission was to move the U.S. away from Vietnam and all things associated with it.

Turner had cleaned out the bloated Asia Division, which was still full of personnel who had been involved in CIA operations in Vietnam. He also removed many people with decades of experience in other areas. It is always hard to figure out where to stop a house-cleaning, and Turner saw his charter as extending to most of the "old" Agency hands of the 1950–70 Cold War. That meant a blood-bath in the Directorate of Operations, which housed the spies.

In a sense, Turner's mission was a necessary task. Intelligence agencies need periodic purges to let in new blood, and the failure of Vietnam needed to be expunged. The problem was that it wasn't clear whether Turner was getting rid of deadwood or destroying U.S. covert capabilities. During the first two years of the Carter administration, the conventional wisdom was that the CIA's problem from its beginning was that it was too spooky. The problem by the last two years of the Carter administration was that all the spooks were gone. Mired in the Iran crisis and Afghan war, the Carter administration did not have deep wells of intelligence talent to draw on, and Turner seemed to be very much out of his league.

Between the Church reforms and Turner's assault on clandestine services in 1977 and 1978, the U.S. was doing much more than working with the Saudis. The U.S. was relying on them, and the Saudis knew it. The perception grew among Saudis that they were being called on to save the United States.

The Saudis chose not to finance this operation directly from government coffers. Rather, the Saudi government tapped into vast reservoirs of private resources, in order to maintain deniability and to help build consensus outside the government in Saudi Arabia for the adventure. Families like the wealthy bin Ladens turned over vast sums of money to help finance the mujahideen who were fighting the Soviets.

Reagan's goal was to boost Carter's policies to reassert the containment of the Soviet Union, then use that encirclement to strangle them. His first move was to replace Turner with the Wall Street lawyer William Casey as head of the CIA. Casey was a spook's spook. He was brilliant, iconoclastic, and incoherent. People could sit in a room with him for an hour while he held forth and literally not understand a word he was saying, or, when they did make out a few words, have no idea how they fit together. Was this the ultimate deception campaign, or did Casey have the worst speech impediment in the world? There was no doubt, however, that Casey thought big and with such incredible complexity that no one could quite unravel what he was doing.

Casey was essentially put in charge of a conscious strategy to break the Soviet Union. There were many aspects of this, including forcing the Soviets into an arms race they couldn't afford, underwriting Lech Walesa's Solidarity movement in Poland, and supporting resistance by Russian Jews. Afghanistan was simply part of this increasingly aggressive pattern of pressure on the Soviets. Around the beginning of Reagan's second term, Casey gradually intensified support for the guerrillas in Afghanistan and created a cadre of covert operatives, dramatically increasing U.S. support flowing in through Pakistan.

What Casey did not do, and did not want to do, was cut out the Saudi connection or discourage young Muslims from traveling to Afghanistan to carry out jihad. This was the backbone of his global strategy. Casey encouraged religiously oriented resistance wherever he could find it—Poland, Afghanistan, and inside the Soviet Union itself. Casey saw religion as a framework around which to construct resistance to the Soviet Union.

The Afghan war was long and brutal. It drained the Red Army of its strength and credibility and became an important, but not decisive, factor in the collapse of the Soviet Union. It also created thousands of hardened, experienced Islamist soldiers, many trained by American Special Forces personnel, now armed with captured Soviet weapons as well as American weapons. These men could field-strip an AK-47, conduct maintenance on a Stinger, and still not miss the call to prayer.

These Islamic warriors had come for many reasons, receiving training in Pakistani base camps before being infiltrated into Afghanistan to work with Afghan rebels. Whether they were Saudi or Egyptian or Pakistani, they were bound together by their hatred of the Soviet Union, which was fueled by their Islamic religiosity. Their American advisors knew this and encouraged it. It was even publicly romanticized, in movies such as *Rambo III,* which portrayed a burned-out Vietnam veteran redeemed while fighting alongside heroic Afghan resistance fighters. Americans prefer their wars to have a moral dimension that transcends geopolitics.

The heroism of the Afghan resistance should never be underestimated. Nothing can be understood about Al Qaeda today if we don't understand the crucible of Afghanistan. The Soviets were merciless in their attempts to suppress the guerrillas, whose supplies were, in actuality, sparse while their weapons were what you'd expect in a guerrilla war. Nevertheless, the resistance continued for a decade. Many died, but those who remained were rock hard and fanatical.

The experience in Afghanistan will be seen as a key event in the history of Islam. With the Islamic world having been occupied by the British and French, manipulated by the United States, and crushed by the Israelis in several wars, the Afghan war was the first time in centuries that an Islamic force had defeated a non-Islamic force. The Soviet force was not only non-Islamic but atheistic. It was not just any country but a superpower. It was not just a superpower but one that collapsed after the defeat. It was not hard for a believer to draw a divine teaching from Afghanistan: Courage and faith in the face of extraordinary odds will yield extraordinary rewards.

Most important, this was seen as an Islamic victory rather than an Afghan victory. The soldiers that defeated the Soviet Union were a multinational force of Islamist fighters, at least in part, and certainly in Islamic legend. The money that paid for the war was drawn from Islamic coffers. The United States was not seen as the savior of the war;

rather, it was perceived as its beneficiary. The idea grew that the Islamic fighters had given the Americans their victory over the Soviets. There was a suspicion—well-founded, as it turned out—that the United States was not particularly grateful or gracious in victory. In fact, it appeared as though the United States had used the Islamic fighters and would now discard them. On this last point, they were correct.

The United States saw the war very differently, of course. Afghanistan was seen as only one of the reasons for the fall of the Soviet Union. The United States saw itself as the driving force in organizing the resistance. Without the U.S., the Soviets would have defeated the jihadists. From the American point of view, the Afghans—and the Islamic world—owed the United States a debt of gratitude. As for the foreign fighters that had been imported, the fact of the matter was that the U.S. didn't give them a second thought. As with other wars, the Americans were casual with former allies, assuming without basis that the Islamic fighters would maintain a bond with the U.S. This was the key disconnect.

Desert Storm and the Birth of Al Qaeda

The United States rapidly lost interest in Afghanistan. As George Bush Sr. came into office, his focus was on Eastern Europe and managing the end of the Soviet Union. The Bush administration missed the critical event that led to September 11: the decision to deploy forces to Saudi Arabia to reverse Saddam Hussein's invasion of Kuwait in 1990. It regarded the invasion as simply an isolated rogue state overrunning another country of some interest to the United States. The people around George Bush—Dick Cheney, Brent Scowcroft, and Jim Baker—believed that the decision to intervene would be treated by all Saudis and Muslims as an act of American solidarity, saving an Islamic state, Kuwait, from obliteration. Bush expected gratitude. He never anticipated rage.

Desert Storm was not only about Iraq. Throughout the war in Afghanistan, the United States had a parallel concern about Iran, a concern that was shared by the Saudi government. The United States was afraid of the spread of radical Islam, as defined by the Islamic Republic of Iran. The passions generated by the combination of Western revolutionary republicanism and Islamic law stunned the United States both with its anti-Americanism and with the powerful sense of national unity it engendered. Having experienced communism as a revolutionary force, the Americans certainly did not want revolutionary Islam sweeping the Middle East.

The Saudis, being more knowledgeable than the Americans about Islam, were far less concerned about the fusion of Islam and Western revolutionary tradition than they were about the rise of Shiite power via the new Iranian state. Like most religions, Islam has its schisms. One of the defining schisms is the distinction between the Sunnis, the majority faction, and the Shiites. The Shiites are a minority in the Islamic world stretching from Morocco to Mindanao, but in the Persian Gulf region, they are a substantial force. They dominate Iran and are substantially represented in other countries in the region.

The Saudis were not only Sunni but Wahabi, a profoundly conservative variant of Sunni Islam. As such, they have historically been antagonistic to the Shiites. Thus, the rise of Iranian power challenged Saudi religious belief. In addition, the Saudis saw Iran as a threat to their oil fields.

American and Saudi interests ran parallel. They were not quite identical, but they were close enough to engender cooperation. Both governments wanted to contain Iran. Thus, both were focused on the same question: how to contain Iran while also fighting the Soviets in Afghanistan. In the short run, during the 1970s and '80s there was a similar answer: support Iraq. What the Americans failed to understand was that in backing Saudi resolve against Iran, they were strengthening another strand of Islam—Wahabi rather than Shiite— and this Wahabi strand could prove even more dangerous to American interests than Shiite Iran. But not anticipating that was hardly surprising and completely understandable.

The United States crafted a solution to the threat posed by Iran to the region, using the classical method of trying to maintain the balance of power. Lacking any means of controlling Iran in the late 1970s, the United States quietly encouraged Iraq to invade Iran—or, to be more technically correct, the United States did nothing to prevent the invasion. The U.S. gave no indication to Iraq that it would be displeased, offering some quiet, unofficial assurances to the contrary.

The United States had no use for the Iraqi regime and had supported the Shah's Iran in a war against Iraq in the 1970s, ending in a peace that had not been favorable to Iraq. With the Iranian revolution, the Americans were searching for a lever to control Iran, and the Iraqis were looking to redefine their relationship with Iran, and saw the revolution and resulting chaos as their opening. It must be understood that the basic American assumption was that Iraq could not defeat Iran. A long, drawn-out war tying down both sides was just what the United States wanted to see—and the Saudis and other Persian Gulf sheikhdoms were prepared to finance it. Thus, Iraq invaded Iran in September 1980.

Lest we moralize, it is useful to recall that during World War II, the United States sided with a genocidal maniac—Stalin—to stop another genocidal maniac—Hitler. Moreover, the United States used Soviet blood to drain the Wehrmacht and didn't invade France until after the Soviets had sapped the strength out of the Germans. Furthermore, the alliance with Stalin strengthened him so much that the Soviets emerged from the war a superpower. In the 1970s, Nixon forged an alliance with Mao Tse-tung to contain the Soviet Union. Strange alliances born of necessity have always been a hallmark of American foreign policy. So has solving one problem even if the solution creates another danger later.

The Carter administration wanted to motivate Saddam to fight, but he had little to gain simply by fighting Iran. What Saddam wanted was to become the dominant power in the Persian Gulf. Absorbing Kuwait, which had been historically part of Iraq under the Ottoman Empire until the British carved it out for their own interests, was a key goal, but so was dominating the region politically. He knew that if he defeated Iran, Iraq would be the dominant power in the region.

He was also quietly assured by the United States that it would have no objection to his claiming his prize—Kuwait—once he defeated Iran. The assurances were very quiet and very deniable.

The United States then did everything it could to make sure that Iraq could never claim the prize, shifting its weight back and forth during the Iran-Iraq war, in classic balance-of-power style. The famous Iran-Contra affair engineered by Bill Casey was part of this strategy, with Americans delivering Hawk surface-to-air missiles and TOW antitank missiles to Iran in order to help stave off an Iranian defeat—while also arranging for supplies to Iraq. Under the circumstances, it was a clever move until better options emerged.

The Iran-Iraq war lasted nearly ten years and cost millions of lives. In the end, Iraq won—or, more precisely, was less exhausted than Iran. After some months of recovery, Saddam turned to collect his prize. In his famous meeting with U.S. Ambassador April Glaspie on July 25, 1990, just before the invasion, Saddam calmly explained his intention to invade Kuwait, and Glaspie, not informed by the State Department that the policy had changed, proceeded to give Saddam the reassurance of American support that had been the U.S. policy transmitted by ambassadors and back channels for a decade. As it was put in a cable to Washington, "The ambassador said that she had served in Kuwait 20 years before; then, as now, we took no position on these Arab affairs." At another point, Glaspie reported that she told Saddam that "we have no opinion on the Arab-Arab conflicts like your border dispute with Kuwait." Many other things were said, including mild admonitions not to use force, but after saying the U.S. had no opinion on the subject, anything else was extraneous.

Glaspie was never considered a truly skilled diplomat, and what she was doing in the extremely delicate Baghdad embassy was unclear. She was certainly pilloried for the way she dealt with Saddam, but the fact is that what she was saying to Saddam was entirely consistent with previous conversations she reported, for which she had not been chastised by the State Department. Glaspie was following the consistent U.S. policy of warning against attacking Kuwait while hinting that the United States really had no position on the subject. These winks had kept Saddam in the war against Iran, but the United States had not yet done the difficult and dangerous work of disabusing Saddam of the notions he had been allowed to develop.

What Saddam didn't know, and what Glaspie hadn't been told, was that the United States had never expected Iraq to win and certainly was not prepared to let Saddam collect his war prize. One of the problems of a covert foreign policy is that sometimes your own team doesn't understand the subtleties. Glaspie either didn't understand the game or was unwilling to act on her own without new instructions— and those weren't coming, since that would involve admitting the original plan. Her basic message to Saddam, lacking any clearer instructions from Washington, came across as "Cool. Whatever." Washington realized that the situation was about to get out of hand. On July 28, Bush warned Saddam against an invasion but also said he wanted better relations with Iraq. Saddam read this as the old Washington line: stern warnings with a wink and a nod. Except this time, Saddam made it clear to Glaspie that, in her words, diplomacy had been tried and that he was now using "unadulterated intimidation."

The American decision to resist the invasion was nearly automatic. What was important was to have Saudi permission for basing troops in Saudi Arabia. The Saudis understood the political risks they faced by having U.S. troops on their soil, but they also understood the risks they faced if the U.S. didn't send troops. The Saudis decided to permit the United States to launch first Desert Shield—the defensive operation—and then Desert Storm.

To the Wahabi religious in the Kingdom, the decision was outrageous. The Arabian Peninsula was the birthplace of Islam, where Muhammad launched the campaign that created the Islamic empire. It is the home of Mecca and Medina, the holy cities of Islam. The presence of Christian troops on this soil—at the invitation of the Royal Family, no less—was a fundamental violation of the law. Moreover, regardless of Saddam's foul nature, allowing Christians to invade Muslim lands from Saudi Arabia was unacceptable.

In the past, such abominations were greeted with impotent rage. This time, Afghanistan made things different. Those Afghan veterans who could were arriving home in Saudi Arabia and elsewhere, having fought and won a difficult war. Viscerally, they did not share their elders' sense of vulnerability and dependency on the United States. They believed they could deal with this matter themselves. Like all soldiers who had seen serious combat, they viewed those who had never fought, bled, and killed with a degree of contempt. They saw the leaders of Saudi Arabia as both corrupt and weak.

The returning fighters drew some conclusions from their experience. First, Islamic countries are not by nature weak. They are able to defend themselves and their interests if they are prepared to sacrifice. Second, the current leadership of the Islamic world was weak and corrupt and could not possibly lead this fight. Finally, the United States, as the only remaining superpower and a Christian state, had to be humiliated if the psychological dependency on the United States was to be broken—and, more important, in order to generate confidence among the Islamic masses.

These young men had come to know the Americans and how they fought. They understood American power clearly. They also felt that they had identified American weaknesses. They learned how the U.S. carried out covert operations, how their intelligence systems worked. The Americans had not hidden much from them, believing that the mujahideen couldn't learn anything useful. They were wrong. The young men who fought in Afghanistan were not the poor and dispossessed. Like Osama bin Laden, they came from all walks of life—some of them wealthy—and were educated at least in Islamic studies, but, as with bin Laden, in secular fields as well. They could see and learn.

They also had the Saudi financial network that supported the mujahideen in Afghanistan and around the world. It had never been shut down. Nor was the recruitment network that had been created by Saudis, at the behest of the Americans, closed. It continued to operate long after the Americans lost interest in it and after the Saudi

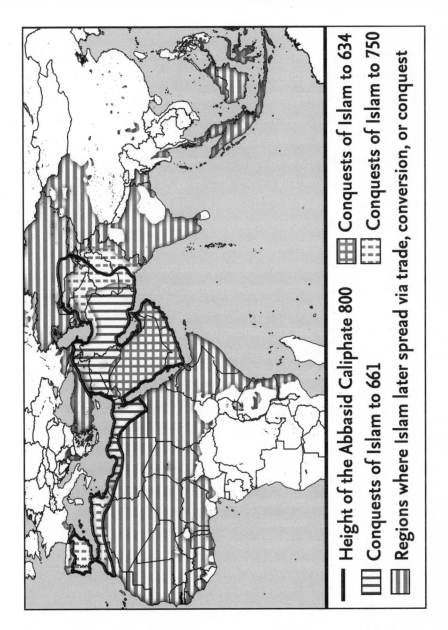

government had turned its back on it. It continued to pump money and men into the jihadist machine.

The mujahideen therefore understood that they needed to undertake a long-term program that would strike hard at the United States in order to provoke a response that would ultimately topple corrupt

Muslim regimes. It was their intention to manipulate the United States into a full-scale assault on the Islamic world, discrediting U.S. allies in the region, sapping American strength, and ultimately paving the way to the Caliphate. They had the financial relationships, the trained personnel, and popular support. They thought they had the future in their hands.

Ten years later, on September 11, 2001, after numerous probes and feints, the plan was implemented. It was implemented by men who emerged from the last battles of the Cold War to wage the first battles of the next war.

CHAPTER 2

Al Qaeda's Strategy and Operational Principles

AL QAEDA WAS BORN out of the end of the Afghan war. Thousands of young mujahideen, or holy warriors, had gone to Afghanistan to fight the Russians, urged to do so by their own governments, religious leaders, and the Americans. They came from everywhere in the Islamic world, among them the brightest, most idealistic, and most courageous. Many died, and all were scarred by combat against a brutal enemy whose actions were not encumbered by CNN crews filming the fighting.

In many ways, the fate of the survivors was much worse than what happened to America's Vietnam veterans. The latter came home to a country that treated their sacrifice with indifference and contempt. The mujahideen, in many cases, weren't able to go home at all.

When the Afghan war ended, those who remained alive were a special breed. They had been hardened by the war physically and spiritually. Their contact with the relatively primitive Afghan tribesmen, whose faith was both simple and violent, intensified their own personal beliefs. These were men who prayed with an intensity that was rare in the Islamic world, and who also knew how to handle hand grenades and rocket launchers. Before the war, countries like Saudi Arabia and Egypt had been afraid of the Soviets, wanted to please the United States, and—in some cases—were frightened of the religious fervor of these young warriors. The governments thought these passionate young men would be much better off getting killed in Afghanistan than staying at home and causing trouble. After the war, the last thing that most Islamic regimes wanted was to have these men return home.

The United States, which had been instrumental in arming, training, and deploying these men, lost interest in Afghanistan once the Soviet Union withdrew its troops and began to collapse. Afghanistan was not of great strategic interest to the U.S., and the cost of maintaining its network of operatives—let alone its secret army—was high. The first Bush administration made a decision that was obvious at the time and disastrous in retrospect: to pull the plug on the Afghani operations. It shut down all operations and left its erstwhile allies dangling in the breeze.

Many of these operatives had been functioning covertly in Afghanistan and Pakistan. Their own passports and identity papers had been replaced by Afghan and Pakistani documents. That was standard operating procedure for everyone's protection. However, as the United States shut down its operations, it did not return the original papers—which were in Washington or had been destroyed—nor did it make any provisions for returning the Islamic international brigade to their homes. This was partly due to U.S. indifference. Even more, however, it was a response to the pressure of allied Islamic governments, which didn't want these holy warriors back.

The best of them, a few thousand perhaps, were left stranded thousands of miles from their homes in a foreign country that was in shambles. There is a Western medieval term: paladin, meaning a knight who is somewhere outside of the normal social structure. Skilled at war, he is available for hire, as long as the cause is just. The paladin is also seen as a force for good, serving and protecting the faith as he travels homeless through the world. The end of the Afghan war created a band of paladins, bound together by the shared agony of Afghanistan and their betrayal by their own government and the Americans. Homeless but skilled in war, they were stranded in a strange land. But it was a land where their skills were needed by the factions fighting one another in the long civil war that followed victory over the Soviets.

In due course, some were able go home either because they were well connected or because they obtained forged papers. The rest remained scattered. They were bound together by the memory of war, the sense of victory, and the profound feeling of betrayal. The sentiment was aimed not only at the United States—the U.S. was to them just a Christian country that was using them, something that was not unexpected. The much deeper wounds of betrayal were attributed to their own governments—particularly the Islamic monarchies of the Arabian Peninsula that they labeled "hypocrites."

This is a subtle aspect of the warriors' psyche—but crucial to understanding them. They did not regard this as simply a personal betrayal. For them, it represented the fundamental disease of the Islamic world. The outside threats to Islam (the Soviet Union and the United States) were manageable, but the real problem was the internal corruption of the Islamic world. Until that was dealt with, the Islamic world could never deal with Christians, Jews, Hindus, and Communists who were using, abusing, and oppressing the Islamic world for their own ends.

It is vital to remember that the Afghan warriors were among the best and brightest. Like the International Brigade that fought in the Spanish Civil War, many were well educated. Obviously, all had traveled a bit, and all knew the arts of warfare. They knew more than a little about the world and its history and could analyze events through their religious prism. A theory developed among them as to what was wrong and what was to be done.

The Problem

From their point of view, the problem of the Islamic world went back to the Christian Crusades and the loss of the Caliphate. Islam, which originated in the Arabian Peninsula, had swept through North Africa and the Indian Ocean basin in a series of brilliant political and military maneuvers. At various times, this vast empire covered points from the Pyrenees to the Philippines, as far south as Zanzibar and as far north as Grozny and Vienna. The range of the empire over time was far grander than the Roman Empire ever was.

At the heart of the empire was the Caliph, a ruler who combined political, military, and religious authority. His task—and that of the political and religious bureaucracy through which he governed—was to hold the Caliphate together, to protect it from foreign encroachment, and to extend its sway. In one sense, it was simply one of many human empires and behaved like it. In another sense, like the Holy Roman Empire in its earliest conception, it represented a divine presence in the world.

It was the intention of the mujahideen to resurrect the Caliphate and ultimately to raise it to the greatness it once had. This did not strike them as at all improbable. Empires come and go. They had—in their minds—brought down the Soviet Union. Israel had been resurrected after 2,000 years. The United States, a relatively unpopulated continent 200 years ago, was now a global empire. In 1600, Britain was a savage island of warring tribes, and 250 years later, it ruled the world. The Islamic world had much fewer challenges than any of these. Nothing had to be invented. The pieces simply had to be put together again.

The pieces had fallen apart for two reasons. The first was the intense military and political pressure placed on the Islamic world by Christianity, something that had dramatically intensified in the twentieth century after the collapse of the Ottoman Empire, the destruction of the last multinational Islamic empire. The second was the collaboration—in various forms—of Islamic rulers with the Christians, as well as with Jews and Hindus. Even apparently devout Muslim rulers were constantly complicit with non-Muslim states.

What was needed, therefore, was a massed Islamic movement that would overthrow these regimes and replace them with genuinely Islamic regimes. The mujahideen knew that there would not be a sudden overthrow of a dozen regimes. What they needed was at least one regime that would serve as an example to the rest of the Islamic world and the core operating base around which to build a broader movement.

The country that could most readily serve as the springboard to the Caliphate was Afghanistan. If a government of the faithful could be established in Afghanistan, then it could serve as both the core and the base of operations. For "the base"—or "Al Qaeda" in Arabic—to be established, a movement of the faithful, built around pious students—or Taliban—had to be created. The religious students could run Afghanistan, and within Afghanistan, the base could be established. In other words, the Taliban would govern Afghanistan while Al Qaeda was established to wage a war in the rest of the world.

The first part of the mission, therefore, was to establish the Taliban—understood not so much as a political faction but a religious imperative—as the rulers of Afghanistan. This was not an easy task. Afghanistan was fragmented among many factions, tribes, and personalities, though they all shared a faith that was intensely and simplistically Islamic. However, their politics and military capabilities made unification difficult if not impossible. In addition, many of the factions were exotic outgrowths peculiar to Afghanistan. There were major powers nibbling around the edges of Afghanistan. Iran lay to the west. It was Shiite and supported a minority Shiite presence in Afghanistan. The Iranians had deep contempt for the backward Afghans and despised their brand of Islam. They had commercial and military interests in the country and meddled continually. To the north, there were ethnic Uzbeks and Tajik, still influenced and funded by Russia, called the Northern Alliance. To the east there was Pakistan. The border between Afghanistan and Pakistan was completely arbitrary. Tribal lines crossed international lines, and no one was ever quite sure where the lines actually were. Under these circumstances, the most probable outcome was that the Taliban would fail and Al Qaeda would be lost.

Events inside of Pakistan changed the dynamic. Pakistan had been established as a secular, democratic state housing the Muslims in the subcontinent's division after Indian independence. It had evolved into an Islamic state governed by Islamic law. The key to Pakistan was its military—and its military intelligence service, known as Inter-Service

Intelligence, or ISI. As with many postcolonial countries, the only thing modern about it was the military-intelligence complex.

The military, and especially the ISI, had become heavily influenced by radical Islamists for several reasons. The primary mission of both organizations was to protect Pakistan from India. From the beginning, Indo-Pakistani tension was framed in religious terms. The military and intelligence people came to see themselves as Muslims. Second, the rule of secularists like the Bhuttos had deeply threatened the nation through corruption and ineptitude—and a female leader was anathema to a powerful segment of the nation. The military and intelligence people came to associate secularism with disintegration, and they saw Islam as the means for maintaining unity.

When they looked across the frontier to Afghanistan, they saw a nation that had been occupied by the Soviets, thereby putting Pakistan into a vise between Soviet and Indian forces—making Pakistan heavily dependent on the United States. Pakistani military and intelligence leaders wanted to secure their western flank. They saw in the Taliban movement the only tool available to unify Afghanistan into a long-term buffer for Pakistan. Moreover, many ISI leaders, who had worked under CIA control during the Afghan war, were close to leaders of the mujahideen who were advising and fighting alongside the Taliban. There was much history there. Therefore, Pakistan did everything it could to bring the Taliban to power in Afghanistan. And they succeeded.

The mujahideen's second mission was to make Al Qaeda operational. But this was simply a means to an end. Afghanistan was a usable base because it was so remote and so primitive. The mujahideen did not believe that the Caliphate could govern from Kabul, Kandahar, or Jalalabad. Afghanistan was useful as a base, but it could not serve as the core of an international Islamic revival. It provided refuge, and facilities for training and planning, but the foundations of the Caliphate would have to be established elsewhere.

From the standpoint of the mujahideen, the problem was that the militant and religious trends in Islam had diverged. The villain, in their minds, was Gamal Abdul Nasser of Egypt, who had overthrown King Farouk in 1955. Nasser, quite simply, was the driving force that gave rise to the secular, socialist military leaders in the Arab world. Men like Iraq's Saddam Hussein, Syria's Hafez al Assad, and Libya's Muammar al-Qaddafi emulated Nasser. Nasser had taken his bearing from Kamal Ataturk, who had founded the modern Turkish state. He—and Nasser—believed in the European concept of modernity— of a nonreligious or barely religious regime focusing on economic development and social equality. Nasser, also a socialist, was heavily influenced by Soviet-style central planning that focused on industrial- ization. Finally, Nasser was a militarist who believed that the army was the most modern institution in Egypt, and that it should be used as an instrument of both administration and change.

Leaders such as Saddam, Hafez al Assad, and Qaddafi also shared another characteristic with Nasser: Arabism. Nasser believed in Arab unification and history more than he did in Islam—or the Caliphate, for that matter. His goal was the creation of a united Arab state built around ethnicity, not an Islamic state built around religion.

Perhaps the most important influence of Nasser was on the Pales- tinian movement. Yassir Arafat and most of Fatah and the Palestine Liberation Organization, which dominated the Palestinian movement until the 1990s, took their bearing from Nasser. They were secular socialists, and since they had no army, they supported terrorism as an instrument of change. Organizations like Black September, Popular Front for the Liberation of Palestine, General Headquarters, Palestine Liberation Front, and so on, all shared the Arabist perspective of Nasser. None of them was Islamist. Indeed, many were completely atheistic.

The secular revolutionaries were a problem to the mujahideen, and the religious even more so. The religious regimes were concen- trated in the Arabian Peninsula, which was dominated by Saudis who had been brought to power through British patronage after World War I. The Saudis themselves were religious, of the conservative

Wahabi school. But their religiosity had been known to compete with the sybaritic lifestyles they adopted in Geneva and London. They used Islam as a tool for uniting their kingdom. But their ambitions did not run to the Caliphate nearly as much as they ran to financial benefits from their oil wealth. Threatened by the secular revolutionaries generated by the Nasserite movement, all of the religious sheikhdoms had developed a heavy dependency on the United States. They had become complicit with the United States in the same way that the Nasserites had become complicit with the Soviet Union.

Al Qaeda was, therefore, trapped between the secular revolutionaries backed by the hated Soviets, such as Al Fatah and the Baath Party governing Iraq and Syria, and the monarchies, such as the Saudis, backed by the United States. In their analysis, both had to be destroyed. However, by the time the Afghan war ended, the Soviets had been defeated, the Iraqis had been run back from Kuwait, and the dynamism of the secularists had declined tremendously. By the early 1990s, the pendulum had swung toward religious regimes—or, as the mujahideen put it, the hypocrites. And the greatest hypocrites were the Saudi Royal Family, which had allowed the United States to use holy ground for its war against Iraq.

The Strategy

Anti-American feeling had been endemic in the Islamic world. It had been preceded by anti-British feeling, anti-French feeling, anti-Dutch feeling, and anti-Byzantine feeling. Waves of aggression from inside and outside the Islamic world had created a sense of victimization that had penetrated the marrow of Muslims. There were reasons for anti-Americanism, ranging from U.S. support for Israel, to perceived U.S. support for India, to support for a variety of repressive regimes in the Islamic world. But resentment had less to do with anything the United States had done than the fact that it was heir to centuries of grievances.

Had resentment been a sufficient driver, the Islamic world would have boiled over centuries before. The reason it hadn't was that there were two scales operating. One was the resentment scale—which had already swung into the red centuries earlier and had stayed there. The other measured the sense of helplessness. What had kept the lid on the Islamic world as a whole was not a lack of anger but the sense of Islamic impotence, the sense that Islam's enemies were overwhelmingly powerful. The sentiment for an Islamic renaissance was there. What was missing was any hope for effective action.

This was the perception of Osama bin Laden—who tried to turn general principles into a working organization—and his fellow mujahideen gathered together in Al Qaeda. From where he sat, the fuel for an Islamic rising against their own corrupt governments was already in place. What had to be generated was a sense of hope. The key to this did not lie in attacking the existing governments in the Islamic world. The only strength and resilience that they had came from their association with the current great power—the United States. Therefore, if the United States could be shown to be weak and vulnerable, the credibility of Islamic states would be completely undermined. This, coupled with built-in resentment, would set the Islamic world on fire and open the door to reestablishing the Caliphate.

This is the key strategic point. Al Qaeda was not motivated by hatred of the United States, American popular culture, or American democracy. Its focus, instead, was on the Islamic world and its governments. Al Qaeda viewed the United States as the main Christian global power. As such, it had assumed a position as guarantor of existing regimes in the Islamic world. Put differently, even if the United States wasn't directly responsible, it was viewed as the protector of these regimes by the Islamic masses.

Already in the Islamic world, there was a latent sense that the United States lacked both the power and the moral character to impose its will in the long run. A series of incidents had made this point. The U.S. defeat in Vietnam; the humiliation of the Iran hostage crisis; the withdrawal from Beirut in 1983 after the Marine barracks was destroyed; the withdrawal from Somalia after a handful of Americans were killed; the failure to destroy Saddam Hussein in 1991—all combined to create a perception of the United States as having tremendous potential power to strike a hard first blow but an inability to force a conflict to successful conclusion. From Al Qaeda's point of view, the latent perception of the United States in the Islamic world had to be turned into a self-evident truth. The United States had to be struck by a blow that was both enormous, easily understandable by the Islamic masses, and against which there was no ready defense.

In Al Qaeda's view, an Islamic rising could occur only when there was hope of success and a clear sense that the Islamic world was under attack by the world's major religions. Al Qaeda believed that Jews and Hindus were already attacking Muslim soil (it should be noted that given the geographical focus of Al Qaeda, more attention was paid to Kashmir than to Israel). If the major Christian power, the United States, could be induced to join in the attack, if the United States could be forced to go to war against a wide range of Islamic countries, the resentment scale would go off the charts.

Al Qaeda rejected the secular Arab movement while adopting its operational style—terrorism. The practice of terrorism is a relatively modern phenomenon. Understood as massed and inescapable death and destruction, terrorism really didn't become practical until the invention of modern explosives. Modern explosives empowered individuals and very small groups to do damage disproportionate to their own number—and to do this while surviving the explosion.

The essence of terrorism is this: In a society with many unguarded targets, a group with courage and explosives is extraordinarily difficult to stop. The fewer operatives, the harder it is to find them. It is this combination of the sparseness of groups and the richness of targets that has traditionally made combating terrorists a nightmare. The material damage caused by terrorists was trivial compared to the psychological, and therefore political, effect. The terror came from an awareness of one's own vulnerability and the sense that terrorists could strike where and when they wanted—that they were in control and held life or death in their hands. The psychological strength of terrorism rested in the idea that no one was safe anywhere—that death was omnipresent. You could not protect yourself, and, more important, the state could not protect you. The frequency of attacks was less important than their effectiveness.

In war, the enemy's next move is usually predictable. War is a game played with most of the pieces on the table most of the time. A general can understand and predict the behavior of his opponent. What gives terrorism its strength is its extraordinary unpredictability. In a world of many targets and very few terrorists, the terrorists always hold the advantage. This was what Al Qaeda wanted to exploit in the United States, but to a degree of effectiveness not hitherto achieved.

This was the strategic origin of September 11. Al Qaeda needed to strike a blow that would be devastating, leaving no doubt as to American vulnerability. It intended to breach the threshold between what was tolerable and intolerable for the United States. Al Qaeda had previously attacked embassies in Africa and a U.S. warship in Yemen, and neither had generated the significant response bin Laden had hoped for. September 11 was intended to be so brutal and humiliating that the United States would be forced, unequivocally, to launch a massive counterattack that would validate Al Qaeda's arguments to the Islamic masses. The broader and deeper the attack by the United States, the better.

The September 11 attacks, therefore, were not meant to send a message to the United States. The primary audience was the Islamic world. Bin Laden viewed the United States as an actor that could be manipulated into behaving as Al Qaeda wanted. But this is not to say that he was not focusing on the United States because of its particular moral shortcomings or character. As a non-Islamic society, the United States was full of inequity, but bin Laden's actions were a politico-military maneuver designed to generate pro-jihadist change in the Islamic world.

The Organization and Its Tactics

Al Qaeda knew that it would come under massive and immediate counterattack by the United States. It had planned for the survival of its movement even though it was prepared to lose a good portion of its leadership—including Osama bin Laden—if necessary. It was even prepared to lose Al Qaeda (the base) if necessary. To be more precise, Al Qaeda was not a conventional organization: Beyond a hard core, it did not have a clear membership or structure. At most, it was a loose federation of like-minded people. At base, it was a resource for people who wanted to take action. Its lack of an organized infrastructure, therefore, made it hard to find and hard to destroy.

Osama bin Laden had studied the lessons of the war that raged between Israel and various Palestinian organizations during the 1970s and 1980s. He tried to figure out how the Palestinians, a highly motivated and capable movement, could be so badly defeated. He came up with two defects in Palestinian organizations that, if changed, would make Al Qaeda less susceptible to defeat.

The first concerned internal organization. Traditional covert organizations tended to be organized hierarchically. Even when they contained small operational cells with limited contact with other cells, orders ran downhill as did resources. Lower-level cells were tightly controlled by higher cells. The Israelis had been very successful at attacking the leadership cells or, when the leadership was protected or couldn't be touched for political reasons, attacking the second layer of cells. Because of the traditional, hierarchical nature of the organization, taking out the layer of personnel just below the top caused the organization to become inert. The cells had very little lateral connection.

In military terms, traditional organizations like Black September had centers of gravity—key points that, if successfully attacked, would render the entire organization ineffective. Osama bin Laden studied this problem and selected a different organizational mode.

His goal was to minimize the center of gravity—to try to deny the enemy an accessible point that, if reached, could destroy the entire organization. He created a very fluid organization, designed to absorb punishing blows and to survive inert for extended periods of time if necessary.

The second lesson bin Laden learned was to avoid dependency on the intelligence services of other nations. Contrary to popular opinion, effective terrorism is hard to do. The maintenance of an effective, ongoing terror campaign requires substantial support, particularly in the area of money management, obtaining or forging identity documents, securing safe houses in a number of countries, and recruiting and training personnel. It is expensive, painstaking, and difficult work.

Many terrorist groups in the West in the 1970s and 1980s developed relationships with Eastern European intelligence services—particularly the East German, Czech, Hungarian, and Bulgarian, all under the management of the Soviet KGB. The Soviets' reasons for supporting Palestinian and European groups were that it helped destabilize the West and gained points for the Soviets in the Arab world. It was a low risk/high reward strategy. From the side of the paramilitary groups, it provided various organizations access to a wide range of essential, highly professional services at low cost.

The problem was simply this: As Western pressure on terrorist groups rose, the risks attendant to supporting them rose as well. The Soviets lost interest in supporting these groups. Having become completely dependent on the Eastern European intelligence services for their basic needs, the cut-off left many of these groups unable to organize their own operations. Indeed, when the Soviets really wanted something from the United States, they could turn over intelligence on one or more groups. Palestinian groups became bargaining chips for the Soviets, traded away for more important things.

Osama bin Laden decided that Al Qaeda should never be dependent on any one country for support. This does not mean that Al Qaeda didn't work with the intelligence services of many countries. To the contrary, there is hardly an Islamic intelligence service with which Al Qaeda did not, in some way, collaborate. However, unlike the Palestinian groups, bin Laden never permitted Al Qaeda to become dependent on any one of them. Osama bin Laden was not prepared to make his organization vulnerable to changing winds of foreign policy. He went to the ball and danced with everyone, but he went home with no one.

As Al Qaeda established itself, it probed at American capabilities. On a strategic level, bin Laden wanted to identify the threshold at which the United States would begin behaving as he hoped—charging headlong into the Islamic world. Operationally, he needed to hone the skills of his operatives in planning operations; training, supplying, and financing them; and carrying them out. On a tactical level, bin Laden needed to understand how the U.S. intelligence services worked. His solution for this was a series of unpredictable and escalating attacks on U.S. interests outside the United States.

The attacks on the U.S. embassies in Kenya and Tanzania, along with the attack on the USS *Cole,* were designed to measure the reaction of the U.S. In each case the Clinton administration consistently declined to engage, making essentially symbolic responses to the attacks, using cruise missiles to hit inessential targets. The Clinton administration was caught on the horns of a dilemma. If it did not respond, Al Qaeda's credibility would rise in the Islamic world. If it did respond, it would set in motion the process that Al Qaeda hoped for. Clinton compromised by responding ineffectively, hoping to find a midpoint that would neither inflame the Islamic world nor allow Al Qaeda's credibility to escalate. The analysis was sound, but there was no sweet spot that would achieve both goals. This balancing act would make the Clinton administration appear less competent than it was.

It was during these operations that Al Qaeda developed experience in its primary skill: evading the CIA and allied intelligence agencies. Blowing up embassies or attacking a U.S. warship with an explosives-laden skiff was easy, particularly with a cadre of men who were prepared to go to their certain deaths in the process. The hard part—at which Al Qaeda learned to excel—was to organize these intercontinental operations without being detected.

Each of these operations involved a large number of planners, financiers, and logistics specialists who did everything from obtaining false papers, to securing apartments, to finding explosives. Then, finally, there were men who would carry out the operations. Dozens of people had to be involved in an operation such as the *Cole,* and all of these men had to be able to communicate with one another, meet to hand off material, and deploy—all without being detected. The simplicity of the final operation belied the complexity of what went before.

Since its primary asset was its ability to evade U.S. intelligence, Al Qaeda understood that it had to be very small, in order to be invisible and limit the chance of internal betrayal. It also had to be a global organization, carrying out operations on potentially all continents. It had to be effective, but only with a very limited number of men. Bin Laden turned his weakness into a strength. If he had to have very few operatives or support personnel, the payoff was that his organization was that much more difficult to detect and destroy. On a global scale, Al Qaeda's core operatives never numbered more than a few hundred. It has been noted that Al Qaeda had trained tens of thousands of fighters. But few of these had the sophistication, training, discipline, and language skills needed to carry out covert operations in the United States or Europe. Most of them were not fully trusted by Al Qaeda. The number of effectives Al Qaeda had available was actually quite limited. This made detecting and blocking their operations a nightmare.

The tension between global operations and aversion to growth also had an interesting paradoxical effect on Al Qaeda. Al Qaeda was a strategic risk-taker, but not a tactical one. It had too few men and resources to be able to take risks. It could not afford failed operations. This meant that each operation had to be successful both in terms of being carried out and in terms of achieving the political goals intended. Failure would mean losing a substantial part of its organization, forcing rebuilding and creating a long hiatus in operations, thereby undermining its strategic goals.

It followed from this that Al Qaeda itself (as opposed to linked jihadist organizations) would carry out a very limited number of operations, heavily dependent on surprise. Should any part of the operation be detected, it would be aborted. Evading U.S. intelligence, therefore, became the centerpiece of Al Qaeda's operational planning.

Understanding U.S. intelligence in the broadest sense was not difficult for Al Qaeda. Many of its members were intimately familiar with CIA operational principles from Afghanistan. Many had had at least indirect access to image intelligence collected by U.S. technical intelligence. They had also encountered at least the output of U.S. signals intelligence. They knew that the U.S. could intercept a wide range of communications and identify enemy operations in the field, because they had benefited from that intelligence in Afghanistan. Obviously, this did not give Al Qaeda tactical information—what the orbital and maneuvering characteristics of U.S. satellites were, how long it took to analyze intercepted phone calls, and so on. But they were well aware of the technical capabilities of U.S. intelligence.

In addition, they had sources inside foreign intelligence services that had been in close collaboration with U.S. intelligence. The two keys were the Pakistani ISI and Saudi Arabia's General Intelligence Department. Both of these organizations had been intimately involved in creating the mujahideen movement in Afghanistan and maintained their contacts long after the war ended. The ISI was implementing a policy of the Pakistani government to build Pakistani influence in Afghanistan after the war. Therefore, operatives of the ISI remained in close contact with both Taliban and Al Qaeda. Turki al Faisal's intelligence organization had been instrumental in recruiting and financing the fighters who went on to Afghanistan. Saudi intelligence also maintained liaisons with the Saudi fighters who remained on in Afghanistan. The Saudis tried to keep an arm's-length relationship, but unlike others they did maintain the relationship.

Both the Saudis and Pakistanis had, at various periods, close relations with the CIA, collaborating on a host of issues. They had a front-
row seat to the capabilities of U.S. intelligence. U.S. aircraft were
operating out of Saudi Arabia in cooperation with the Saudi Air
Force. The Saudis knew when U.S. aircraft sortied against the Iraqi
no-fly zones. That meant that they could at least intuit—and most
likely had detailed knowledge of—the kind of intelligence that triggered these sorties. They had AWACS aircraft of their own and knew
what they could do. They could extrapolate about the capabilities of
U.S-operated AWACS and other intelligence platforms.

It was not the details of the Iraqi sorties that interested Al Qaeda.
They knew that the United States collected enormous amounts of intelligence. Indeed, they knew through their Pakistani and Saudi contacts—
as well as from their own experience with the Americans—that over
time the Americans would know everything there was to know. What Al
Qaeda needed to know most was how rapidly this collected information
was turned into intelligence and how quickly the U.S. responded. The
Saudis and Pakistanis who were sympathetic to Al Qaeda and who had
long-standing relationships with many of its members knew the answers
to these questions and were willing to share them.

Nevertheless, Al Qaeda needed a clearer understanding of the
details of American responses. During the Cold War, the Soviets flew
bombers up and down the coast of the United States to map out U.S.
radar stations and to observe how quickly U.S. fighters would scram-
ble to intercept them. Al Qaeda resorted to a similar process. Over
time, they found what U.S. intelligence was watching and what it
wasn't, what the United States would respond to and what it wouldn't.

Part of this was learned from the successful operations carried out
against U.S. interests, and part was the result of deliberately pinging
the system in a variety of ways to find out what the response would
be. Phone calls would be made mentioning fictional operations against
embassies, while operatives outside those embassies watched to see if
alert levels were raised. Individual members of Al Qaeda were given

false information about hijackings, while operatives observed if airports had increased security.

These information operations served three purposes. First, they served to map out U.S. capabilities. Second, they served to test the security of their own system, identifying potential leaks and identifying safe modes of communication. Third, they exhausted U.S. intelligence. A constant barrage of false positives renders intelligence systems insensitive—they just start ignoring things. As inevitably happens when facts about a real operation leak out, analysts can't distinguish the false from the true and disregard the real information. Thus, the process of mapping out U.S. intelligence served to increase Al Qaeda's security.

The means for distributing false information were varied. The car abandoned at Logan Airport on 9/11 was filled with tantalizing leads producing little. Internet chatter constantly identified plausible targets and dates, without anything happening. People with limited contact with Al Qaeda were hired to videotape targets like the Golden Gate Bridge. When detained, they could not identify who had hired them or why. Nothing could be ignored. Everything had to be acted upon. The system became overloaded, and analysts became exhausted.

Osama bin Laden and the rest of Al Qaeda knew precisely what they were doing. The tendency to undervalue the sophistication of Al Qaeda because they used low-tech weapons is a fundamental weakness in the U.S. mind-set. It fails to grasp how thoroughly Al Qaeda planned its operation, and how well it understood its own strengths and weaknesses.

Most important, the U.S. mind-set ignored how the strategic and tactical sides of the equation fit together. Al Qaeda had a clear image of what it was trying to achieve strategically. It also understood its own tactical weaknesses and tried to turn them into strengths, which is why the hijackers succeeded on September 11. It is also why Al Qaeda was able to evade and survive after September 11, proving to be a formidable enemy, even for the United States.

At the same time, it must be noted that thus far, several years after the September 11 attacks, Al Qaeda has failed in its fundamental goal. First, there has been no massive rising in the Islamic world. Second, no Islamic regime has been toppled by jihadist forces. The Caliphate is no nearer to realization. Thus, as effective as Al Qaeda has been operationally, its fundamental failure shapes the rest of the war.

CHAPTER 3

American Strategy and the Rule of Unintended Consequences

AL QAEDA HAD A VERY CLEAR IDEA of where it was heading, and it knew that one of the stops it would have to make would be in confronting the United States. The United States also knew where it was heading, but the last thing on its agenda was a deep and broad confrontation with the Islamic world. In spite of the fact that the United States had been involved in four major engagements in the Islamic world—Kuwait, Somalia, Bosnia, and Kosovo—as well as numerous minor clashes, and in spite of a continual drumbeat of Al Qaeda operations against the United States, the U.S. did not see any systematic threat in the Islamic world. There were problems, but the last thing on the minds of the Americans in the 1990s was war—with anyone.

The United States never expected the Cold War to end when and how it did. It did not know what to make of the world after the Cold War ended. For a while, the first Bush administration wasn't even certain that the Cold War was over. When George H. W. Bush made his now-famous "New World Order" speech, he was trying to come to grips with what the new world order might actually look like. The nature of the world slowly dawned on Bush and then on Bill Clinton. It was a world in which war had been replaced by business, and conflict by cooperation.

The prevailing view was that the fall of the Soviet Union was more than simply another punctuation mark in the long history of the world that had begun when Spain and Portugal created the first global empires. The fall of the Soviet Union represented a fundamental redefinition of the international system in the U.S. mind-set. The traditional understanding of the nation-state had been rendered irrelevant. War and geopolitics no longer governed the world. Except for a few rogue states, everyone was in fundamental agreement about what was important: economic growth and prosperity. Modern prosperity was global in nature, and all reasonable people and nations would want to participate in the global adventure.

The End of the Cold War and the Fantasy of the New World Order

A book published in 1992 called *The End of History,* by Francis Fukuyama, argued that the end of the Cold War marked the triumph of liberal democracy, at least as a universally acknowledged moral principle. The book did not claim that change would cease, but it did say that history, as a clash of fundamentally different ideas and ideologies, was at an end. It also argued that the institutions built up during the Cold War would now oversee the rational administration of the world. Fukuyama's book was not only a best-seller. It was widely accepted and believed.

The idea that conflict in the international system had been abolished was not new. After every major war—what we might call systemic war in which the entire international system convulsed—there was a belief that in the future war could be contained. After the Napoleonic Wars, there was the Congress of Vienna. After World War I, there was the League of Nations. After World War II, there was the United Nations. After the Cold War, there was the New World Order.

In each of these wars, a coalition had defeated an enemy. The coalition had come together to fight the enemy. In the course of uniting, they had submerged other differences. As an example, the vast differences between the United States and Soviet Union didn't seem that great in the face of Hitler. When the war successfully concluded, it was believed that the coalition that had won the war would now stay together and manage the peace as they had fought the war. The Congress of Vienna, the League of Nations, and the United Nations all were expressions of this belief, but the peace that followed the wars was a temporary condition, an illusion. It lasted a while, but in the end it always failed. Without a common enemy to hold the coalition together, it was only a matter of time before the old differences resurfaced and the coalitions collapsed. With it, the idea that war had been abolished and that reasonable men could manage the peace also collapsed. In the end, new alliances were formed and new wars occurred.

The Cold War was fought by a coalition of nations under the leadership of the United States. The United States had two things going for it. First, there was geography. The Soviets could be surrounded. The U.S. could not. Second, the United States was a maritime power, whereas the Soviet Union was a landlocked power. Soviet soil was as productive as American, but the cost of shipping by sea or river was always enormously lower than shipping by land. The American coalition was held together by prosperity, driven by efficient social systems, and supported by the inherent advantage that maritime trade brings. The Soviet alliance was torn apart by the built-in inefficiency of socialism and the accident of geography.

To capitalize on its advantage, the United States created a set of institutions designed to maximize the benefits to other nations of alignment with the United States. This ranged from NATO to the International Monetary Fund. Some existed to impose containment and others to manage the relative prosperity of the American alliance system.

When the Soviet Union collapsed, the belief was—as had been thought in other cases—that the institutions that had managed the U.S. alliance system could now administer the world of victors. The assumption was that there were no fundamental disagreements about how the world should be shaped, that everyone now had common interests. This was the old optical illusion. States that had submerged differences in order to fight the common enemy hadn't lost those differences, and when the common enemy was gone, those differences reemerged.

The United States and Saudi Arabia, for example, had had a common interest in defeating the Soviet Union. It was an interest that overrode the profound difference that divided them. For a period of time, the relationship continued unchanged. It was partly a matter of the tiger that paced in its cage. When the cage was taken away, it took the tiger a while to realize that it was gone. It was also partly a matter of mutual interest in containing Iraq. But underneath it all, it is hard to imagine two nations with less in common than the United States and Saudi Arabia. The glue that held the United States to Saudi Arabia—or to Germany or Japan—was the Soviet threat. If that threat disappeared, either a new foundation had to be found or the nations would drift apart.

The Post–Cold War World

Following the collapse of the Soviet Union, American strategists were able to relax about foreign policy, for two reasons. First, on an obvious and ultimately superficial level, the one superpower—the United States—and the great powers were essentially aligned, and lesser nations had no desire whatsoever to resist the new order. Certainly, there was trade friction and in some areas ethnic conflict, but the major confrontations of the twentieth century seemed in the past. North Korea, Iraq, Libya, and Yugoslavia were considered rogue nations that did not pose a global threat. On a deeper and more serious level, Eurasia, from Central Europe to the Pacific, was in chaos. That chaos was what reassured the United States the most. No Eurasian power would be seeking hegemony for a generation or more. American control of the seas was secure, and with it, the United States. Subjectively, most policy makers probably wanted to work to reduce the chaos—or to go to meetings to discuss how to reduce it. But the fact was that the instability in Eurasia guaranteed American security.

It was in this context that the first major post–Cold War conflict took place. When Iraq invaded Kuwait in August of 1990, the issue was no longer viewed in terms of great-power politics, even though that was its origin. It was viewed, instead, as if it were simply the case of an isolated, rogue power invading a neighbor for money and oil. The American view of the invasion was relatively simple. First, it was unacceptable that one nation invade another, particularly one with which the United States had a security agreement. Second, it was not in the United States's interest to see Iraq control more of the world's oil reserves than it already had, nor increase its power in the region. Third, the invasion had to be reversed by a coalition of international powers and not by the United States alone in order to share the risk. Finally, none of this should interfere with the more fundamental issues, which involved managing global stability and economic growth. Desert Storm was seen as marginal to the main thrust of U.S. foreign policy, which was the successful management of a harmonious international system.

The strategy that led to Desert Storm tracked perfectly with American assumptions about the post–Cold War world. The operation was seen as enhancing rather than undermining regional and global security. It not only put Iraq back into its box, but it also demonstrated the reliability of the United States as the global hegemon. Just as important, it did not require the United States to rethink its Middle Eastern policy in the wake of events in Europe. The United States would have defended Kuwait against Iraq during the Cold War. The defense of Kuwait was the defense of the conservative, religious monarchies with which the U.S. had been allied during the Cold War. Although the United States was operating in a new strategic environment, defending Kuwait was fully compatible with the old environment. No deep thinking about strategy was needed, which was good, since the Bush administration was having a great deal of difficulty absorbing the meaning of the collapse of Soviet power in Eastern Europe.

Every level of U.S. foreign policy dictated intervention. Grand strategy called for stopping Iraq from becoming a regional power.

Cold War strategy called for protecting the Arabian Peninsula. Formal, post–Cold War strategy called for maintaining global stability by using the institutions of the Western Alliance to incorporate former communist states in U.S.-dominated peacekeeping operations. It not only made perfect sense, but all factions within the Bush administration bought into it. Those who were hard-line Cold Warriors liked it because it defended a Cold War ally. Those who were focused on realpolitik, liked it because it blocked Iraq's emerging power. Those who believed in the end of history loved it because it was an example of the global system operating against a rogue. Even the Democrats who halfheartedly fought against it tended to buy into the multilateralism idea, wishing that it had been theirs.

Desert Storm started a foreign-policy process that began under the Bush administration but was perfected by the Clinton administration. As Cold War considerations fell to the side and realpolitik seemed irrelevant, the argument that the United States had to lead a multilateral coalition to police the world became the basis of Clinton's foreign policy. It continued the Bush administration's policies in Somalia and extended intervention to places like Haiti, Bosnia, and Kosovo. There was no geographical or ideological driver in these interventions. The driver was the idea that the only military threats in the world were destabilizations by rogue leaders or in failed states, and the mission of the United States was to prevent those situations from expanding to destabilize their regions, to prevent atrocities from taking place, and to exercise and thereby improve the new system of international security maintenance.

There was almost no difference between the first Bush and Clinton administrations on U.S. strategy. The rhetoric was somewhat different, but the operational principles were the same. So was the conviction that the U.S. post–Cold War military and intelligence establishments were too large and inappropriate for the kinds of engagements the United States would be facing in the coming years.

Both administrations had an identical view of the world after the collapse of communism. The war that everyone had prepared for, a

Soviet invasion of Germany, had never taken place. U.S. military posture was designed to prevent that invasion. That meant that the United States was focused on armored warfare, tactical airpower, and control of the North Atlantic. This, combined with the potential use of nuclear weapons to create sufficient uncertainty in the Soviets' minds about U.S. actions should it invade Germany, would serve as a deterrent.

The post–Cold War model of war was seen as much less threatening, more diffuse, and less intense. The military and intelligence posture designed to deal with the Soviet threat was unnecessary. Indeed, the fundamental threats to American national security no longer arose from military challenges. They arose from economic challenges from countries like Japan, who could compete with American production. The entire sphere of military challenge was degraded to the level of subsidiary threat, while the perception of the national interest shifted to the economic sphere.

Rogue States and Systemic Threats

The post–Cold War United States was focused on a series of rogue states—North Korea, Libya, Yugoslavia, Iran, Cuba. These were no longer part of any large-scale coalition that could threaten the existence of the United States, but simply fragments, leftovers that could cause problems. The worst threat they would pose would come if they developed nuclear weapons. The second-tier threat was that they would invade neighbors. The third-tier threat was that they would violate the human rights of their own citizens. All of these were considered containable and manageable by using international institutions like the United Nations.

What neither the Bush nor the Clinton administration understood was that the pressure of its assertive policies, designed to manage the international system, was triggering unexpected responses—particularly in the Islamic world. From the beginning, with Desert Storm, the U.S. was involved in a complex series of interactions deep inside the

Islamic world, as well as along the Islamic world's frontiers with the non-Islamic world. For example, the intervention in the Balkans was seen by the United States as ideologically neutral—an attempt to stabilize a region that was threatened by a rogue power. In fact, this action was perceived in the Balkans as an intervention in a struggle between Islam and Orthodox Christianity.

Christians in Bosnia and Kosovo saw the United States acting on behalf of the Muslims. The Muslims, however, saw the interventions as carefully timed to follow Christian atrocities. In other words, the United States permitted Christians to brutalize Muslims and, once that was completed, intervened under the pretext of protecting Muslims. Similarly, the U.S. intervention in Somalia, which was designed to feed the hungry, was seen by the Somalis as an intervention on behalf of one faction and against others.

There was a huge disconnect between American intentions and regional perceptions. The American perception of itself was that it had an interest in stability but no interest in the governance of the region. The players in the region, however, saw the United States as using the cover of stability and human rights as its justification for intervening on behalf of factions with whom the U.S. had made political arrangements. The United States, particularly during the Clinton years, seemed unable to grasp the distinction between what it thought it was doing, what it wanted others to think it was doing, and what others actually believed the U.S. was doing.

The core defect of the American strategy in the 1990s is that it did not come to grips with the fact that there was no such thing as a neutral intervention. Every intervention, regardless of the rhetoric behind it, favors someone and hurts another. Intervening in any country reshapes its politics and creates winners and losers. The United States will be perceived as having intervened in order to make sure that the people it wanted to win actually won. That the United States frequently didn't have a horse in the race made the situation even more confusing in the region. Desperate intellectual gymnastics took place in the Balkans by analysts trying to create a rational explanation for

U.S. interventions in conflicts where it appeared to have no real interest. An intense debate involving extraordinarily bizarre explanations resulted. It was and remains an article of faith in the Balkans that the United States had an extremely clever and well-hidden interest for its actions.

Obviously, U.S. policy makers understood that the rhetoric of peacekeeping always differed from the reality on the ground. They understood that their intentions—maintaining regional order—were close to but not quite identical to their rhetoric—protecting human rights. They also understood—certainly after Somalia—that these interventions could generate severe opposition and resistance in the target countries.

This was a price the U.S. was prepared to pay. It did not want to see instability in these regions not only because it threatened U.S. interests, but because the U.S. wanted to be seen as an effective global manager. In this role, the United States could deal with more pressing issues, such as the international economic order and forging the coalition that enabled American power.

The U.S. saw these interventions as low risk. If there was blowback, as in Somalia, the U.S. could always withdraw. But even if there was resistance, the U.S. viewed this resistance as localized. Without a Soviet Union and without a centrally organized geopolitical force that could organize resistance to American intervention, the United States felt that there was no systemic threat to the U.S. or its interests. The prize—growing recognition of American power, avoidance of regional hegemons, increased stability—was worth the low risk.

This was the first of two dimensions of American strategic miscalculation of the 1990s. The United States assumed that other countries would be willing to trade a degree of national autonomy in exchange for stability and prosperity. To a great extent, this was true. But underneath their accommodation to the American reorganization of the post–Cold War world, there was also a deep-seated fear. Most of the world's great powers—France, Russia, Germany, China—understood two things about the situation. One, there was a heavy element of inevitability to American power. Second, there were in fact substantial benefits to them. But they also understood a third thing.

These other great powers understood that the enormity of American power had made the U.S. unpredictable. Unlike countries that are locked into constrained circumstances and therefore have few foreign-policy options, the United States had an enormous menu from which to choose. One could never predict what the U.S. would come up with next, what one would be drawn into, or when, in fact, one might become the next target. Like a giant adolescent with enormous strength, the U.S. was dangerous regardless of its intent. Other nations preferred a more contained and controlled United States, and were prepared to take advantage of opportunities to reduce American power and force the U.S. to choose from a more limited agenda. The U.S. did not fully appreciate the interests of the great powers (France, Russia, Germany, China), nor did it anticipate their response to serious American problems. The United States assumed a broadly shared interest with the great powers, not realizing during the 1990s that its own actions constituted a systemic threat to them. Put simply, the great powers were waiting for the United States to trip, and they were prepared to help the process along. They were not prepared to openly challenge the U.S. yet openly expressed fears of growing American power.

The second dimension of American miscalculation was in the Islamic world. A large number of U.S. interventions in the 1990s involved the Islamic world—Iraq, Somalia, Bosnia, Kosovo. For the United States, the Islamic nature of these interventions was incidental. For a movement like Al Qaeda that was trying to re-create the Caliphate—a transnational Islamic state—the recurring U.S. military interventions in the Islamic world represented both a direct challenge and, more important, an opportunity to mobilize support by labeling the United States an enemy of Islam.

U.S. strategy was based on the assumption that there was no systemic opposition. In fact, there was such opposition on two levels— Cold War allies who thought the U.S. was becoming too powerful, and Muslims who saw an opportunity for fomenting risings. These two forces were not setting a trap for the United States, nor was the U.S. seeking a confrontation. All sides were playing out the hands that had been dealt to them. But this is what accounted for the rise of Al Qaeda as well as the behavior of erstwhile American allies following September 11.

The policies that led to this were adopted by both Democratic and Republican administrations. The idea that the end of the Cold War had created a global economy that was infinitely more important than either military or political power was shared throughout the American political and economic elite. In their interactions with other countries' business leaders, it appeared that the global economy was a universally shared value. In fact, there was a deep-seated geopolitical resistance in place that was increasing with each passing year.

Globalists argued that economic well-being transcended all other considerations. In fact, as had historically been the case, people valued national autonomy as much as prosperity. The prospect of being submerged into a transnational system in which the nation lost its autonomy to distant bureaucracy brought a great deal of unease in the industrialized world. In the Islamic world, it was anathema. The U.S. government thought that all reasonable people would welcome transnational prosperity and stability. Many certainly would. Others were prepared to resist—some to the death.

It is not at all clear that had the United States recognized the forces that were being unleashed, it could have followed a different policy. The menu of options was actually quite limited. The collapse of the Soviet Union had left behind this situation, not unlike those after the two world wars and the Napoleonic wars, and the United States had responded to them in a completely predictable way—a way in which there had been general consensus among both leaders and the American public. It was an unavoidable path. The United States was the victor in the Cold War and had to deal with the implications. The unintended consequences (resistance from other global actors) were also unexpected, which was the critical problem. U.S. policy might not have been changeable, but the American perception of what it was doing could have been clearer.

The United States, Al Qaeda, and Terrorism

When Al Qaeda came on the scene, its most important characteristics tended to be overlooked by terrorist experts. They were treated as part of a continuum of terrorism stretching back to the 1960s rather than as a singular phenomenon requiring a unique understanding. Everything about Al Qaeda was different, but as long as the term "terrorist" was used, it was easy simply to lump them into prefabricated categories that misled observers in significant ways. It tended to treat them less as politically astute operatives and more as psychological defectives, a massive and major error.

The United States could never quite deal with terrorism as a rational strategy by an enemy. Terrorism in the United States remained framed by the metal detector at airports and the image of the terrorist as a dangerous but inconsequential nuisance. It also generated a group of people who were in the business of thinking about terrorism.

The problem was rooted in the very term "terrorist." First, it treated the people who used terrorism not only as moral monsters but as people whose primary goal and primary driver was psychological. In doing so, analysts immediately began to undervalue the rationale that was driving the terrorists. Their motives may have been exotic, but they had a clear understanding of their environment and were adept at matching means to ends. They were not imbeciles, a point obscured by the term.

Second, use of the term "terrorist" appeared to refer to a class of actors who were, in reality, wildly different in nature. It obscured not only obvious differences—between someone blowing up the mathematics building at the University of Wisconsin and a Tamil Tiger—but also critical differences within movements. The Popular Front for the Liberation of Palestine and Hamas might both commit terrorist acts and be part of the Palestinian movement, but their interests and intentions were extremely divergent. The term "terrorist" tended to hide critical differences and therefore made it extremely difficult to defend against them.

Americans historically have a tendency to underestimate the intellectual and personal qualities of their enemies. Then, after they encounter the enemy, they vastly overestimate him. Japan is a case in point. Prior to Pearl Harbor, there was a tendency to dismiss the technical capabilities of the Japanese. Afterward, the U.S. overestimated their strength to the point of despair. The American mind-set changed similarly in Vietnam. With the Soviets, the view at the beginning of World War II was that they would collapse in weeks. The view ten years later was that they were vastly more powerful than they actually were.

The concept of terrorism took this problem and magnified it many times over. Before September 11, there was a tendency to vastly underestimate Al Qaeda's capabilities. This was particularly true because of Al Qaeda's efficient use of simple technologies. After September 11, the United States flipped its evaluation, vastly overestimating them. Both extremes were a result of a generation-long approach to terrorism that obscured more than it revealed.

When U.S. forces first deployed in Saudi Arabia in order to face down Iraq, they were confined to bases. The reason was that the Saudis were afraid that public awareness of the American presence on their soil would generate a massive reaction. On one rare occasion when U.S. troops went off base, a small group visited a Saudi coffee shop. There they were taunted by Saudis, who told them that the Saudi government had merely hired the U.S. Army, just as they hired engineers or servants. The U.S. soldiers responded vigorously, and were later brought up on charges.

The incident resulted in a sharp encounter between Norman Schwarzkopf and the Saudi command. Schwarzkopf demanded that the Saudis take steps to stamp out the perception, encouraged by the government, that the Americans were simply hired mercenaries under Saudi control. What Schwarzkopf and the rest of the U.S. government didn't grasp is that the story was spread among the Saudi population because the Saudi government harbored a desperate fear: that the presence of U.S. forces in Arabia would trigger an uprising. In fact it did generate a rising, but not an immediate one. It triggered Al Qaeda. The U.S. did not clearly recognize the unique political foundations of this group.

When Al Qaeda began operating, as far back as the first World Trade Center bombing, the tendency was to lump it into the terrorism bucket and to consign it to the study of the terrorism experts. The experts understood that Al Qaeda had a different ideology from those of the 1970s crop, but they didn't understand the extent to which Al Qaeda differed from other terrorist groups. Al Qaeda did not see itself as primarily making symbolic gestures. Rather, it saw itself as trying to put into motion certain political processes that would result in achieving its political goals.

The most important thing that was missed by the terrorism experts, who were studying Al Qaeda's methods instead of its ends, is that it had a much more sophisticated understanding of the Islamic world than did the left-wing movements in the 1970s and 1980s. These were not Qadaffi- or Assad-financed groups, trained by communist bloc personnel. Those groups were alien transplants into Arab culture—along with the idea of pan-Arabism. Al Qaeda grew from the natural soil of Islamic—not Arab—culture and had roots going back centuries. Its dreams were alien to Americans, but far more natural to Muslims than the ideologies of groups like the Popular Front for the Liberation of Palestine. Put bluntly, Al Qaeda's message had legs, and the likely effect of its actions was much more threatening to the United States than that of previous terrorist groups.

This threat was not confined to the United States. Israel had likewise massively underestimated the capabilities of Hamas. Believing they were dealing with merely another iteration of old terrorist groups, Israelis failed to understand that the combination of operational sophistication and religious dedication made these groups fundamentally different from what went before. Timothy McVeigh and Al Qaeda both blew up buildings, but they had nothing else in common.

Therefore, even as Al Qaeda attacked embassies and warships, the political leadership turned to the terrorism experts who focused on its operational and tactical techniques, rather than on the vision it was pursuing. Put very simply, by neglecting its vision and the credibility of its hopes, and focusing on the explosives, the United States missed the significance of Al Qaeda. This was one of the origins of Clinton's halfhearted countermeasures after the African embassy bombings and the USS *Cole* incident—for him it was simply another terrorist group.

As a result, the United States helped create conditions in which Al Qaeda could flourish. It should be noted that this is a far cry from "creating Al Qaeda," as some extreme critics of the United States have charged. It was an act of omission, not commission, that had this effect. In the end, the rise of Al Qaeda did not depend on the U.S. Al Qaeda came out of deep processes in the Islamic world and would have emerged regardless, because its vision is one of the tenets of that world. The United States, for its part, was following its own historical imperative, looking for prosperity and security and imagining it had found it in the post–Cold War world. The resulting collision resonates, to say the least.

CHAPTER 4

The Anatomy of Intelligence Failures

THERE IS A SAYING in the American intelligence community that only its failures are ever noticed, because its successes are secret. That sounds good, and on one level this is true. But the intelligence community is being much too easy on itself. Intelligence specialists are frequently successful, but their successes are usually about the minute details of events and not about the earth-shattering shifts that transform the world. If the President wants to know what a particular world leader is telling his mistress, U.S. intelligence excels at that. But if the goal is to tell the President the next big thing, the intelligence community has had a much harder time of it.

Since World War II, the U.S. intelligence community has failed to predict the North Korean invasion of the South, the Chinese intervention in Korea, Khrushchev's plan to place missiles in Cuba, the fact that U.S. strategy in Vietnam would fail, the fall of the Shah of Iran, the collapse of communism, or the breakup of the Soviet Union. Therefore, the general shock at the fact that the U.S. intelligence community failed to predict September 11 is rather surprising. U.S. intelligence has never been very good at forecasting the big things.

Historically, U.S intelligence has had two traits. First, harking back to the OSS, it was action oriented. It did not simply watch things—it did things. The people who got things done naturally and inevitably had greater standing than those who simply gathered information and much greater standing than those who sought to understand it. Second, U.S. intelligence was source oriented. It insisted on intelligence from people or devices "on the ground." That sounds reasonable until you consider that all information is inherently incomplete and refusing to make an analytic call until you have fully sourced your analysis means you will tend to make calls late or not at all.

For example, the obsession in the CIA during the Cold War was penetrating the Soviet elite. Every effort was made to recruit or tap into the communications of the Soviet Politburo, Central Committee, Soviet military leadership, and so on. This was extremely useful in learning about Soviet plans during the Cold War, but it did little to provide intelligence on things that were unplanned—such as the collapse of the Soviet Union. The ultimate goal of the CIA was to know what the Soviet leaders knew. But in the end, the Soviet leadership turned out not to know a great deal, including the real size of the Soviet economy. During the critical mid- to late eighties, the Soviet leadership was literally the last to know what was happening.

The failure to anticipate first-order events is hardwired into the U.S. intelligence system, owing to three factors. First, there is the organization of the U.S. intelligence system. Second, there is the obsession with the collection of information rather than with its analysis. Finally, there is a "committee system" that tries to achieve a compromise among stakeholders and, as a result, produces analyses that are marked not by bold insight but by coalition building. It is a system designed to produce small facts rather than broad visions, and it can tell you a million things about Al Qaeda. But it has a great deal of difficulty not only building the big picture but filling in the blanks through logic, inference, and intuition. In a world where the most important intelligence is hard to find, the CIA won't often be wrong, but it will frequently be silent on the things that are really important. Understanding the three weaknesses of the intelligence community is the key to understanding how, with a budget of about $40 billion a year, it missed the big ones.

Part of the answer is contained in the CIA's basic statement, called "Vision, Mission, and Values of the Central Intelligence Agency," which identified the following basic missions:

> We support the President, the National Security Council, and all who make and execute US national security policy by:
> Providing accurate, evidence-based, comprehensive and timely foreign intelligence related to national security; and
> Conducting counterintelligence activities, special activities, and other functions related to foreign intelligence and national security as directed by the President.

The issue is laid out in the vision. If intelligence is to be evidence based, what is the standard of evidence for triggering the "special activities"? And if the CIA is carrying out special activities based on its own analysis and provided to the President, then what will the criteria of failure be and who will enforce them?

The Organization of the Intelligence Community

The term *intelligence community* is the starting point of the problem. There shouldn't be an intelligence community, nor was there supposed to be one. There was supposed to be a single, integrated Central Intelligence Agency, which was to be the pivot of U.S. intelligence, and whose director was supposed to wear two hats: Director of the Central Intelligence Agency, and DCI, or Director of Central Intelligence, which placed him over all government intelligence operations, under the rules laid down by the National Security Act of 1947, which created the contemporary U.S. intelligence system. This is something that never really happened.

The real impetus to the creation of the CIA was Pearl Harbor and the hearings that were held at the end of the war about what went wrong. The United States government "knew" about the Pearl Harbor attack, meaning that individuals in the U.S. Navy, Army, and State Department each had small bits of information in their possession that, if integrated at a central point and viewed by a single integrated team, would have yielded the answer. As it was, the Navy and Army maintained their own intelligence services that focused on the things they were interested in. The State Department ran its own intelligence shop, and the President, FDR, ran his own agents around the world, some through the Commerce Departments and some on his own. The FBI was involved as well, in a kind of unsystematic, unpredictable way.

All of these organizations were obsessed with collecting information. There was no clear system for sharing and aggregating information, nor for analyzing it. From the earliest intercept of the Japanese codes, to the final report from an Army radar station reporting incoming Japanese bombers, none of the information was channeled in the right direction, certainly not in time to do any good. Nobody was thinking of intelligence as a system, and therefore there existed no system of intelligence.

After World War II, looking at the foul-up at Pearl Harbor, the United States created a new organization, unprecedented in U.S. history—the Central Intelligence Agency. There had been other intelligence agencies—George Washington was an intelligence junkie using a wide range of sources, and Abraham Lincoln used Allan Pinkerton to organize the Army's secret service. The military always maintained some sort of intelligence apparatus—but there had never been a formal, centralized intelligence organization.

The CIA is divided into two main directorates. The Directorate of Operations operates the espionage system and at times carries out covert operations—which are not actually part of an intelligence organization's brief but usually fall into its lap. The other, the Directorate of Intelligence, houses the analysts, who study the material delivered to them by the DO.

There is and always has been a barely permeable curtain between the DI and DO. The need for secrecy means that the DI is kept out of operations. It receives product and is able to task, but virtually everything it receives is filtered from the DO. This means, in effect, that if you think of the CIA as an organism, the sensing parts are kept at a substantial distance from the thinking parts. The result of this is a constant desynchronization between intelligence gathering and intelligence analysis.

But it gets more complicated. The CIA specializes in human intelligence, or humint. If information is received from a human source, the CIA owns it. But there are other ways of gathering intelligence. For example, signal intelligence, or sigint, is any information that is gathered through intercepts of radio programs, cell phone calls, and the like. Sigint belongs not to the CIA but to the National Security Agency, which has a much larger budget.

There is also image intelligence, or imint, which are pictures gathered by satellites or strategic reconnaissance aircraft like the U-2. The satellites themselves are owned by the National Reconnaissance Office, which also owns the NSA satellites that could pick up sigint. NRO is responsible for developing and operating the satellites. Sigint goes directly to NSA. Imint used to go to NPIC (National Photographic Interpretation Center), until it was merged with DMA (Defense Mapping Agency) into a single agency called the National Imagery and Mapping Agency (recently changed to National Geospatial-Intelligence Agency of NGA). Of course, the CIA operates its own imint shop, as do the military services.

The Pentagon operates its own intelligence service, the Defense Intelligence Agency. DIA receives a great deal of its intelligence from CIA, NSA, and NGA, but it runs its own human intelligence service, Defense Human Services. They are supposed to be focused on enemy military capabilities, but with an enemy as diffuse as Al Qaeda, the distinction between military intelligence and the kind of political intelligence the CIA is charged with collecting becomes academic very quickly.

In addition to DIA, each military service runs its own intelligence unit. The Army has Military Intelligence, the Navy has the Office of Naval Intelligence, and the Air Force has the Office of Special Investigations. These focus on the specific areas of interest of each service, and particularly on tactical intelligence. The problem is that in fighting a guerrilla war and a terrorist war, all intelligence is tactical, so responsibilities quickly become confused.

Surrounding all of this is a series of domestic services, particularly the Federal Bureau of Investigation. The FBI is charged with domestic law enforcement and with counterintelligence (the CIA also maintains its own counterintelligence capability). Separating intelligence from counterintelligence is not a bad idea. The British maintain MI5 and MI6 as separate units. If the intelligence arm is penetrated by the enemy, it is more likely to be detected by an external agency, completely separate, than by an internal agency with a vested interest not to rock the boat or—worse—one that might be penetrated itself.

However, few countries link their counterintelligence services as closely with routine law enforcement as the United States does with the FBI. The FBI not only monitors foreign intelligence operations and terrorism in the United States but handles stolen-car rings, kidnappings, and virtually any other crime that can be imagined. The FBI is a law-enforcement agency with a counterintelligence and counterterrorism mission tagged on.

This is a critically important fact to understand. A law-enforcement agency has two complementary mind-sets. First, in the United States, laws generally can be enforced only after they are broken. The FBI is a criminal investigation unit, which means that they solve crimes that have already happened. Second, they are prosecution oriented. They are policemen, primarily evaluated by the successful prosecutions carried out based on their investigations.

Intelligence is about events that have not yet happened and might never happen. It is certainly not about making arrests. They are important, but the primary mission of intelligence is to understand what is happening around it and to predict what will happen. The inclination of intelligence must be to watch and wait. The institutional bias of the FBI is to solve crimes, which causes it to behave in two ways. First, it becomes interested in things after they have already happened, and second, it tends to act as quickly as it can to arrest the perpetrators—so quickly that at times important, unindictable relationships tend to be overlooked.

The FBI is only the largest of a number of law-enforcement organizations that intersects intelligence. The Secret Service, for example, is involved with protecting the President and tracking anything that has to do with currency and child pornography. Since tracking currency transactions is essential to counter Al Qaeda operations, the Secret Service, the country's original intelligence service, has a diffused focus.

The Drug Enforcement Administration is responsible for global monitoring of drug trafficking as well as for domestic law enforcement. Its responsibilities for heroin trafficking make it a major intelligence gatherer in places like Afghanistan and the Bekaa Valley of Lebanon. Indeed, when political interest in these regions declines, DEA is more likely to be operating than the CIA. DEA agents are frequently pressed into service in countries where the drug trade is heavy and when political interest rises.

Alcohol, Tobacco and Firearms is responsible for moonshiners and weapons traffickers. The former does not touch much on Al Qaeda, while the latter can be extremely significant. Tracking money is the Treasury's job (with the help of the Secret Service), but it is not well known that tracking weapons in the United States is also the job of the Treasury Department. In 2003, ATF became the Bureau of Alcohol, Tobacco, Firearms and Explosives and became part of the Department of Justice.

FBI, Secret Service, DEA, and ATF are all primarily law-enforcement agencies. Most of their personnel are engaged in law-enforcement activities, and they are not organized as intelligence agencies. Prior to September 11, none of them had large numbers of skilled and trusted analysts on staff for sifting through the information gathered. That was acceptable, since most of the information they gathered wasn't shared inside their own organizations, let alone with other agencies. Since their primary purpose was to make arrests, the information they accumulated was held closely to facilitate prosecutions. If there were no prosecutions to be made, the information was of little interest.

There are also the border guardians—the Immigration and Naturalization Service, the Customs Bureau, the Border Patrol—all of them having a critical role in tracking what enters the United States, but none of them having the resources or charter to focus on potential terrorists. These organizations were not traditionally charged with law enforcement or intelligence as their primary mission, but rather with ensuring the efficient processing of humans and cargo moving into the United States. Law enforcement came second and intelligence a distant third.

The State Department has a fairly small intelligence unit, mostly consisting of analysts sifting through embassy reports and the crumbs that the CIA and NSA let them have. However, there is another critical group within State—Diplomatic Security Services, charged with protecting U.S. embassies around the world. This not only gives them a counterintelligence role, it puts them directly on the spot when U.S. embassies are hit.

Last, but far from least, was the Office of Special Plans in the Defense Department. An office like OSP had been maintained in the Department of Defense for decades under different forms and names. It was a small group of intelligence analysts who were considered to be (and considered themselves) particularly brilliant. Unlike the DIA, which had a clear institutional function, OSP and its predecessors were more informal. It served as a second check, a Red Team, on intelligence that was reaching the Secretary of Defense. It was more than just an analyst cell. It also maintained contacts with sources around the world and particularly in areas of pressing interest. It frequently had a very different view of the world than the rest of the intelligence community.

OSP had the virtue of being small and therefore unencumbered by complex progress, but it also had the vice of self-assurance when it wasn't warranted. Headed by Abe Shulsky, who was particularly close to Deputy Defense Secretary Paul Wolfowitz, OSP had resources, access, and credibility. Its read of the situation could trump the rest of the intelligence community's so far as the Secretary of Defense was concerned, and, depending on the credibility of the Secretary of Defense, it could shape the choices being made in the Office of the President.

Rather than a single integrated intelligence service, as was envisioned in the founding of the CIA, the United States had, on September 11, a chaotic hodgepodge of completely uncoordinated agencies all charged in one way or another with dealing with intelligence. Some of them focused on collecting one type of intelligence, while others focused on collecting intelligence as a sideline, while tracking stolen-car rings, pot growers, or cigarette smugglers.

There was no single place where all this intelligence was gathered and reviewed. Given the overlaps, gaps, and lack of systematic control or process, it was possible to drive four hijacked planes through the system and deploy nineteen hijackers without being noticed. The statement "the U.S. government knew" about anything is meaningless. Certainly, buried somewhere in the files of all of these agencies, one could find anything and everything, but that is a far cry from anything being known.

The U.S. intelligence community was an accident waiting to happen on September 11, 2001. It was not a matter of personnel. There were plenty. Nor was it a matter of motivation. The dedication of the employees was in the same range you might find in any American corporation, from timeservers to the incredibly committed. The problem rested with the fact that the basic law that had created the centralized intelligence system that the CIA was supposed to dominate had been utterly disregarded by politicians and the public.

On a deeper level, in the 1990s, some serious figures argued that the CIA was no longer necessary. New York senator Daniel Patrick Moynihan introduced a bill called "End of the Cold War Act of 1991," which called for the abolition of the CIA. That wasn't going to happen, but others argued that the CIA's mission should be shifted away from political and security intelligence and toward economic intelligence. Fixing the CIA's manifest defects was not likely to happen when there was a general feeling among the public and politicians that the CIA might have outlived its usefulness.

Al Qaeda, which had extensive experience with U.S. intelligence during the Afghan war, certainly knew about these weaknesses. It knew how the visa system worked. It knew how NSA intercepted phone calls and how to keep the CIA from planting people in its cells. It knew these things because the U.S. had shown them the book—a book that did not evolve much in the 1990s. The same things they had learned in Afghanistan in the 1980s were still operant in 2001. If anything, it was all looser, since the Cold War was over, the U.S. had no real enemies, and its guard was down.

The Myth of Sourcing

The crazy-quilt structure of U.S. intelligence was destined to fail. It was virtually impossible for so many entities, with areas of responsibility divided arbitrarily based on random historical circumstances, to deal effectively with the unexpected. Put differently, the U.S. intelligence community was configured to deal with the routine and the expected. It was not designed to deal with the extraordinary—and was particularly weak in dealing with the extraordinary that hit the seam between agencies.

Immediately after September 11, the Bush administration began to try to integrate the disparate services. Unfortunately, it didn't go as far as to abolish the differences and integrate them all into one service. It did not deal with the fundamentally different orientations of the various agencies, nor did it address overlapping responsibilities. It assumed, as Washington likes to do, that the problem was simple bureaucratic inefficiency and that forcing the agencies to work together would be the solution.

The one issue everyone agreed on was that the United States needed to increase its intelligence-collection capabilities. The immediate reaction to the intelligence failure on September 11 was that the U.S. had focused too much on technical means of intelligence— imagery, signal intelligence, and so on—and had neglected human intelligence, or humint. This was a view particularly held in the CIA's Directorate of Operations, which had primary responsibility for humint. They blamed the failure on Stansfield Turner's assault on the DO in 1977 and on limits placed on the recruitment of agents during the 1990s, when Bill Clinton and Congress created a set of rules that said—among many other rules—that recruiting an agent who had violated human rights or engaged in terrorist activities could only be done with the approval of the Deputy Director of Operations in Langley. This was not only a lengthy process but one discouraged by the DDO. Since recruiting Al Qaeda meant, by definition, recruiting terrorists, it cut down on human sources enormously, and that was assuming that Al Qaeda could be recruited in the first place.

This was not a trivial problem, but it was not the heart of the problem either. Indeed, as weak as the DO's humint network had become, it was still an impressive capability. Human intelligence flowed copiously from around the world, and when integrated with technical intelligence, it could provide deep understanding of the world. The key words here are "could" and "integrated."

If you look across the array of agencies charged with intelligence, you notice that the vast majority of them are concerned with collecting intelligence. Very few are charged with analyzing it. Whether they were law-enforcement agencies like the FBI and DEA, or technical intelligence agencies like NSA and NGA, their primary commitment was to the collection of intelligence. Over 90 percent of the roughly $40 billion a year spent on intelligence by the United States goes to the collection side of the business. Less than 10 percent is spent on analysis.

Collection is the obsession of U.S. intelligence. The debate that broke out after September 11 was about the type of intelligence that should be collected. The conventional wisdom was that there was insufficient humint. In fact, when the postmortem on 9/11 was done, it emerged that the information about Al Qaeda's planned attack had been collected before the attack but was sitting in the files and databases of all of the agencies and all of their offices.

The problem was that despite effective collection, no one had put the pieces together. This was not just attributable to the bureaucratic nightmare U.S. intelligence had turned into, although that contributed to it mightily. It was rooted in the imbalance between intelligence collection and analysis that had been built into the U.S. intelligence system from its founding. The most bizarre collection schemes imaginable could get funded. The simplest analytic requirements—from enough language specialists, to enough analysts cleared to move outside of their compartments—had to struggle for funding.

The tendency of the intelligence community was to solve analytic problems with technical solutions. For example, the vast amount of phone traffic intercepted by the NSA could not possibly be read without the support of computer-based analysis that could search through the digitized data looking for things that analysts should review. Or, as another example, it was obvious that the FBI needed, but didn't have, a comprehensive, secure database for sharing intelligence within the FBI and between the FBI and other agencies. In the wake of September 11, vast amounts of money were spent on these technical support systems.

However, in the end, that is all these technological fixes were— they were support systems to allow the analyst more time for reading, discussing, and thinking, in order to make the kind of unexpected, insightful connections that only human beings can make (what true intelligence is all about). More money was being spent on technological support to analysts than on improving the quantity and quality of analysts. The intelligence community was prepared to spend vast sums on technological solutions to what was ultimately a human problem—smart analysts.

The problem was that the business management practices that the best and brightest in the intelligence community liked to use did not see analysts as highly leverageable expenditures, to use the jargon.

Money spent collecting and distributing huge amounts of data appears to be leverageable. A dollar spent building a database increases the efficiency of thousands of people. Analysts do not work in a leverageable environment. They are simply people thinking. That appears to be inefficient to managers, who would like to find a machine that allows one person to think for twenty.

Analysis is the bottleneck of intelligence. It is also the process that turns information into knowledge. Analysis is made even more complicated by compartmentalization, a security process designed to minimize the chances that any one analyst will know enough about a subject to damage national security should he go rogue. Like all security procedures, compartmentalization imposes penalties on efficiency. It protects information but also prevents a comprehensive picture from emerging.

If there was a single weakness of the U.S. intelligence postures prior to September 11, it was not a lack of spies or the lack of sophisticated intelligence-gathering systems. It wasn't, in the end, even a weakness in collating intelligence. At the end of the day, the core weakness was a profound lack of language skills and trained and sophisticated analysts to figure out what was being said. Together, these weaknesses were fatal. The lack of language skills meant that translation of critical material was always delayed. The insufficiency of analysts meant that no one could pull this together into a comprehensive picture.

There was a further serious defect in the analytical system—an obsession with sources. That sounds like a paradox, since we assume that intelligence is about gathering information. But that is too simple. Intelligence analysis is about using sources, but it is also about filling in the blanks where no sources are available or where the sources of information are unreliable.

The former head of Saudi intelligence, Prince Turki al Faisal, once said that the problem with penetrating Al Qaeda was its vetting system. Al Qaeda would not admit—certainly not into its decision-making cells—individuals who had not been known to the plotters for years prior to the creation of the organization. Since Al Qaeda had a pool of thousands of experienced fighters to draw on from Afghanistan—as well as their families—this was an ample source of recruitment. It also made planting a mole inside of Al Qaeda extraordinarily difficult. That meant that good intelligence was not flowing from inside Al Qaeda. The primary means of intelligence had to be technical—assuming that Al Qaeda wasn't working to block those penetrations (which they were).

This does not mean that a good analyst could not have identified the fundamental threat of Al Qaeda or probable actions.

- An analyst knowing the background of many of the operatives— available in CIA files—would have known the unrelenting nature of these men, the quality of their minds, and the financial resources available to them.
- They would have been able to "nibble around the edges," using intelligence from individuals and groups not far from Al Qaeda to infer the kind of things Al Qaeda would be considering.
- They would have been able to look at Al Qaeda's pattern of operation to determine a pattern of action.

In other words, they would have had to use logic, inference, and intuition to guess. Guessing is not frowned on in the Directorate of Intelligence. It is understood that an inspired guess may be all that is available. However, inspired guesses do not easily make it into final intelligence products.

The final intelligence estimates must be fully "sourced." In other words, every claim must have a clearly defined structure of intelligence undergirding it. If the President or a cabinet member or the Chairman of the Joint Chiefs of Staff asks a question about the reliability of the analysis, the briefer—the person delivering the analysis— must be in a position to assure the customer that each claim is the result of gathered intelligence, and not just an inspired guess. The last thing the briefer wants to say to the President is that the assertion that

Al Qaeda is about to attack was based on a really smart analyst working with limited data making his best guess.

That means that the gut feelings, intuitive leaps, and brilliant insights tend to be left out of the product delivered to the decision makers. What they see is analysis based on the best verifiable information that has been gathered. This creates two problems. First, it isn't the best verifiable information gathered, but the best verifiable information that has come to the attention of the analyst due to the institutional chaos surrounding intelligence analysis. Second—and more important—no one ever gathers all the intelligence needed to make a call. The world is much too large and complex for any intelligence organization to grasp its fullness.

The U.S. intelligence community has, ever since the Kennedy years, practiced what we might call "defensive intelligence." The massive intelligence failure at the Bay of Pigs, which made the intuitive leap that the Cuban public would happily rise against Castro once the invasion came on shore, was a failure from which the U.S. intelligence community has still not recovered. While periodic improvements take place, the intelligence community has used the concept of "intelligence process," a notion borrowed from management theory, to defend itself against criticisms of failure. This has the following steps:

1. The intelligence community develops an estimate as closely tied to verifiable intelligence as possible and therefore inherently limited.
2. It puts the intelligence through a vetting process in which sources are numerically rated for reliability and the intelligence is rated as well—say, on a 1 to 5 scale. The rating is pretty arbitrary, but any external audit will perceive a rigorous process because there are a lot of numbers being used.
3. Huge areas of reality are ignored, because there is no source—that is, no rated, quantified source verifying the fact. Huge parts of reality are ignored because there is no sourced fact backing it, not because the reality isn't there.

4. Inside the DI, lots of people are generating analyses that are getting pretty close to the truth of what is happening out there, but these analyses, although true, are speculative and don't fit into the final product, since they would be difficult to defend.

5. Something unexpected happens and the Director of Central Intelligence proclaims that there was no intelligence failure, because the process worked.

6. Later, it is discovered that lots more facts were available and an analyst had actually written a report that correctly forecast the event.

Getting things right starts to play second fiddle to following the process.

Those restrictions were startlingly obvious after September 11. Al Qaeda was built to be stealthy. It was difficult to monitor with images, it was careful about its use of communications equipment, and it was difficult to penetrate with spies. By definition, the sourcing on Al Qaeda was extremely limited. Lack of intelligence did not mean that Al Qaeda wasn't there, that it wasn't plotting and planning, and that it wasn't ready to act. All of that could be intuited from the very lack of data—the more careful Al Qaeda was being in not emitting intelligence, the more dangerous they were. Indeed, many in the intelligence community were convinced that Al Qaeda intended a major operation against the United States, based on the force of logic. But the lack of sources meant that the final intelligence products had to hedge the findings. As a result, senior figures in the Clinton administration could not draw the obvious conclusion—that Al Qaeda was a major, direct threat to the United States in the relatively near future. Therefore, counteraction, designed to disrupt Al Qaeda, was never a front-burner issue. Kosovo trumped Al Qaeda.

The Intelligence Process as Defect

The problem with sources is not that they aren't useful but that they become a crutch on which intelligence organizations lean in order to evade responsibility. A source can be referenced. A powerful insight can't. If a source misleads, his handler can be fired, and the problem can be contained. If an unsourced judgment is made and fails, then a systemic error has taken place, and that is dangerous. The way the CIA is set up, it is better to be rigorously accurate in the small things, and utterly wrong in the big things, than the other way around. Thus, in the case of Al Qaeda, the insight that there was a global conspiracy targeting the United States was difficult to support because of a lack of evidence. Details, like the presence of one Al Qaeda operative in a European city, could be sourced and was used in briefings. In the end, the CIA knew with certainty that there were a few trees out there but did not draw any "unsupported" analytical judgment about what those trees meant.

The accusation has been made that Langley bends its analyses on political bases, giving the President what he wants to hear. That undoubtedly goes on, but there is an enormously more insidious process under way—the search for consensus. Consensus building is built into the CIA process using a method called "weight of evidence." What this means, simply, is analysis based on best evidence, as defined by a fairly large number of analysts and managers. The result sometimes comes out as the lowest common denominator.

The geniuses want their own ideas put forward and regard everyone else as an obstacle to their greatness. At the CIA, the geniuses pose a huge problem. They see the world in idiosyncratic ways. They violate the carefully built process and consensus. They are irritating and slow down the process. Most of the time, they aren't necessary. But in that rare instance—like September 11—where the process cannot produce the right consensus, it takes a brilliant, intuitive leap to come up with the right answer. The U.S. intelligence community allows professionals and careerists to flourish. But it grinds idiosyncratic brilliance into dust.

The CIA does consistently well on secondary things. It is as surprised as anyone else on the big things. Whether it is the fall of the Soviet Union or September 11, the CIA will be discovered to have the facts in its files. Friends or enemies can prove that it "knew" these things were going to happen. But the fact is that it "knew" about these things only if filing cabinets and databases can think and talk. Conspiracy theories will abound based on what was found somewhere in the Agency or at the FBI. But the fact is that the American intelligence community was constructed in such a way that no one really knew what was in those files, and those who intuited what was going on were never listened to, because intuition never fit in with the intelligence process.

CHAPTER 5

The American Way of War— Planning for Everything Except What Happened

THE AMERICAN RESPONSE to September 11 was to launch a global war against Al Qaeda. This war included major operations in Afghanistan and Iraq, as well as smaller operations throughout the region. These obviously strained the American military by forcing continual action at long distances. But on a broader level, it strained the U.S. military by stretching—and in many ways breaking—the conceptual framework in which the United States had operated since the end of the Cold War. The gap between American military planning and American military conflict is not new, of course. The U.S. planned for a war in Europe but fought a war in Vietnam. This gap dominated the Cold War. But it was never as stark as it was after September 11.

The last thing that U.S. strategic planners expected at the end of the Cold War was to be embroiled in the kind of global war in which the United States is now engaged. September 11 was certainly not anticipated, but it is crucial to understand that the kind of war that would have to be fought in response to September 11 was not anticipated either. Everything that happened after that date was a series of hastily sketched improvisations.

The United States defense community is obsessed with planning. There are contingency plans for everything, and thousands of people in the Pentagon and elsewhere do nothing but update these plans.

This goes back almost a century and covers even the most outlandish possibilities. After World War I, for example, the United States developed War Plan Red, which prepared for a war with Great Britain. There is virtually no scenario, no matter how far-fetched, without a plan—and no plan that isn't reviewed and refined over time.

This is what made September 11 so brilliant from a simple military standpoint. Tactical surprise is always important. However, it is an act of genius to surprise an adversary so completely that he has not even begun to think about how to deal with the threat. And that is where Al Qaeda really hit the United States. Apart from killing thousands of Americans, it left the U.S. defense and intelligence establishment at an utter loss as to how it would respond. There was no plan for defeating Al Qaeda. Everything that followed, most especially the U.S. invasion of Iraq, was a consequence of this fundamental fact.

The End of the Cold War and U.S. Strategic Thinking

As the Cold War ended, strategic planners were at a loss. An enormous military establishment had been created to fight World War II and had essentially been maintained during the Cold War. After the Cold War no one wanted to completely get rid of it, but no one quite knew what to do with it, either. It had been reduced in size, but it remained a significant force in search of a mission that many argued no longer existed.

Many Americans think of the pre–World War II days as a relatively peaceful time during which the "military-industrial complex" wasn't a major social and economic reality. To a great extent that was true, but not as true as many observers think. In fact, throughout its history, the United States has spent a great deal of time at war and an even longer period of time preparing for war. In the twentieth century, the United States spent about nineteen years in war, not counting minor conflicts. If you take the Cold War as a period of war preparation ending in 1990, the total amount of time in war and war preparation rises to about fifty years. The United States spent half of the twentieth century fighting wars or preparing for them.

Looking at the United States from 1776 and the beginning of the Revolutionary War until today, the numbers are not very different. The U.S., throughout its history, was involved in major wars about 13 percent of the time. However, if you include the Indian Wars and the Cold War, the United States has been engaged in combat operations or intense preparation for combat operations 56 percent of the time. War and the preparation for war are neither abnormal for the United States nor a recent development.

As the Cold War ended and the Soviet Union collapsed, Americans believed, for no good reason whatsoever, that a fundamental break with the past had occurred, and that American history had shifted fundamentally. War was going to be a marginal exercise, and peace—with significant trade issues—was going to be the American condition, if not the human condition. If war was no longer a systemic threat, then the armed forces no longer served a strategic purpose. They might be useful, but they were no longer at the center of national security. Indeed, one of the arguments coming out of the Clinton administration was that an entirely new definition of national security was needed, where the traditional nexus of military and intelligence was complemented—if not substituted—by nontraditional considerations, ranging from human rights to trade.

The kinds of military threats the United States became focused on were rogue states, and the military and intelligence communities were ordered to change their focus to accommodate this new reality. The CIA was put under pressure to cut back its politico-military espionage and focus on economic intelligence. The U.S. military was ordered to shift its focus from high-intensity conflict and strategic warfare to low-intensity conflict and "operations other than war."

Contrary to expectations, the end of the Cold War actually increased the frequency of U.S. military operations. Even more important, these operations were all over the place both geographically and in size and scope. From Desert Storm, a multidivisional conventional war requiring the intense utilization of airpower, to smaller-scale operations in Haiti and Kosovo, to cruise missile strikes on Afghanistan, there was no single model for American warfare. The Pentagon wanted a finite set of warfighting models, but there simply weren't any.

There was, however, a single, unifying point in all of these operations. It was the fundamental belief of all planners that no crucial U.S. interest was ever involved in these conflicts. During the Cold War, the potential conquest of Europe by the Soviets or an unexpected nuclear attack by them was a fundamental danger to the United States. There was no way not to deal with it. All of the wars expected after 1990 were seen as secondary or tertiary threats. Secondary threats— Kuwait—were important but not life-threatening to the United States. Not intervening was an option and possibly a good one. Others were tertiary, without any real threat to the United States, like Haiti or Bosnia. It was the nonessentiality of war—the idea that war was an elective activity—that framed the post–Cold War period.

The Search for a Strategy

When Bill Clinton appointed Les Aspin, a congressman with a deep interest in defense matters, as Secretary of Defense in 1993, he was given the mission of defining U.S. military strategy after the Cold War. Clinton was not particularly interested in foreign affairs. His political motto was "It's the economy, stupid." For Clinton, foreign policy was about building international economic and trade institutions, like the World Trade Organization and the North American Free Trade Association (NAFTA). He believed that major military conflict was not a real issue, and that the military interventions under his administration would be isolated affairs, in the context of a coalition led by the United States, designed to stop misbehavior by local political leaders. In holding this view, Clinton was simply extending what had begun to develop in the Bush administration. Just as he maintained Bush's basic doctrines, so too Clinton continued the Bush policy toward Iraq and applied it to places like Haiti and Bosnia.

U.S. foreign policy under Bill Clinton was luxurious. The United States had no pressing needs and few significant threats. The collapse of the Soviet Union meant that the United States was the leading power in the world, invulnerable and invincible. Where Kennedy had to be concerned with Cuba or Berlin because they were inherently threatening, Clinton had no such threats. He could therefore indulge the American appetite for random acts of self-defined kindness. The result was a series of global interventions based less on strategy than on charity. Foreign policy was about doing good things to help deserving people. It was not about the ruthless pursuit of American interests in the world.

U.S. military planning was carried out on the assumption that wars were optional. They would not be forced on the United States by an enemy, nor would the United States ever be put in a position where it couldn't decline combat. As a result, U.S. war preparations did not have to go to extremes. If a potential conflict outstripped U.S. current capabilities, the U.S. always had the option not to go to war.

Les Aspin, understanding that the United States was going to cut back its forces substantially but was not going to cut back its military engagements overseas, had to define a strategic vision that would permit the President to invade a Haiti or a Kosovo at unpredictable intervals. But the U.S. also had to retain enough force to prevent the emergence of regional hegemons—significant second- and third-tier powers that coveted regional dominance and could, over time, become more serious challenges to American interests.

Aspin began a process called the Bottoms-Up Review, or BUR, whose task it was to rethink every aspect of U.S. military policy. Aspin, experienced neither in the military nor in the complex bureaucratic battles of the Pentagon (he was good at the congressional budgeting process), nevertheless had some significant insights. Indeed, he may have had those insights because of his lack of direct experience. Aspin and his team of analysts reached a set of conclusions that can be summarized this way:

1. The United States now had, as its primary interest, the maintenance of global stability as a basis for expanding global economic

prosperity. The mission of the United States military was to maintain global stability through interventions against smaller powers in the context of coalitions. The United States did not have to face any peer rival power—such as the former Soviet Union.

2. The United States, therefore, would have to continue projecting force all over the world—to unexpected places and at unanticipated times. The military force would have to be capable of doing this.

3. The biggest problem, underscored by Desert Storm, was that the U.S. military was so heavy, in every sense of the word, that it would take six months to build up a force capable of launching a substantial attack—much too long, unless the enemy cooperated (as Saddam did).

4. Therefore, the United States had to build a lighter, faster force with a greater emphasis on technology that would be able to deal with the variety of enemies that it would be confronting in the new world.

The military was deeply split on Aspin's vision. The Air Force loved it. Special Operations Command (SOCOM), which contained the covert warriors and special forces units, also loved it, since it increased the amount of technology that would be available to them, making them more lethal and more important. The Army, on the other hand, absolutely hated the results of the BUR. It had built its force around armor and helicopters, both of which took a long time to be deployed and required massive amounts of supplies to operate. The Army saw its role being cut back.

A vision started to emerge from the BUR. U.S. power projection would be built around two foundations: airpower and special operations forces. This was the framework that planners worked from as they mapped out their invasion of Afghanistan almost a decade after these plans were laid.

The Air Force was developing a new concept called Global Reach, a vision in which the Air Force could reach out and blow something up from bases in the United States, using long-range bombers. This would be a huge time-saver, since it wouldn't require the Air Force to first deploy tactical strike aircraft to the theater involved, and it wouldn't require the Navy to maintain carriers around the world or get to trouble spots at twenty-five knots. Global Reach was, as it turns out, a marketing brochure rather than a strategy, but it did place airpower at the center of everything, whether it came from the Air Force or the Navy.

In the meantime, Special Operations Command and the Army's own Special Forces were coming up with solutions for putting boots on the ground faster and more effectively than the conventional Army could. Special Operations saw their mission as delivering lethality quickly. They proposed to do this in three ways. First, their own forces—defined as "high speed, low drag"—could get into a hostile country quickly and execute precise covert operations. Second, Army Special Forces could get in, link up with indigenous forces sharing U.S. interests, and guide that force in battle. Finally—and this was where the Air Force and SOCOM fell in love—special operators could locate targets and call in air strikes against them, and could do so in days rather than months. Particularly in the smaller conflicts of the 1990s, SOCOM saw itself as fighting the war until the Army could get there to occupy the country.

A new model of warfare, resting on three legs, began to emerge. The heavy firepower would come not from artillery and tanks but from aircraft. Ground combat forces would be very light, very fast, and very technologically sophisticated—and organized by Special Operations Command, rather than the Army. Where major ground forces were needed, they could be recruited, trained, and led by the Army's Special Forces within the enemy nation. This would solve the crushing problem of bringing the heavy forces of the Army to the conflict.

This brought the planners to a very basic principle of U.S. warfare going back to the First World War: The United States does not fight alone. It fights with coalition partners, whether drawn from indigenous forces or from nation-states. The reason is demographic. The

U.S. is always outnumbered when fighting on the Eurasian landmass. Technology alone doesn't compensate. It needs allies at every level. The model of warfare envisaged by Aspin decreased the dependency on other nation-states by increasing dependency on indigenous forces. That moved Special Forces to the center of things, because it was their job to raise an indigenous force to do America's fighting.

The Special Forces were created in the 1950s with the mission of conducting guerrilla warfare behind Soviet lines in the event of a European war. It evolved during the Vietnam War into a force that could carry out irregular operations on its own or in conjunction with the Vietnamese or Laotian forces that it had trained. In the 1980s, the Army's Special Forces were integrated into the United States Special Operations Command (USSOC), which also managed the Navy's SEALs and the Air Force's Special Operations groups, Delta Force, and other uniformed special operations units. Needless to say, the Army was uncomfortable with its own Special Forces and hated USSOC.

But the Army's Special Forces were the key to the entire concept. They were built to move in before the main battle was joined, link up with friendly forces inside the country, deliver intelligence to the Air Force, and attack the enemy forces directly. From Aspin's point of view, they were the solution to the strategic problem of the United States. The fact that they could work and play well with the Central Intelligence Agency's Directorate of Operations field personnel served to increase their utility.

The role of the Army was to move in after the USSOC and the Air Force (and/or Navy carrier-based aircraft) had already wreaked havoc on the enemy, to mop up and occupy the country. In this new vision, the Army's combat role would begin at the tail end of the war, if all went well. It would wage the final battles with minimal casualties and garrison occupied territory while the Special Ops boys went on to greater glory. Naturally, Army tank commanders hated this vision of warfare with a passion. It was, however, the version of warfare the U.S. used in Desert Storm and Afghanistan.

Rumsfeld Takes Control

It should be noted that Donald Rumsfeld, before he became Secretary of Defense under the second Bush administration, did not really buy into the full strategic vision on which this new model of warfare was based. The geopolitical foundation of this theory was based on three assumptions:

1. The United States had no peer enemy and would not have one for a long time.
2. The primary mission of the United States would be asymmetric interventions—interventions against small, weak states or non-state players.
3. The United States would always have coalition partners inside and outside the adversary nation.

Rumsfeld didn't doubt that there would be many asymmetric interventions. However, he was not prepared to accept the idea that the United States was free of symmetrical challenges, from countries that could directly challenge U.S. forces with similar capabilities to their own. He was even less sanguine about the likelihood that the U.S would always be operating in an alliance. Therefore, Rumsfeld came up with the idea that the United States needed a force that could do all the things that Les Aspin wanted, but could also do more—and do it with less.

Rumsfeld came into office believing that a peer power would threaten the United States in the next twenty years, and he had a potential candidate: China. His first major decision as Secretary of Defense was to shift U.S. strategy from Europe, where it had been focused out of sheer habit since the fall of the Soviet Union, and refocus it on Asia. Rumsfeld's plans to refocus the U.S. on China led to serious tensions between the two countries prior to September 11, including the force-down of an EP-3 aircraft over the Chinese island of Hainan in the spring of 2001.

Rumsfeld mostly bought into the Aspin vision for technology. He had not, however, fully bought into the light model of land power, because he had not accepted all of the geopolitical premises of Aspin. He was certainly no fan of the Army. However, he was still searching for a force that could challenge China. Rumsfeld understood that the United States would be fighting rogue states and carrying out operations other than war. He simply did not perceive these operations as particularly difficult.

To be more precise, he did not want to build U.S. military strategy around low-intensity conflict. His reasoning appeared sound. Low-intensity conflicts in the Eastern Hemisphere would be frequent, but they would not, individually or as a whole, threaten the physical security of the United States. Nor could they ultimately affect fundamental national interests. The U.S. force could cope with these interventions regardless of how the force was structured. There was no need to optimize the force for a Haiti or a Bosnia.

Rumsfeld focused, instead, on two scenarios. One was the Iraqi invasion of Kuwait and the U.S. counterattack. The other was the development of another great power, most likely China, that could challenge the United States in a generation or two with full-spectrum warfare—the term used to describe the kind of war that was envisioned with the Soviet Union. These would be wars that would require a full range of capabilities, from extremely technical to counterinsurgency. Rumsfeld argued that the United States had to rapidly come up with solutions for dealing with situations like Iraq, while integrating these solutions with a long-term plan for coping with a great-power challenge such as China's.

The problem he had to solve was power projection, the same problem that Les Aspin had tried to wrestle to the ground. Essentially, the United States did not have a large enough standing force to preposition troops—or equipment—everywhere these resources might be needed. In addition, if forces were held in reserve in the continental United States—CONUS—the time it would take to send them into action in the Eastern Hemisphere would be so long that the crisis would likely be over by then.

Everyone recalled the miracle of Desert Shield, the operation that preceded Desert Storm. Saddam chose to halt in Kuwait, but had the Iraqis continued southward after taking Kuwait, they could have overrun the Saudi oil fields as well in a matter of days. The Saudi Army could not have stopped them. And the truth was that it took at least two months for the United States to send sufficient ground forces into Saudi Arabia to have a chance of stopping Saddam's forces. The counterattack turned out to be relatively easy compared to the nightmare possibilities of August and September 1990. Everyone knew—from the President of the United States to Saddam Hussein—that the U.S. could have done nothing to stop Saddam if he had chosen to move south. The U.S. had dodged a bullet.

The real problem for the United States was that its military was like a supertanker. It took a long time to stop it and an even longer time to turn it around. Building systems that would allow the U.S. to deploy forces more quickly would take years to bring on line. That was Rumsfeld's thinking when he took the oath of office as Secretary of Defense. He understood the core weakness of the U.S. armed forces and figured he would spend his time as Secretary of Defense nurturing systems that would solve the problem.

First, smaller forces needed to be available to land in any country, and they had to be extremely light. Second, these forces had to increase their lethality dramatically, by carrying much more effective lethal systems and being able to call on more lethal systems from in theater and from as far away as the United States. What if, for example, a request for an air strike by an army team in Kuwait could be satisfied directly from the continental United States? The U.S. Air Force had the ability to carry out air strikes anywhere in the world. Unfortunately, it took too long to get there and affect the tactical situation. But the time to target was not technically fixed, nor was the use of manned aircraft. What if a hypersonic system could be created that would deliver munitions to distant targets as quickly as in-theater aircraft or artillery could?

This is where Rumsfeld set his sights—on dealing with a peer superpower like the Chinese as well as coping with regional hegemons looking to expand their power. Most important, Rumsfeld mistakenly believed he had time to deal with these issues.

The Al Qaeda Wild Card

Rumsfeld hadn't counted on Al Qaeda, and American strategy in general was blindsided by September 11. It was a fixed idea in American thinking that nonstate organizations could not pose a strategic threat to a major state. They could pose a political problem—both domestically and globally—but they could not, by their own actions, force a strategic redefinition. The United States had observed nonstate actors through the 1970s and 1980s and had drawn the conclusion that (a) dealing with them was primarily an intelligence and security problem but not a military issue, and (b) no nonstate actor could compel a military response.

There were many scenarios in the defense and intelligence communities in which some group would poison the water supply or knock out power grids to major cities. These were not frivolous threats, but it was well known that they were much more difficult to execute than to imagine. Moreover, it was easier to recover from such attacks than might be expected. If the power grid went down, it would be up in a few hours and life would go on. As for poisoning the water supply, it would take a tremendous amount of poison to render significant damage. As for the superfantastic poisons in which one drop would kill an entire city, the secret was that anyone attempting to make or use them would probably be killed in the process.

The same applied to nuclear weapons. There was an urban myth that anyone could walk into a bazaar in Alma Ata and buy a small nuclear device. You certainly could buy something that was claimed to be a device, and it might even have some radioactive components.

But U.S. intelligence kept a pretty close watch on those bazaars and knew perfectly well that while someday something might show up, the chances of a nuclear weapon going unnoticed by some major intelligence agency were pretty slim. They knew that Muslim groups had been trying to buy such systems for a generation and had failed. The overriding sense was a degree of concern but not panic.

From the American point of view, groups like Al Qaeda were basically nuisances. They could cause a few dozen or even a few hundred deaths, but they could not materially affect the functioning of the United States. Indeed, the performance of Islamic fundamentalists since Desert Storm had not impressed the U.S. The first attack on the World Trade Center was a failure. The attacks on the U.S. embassies in Nairobi and Dar es Salaam were nasty but not strategically significant. Even the attack on the USS *Cole* in Yemen was unfortunate but did not strategically affect the mainland United States. The basic read of Al Qaeda was that it was more effective than most of the big-talking groups but not a major threat. Al Qaeda could not conduct nuclear, biological, or chemical warfare on any large scale, and therefore it could not really hit the United States in any meaningful way.

U.S. strategic planning continued on the path laid out by Les Aspin in 1993 and reinforced by Donald Rumsfeld in 2001. Peacekeeping operations were definitely expected. Operations other than war were debated and disliked by Rumsfeld—as were peacekeeping operations—but were part of the menu. Dealing with regional hegemons and great-power challenges was clearly on the main course. The U.S. defense establishment, however, certainly never imagined a challenge posed by a nonstate actor that would require a total reorientation in U.S. strategic policy.

The genius of Al Qaeda's attack on September 11 is simple to understand. It managed to pose a strategic threat to the United States without relying on exotic weapons systems. It did exactly what the U.S. expected of them—hijacking planes—and took it to a new level—suicide attacks. Those suicide attacks were on targets that were so strategic that the fundamental functioning of the United States was threatened. If those attacks continued and were expanded, the economic and political functioning of the United States would have been potentially crippled.

September 11 could neither be ignored nor dealt with through existing strategy. There was no current strategy in place for dealing with a nonstate group using conventional weapons. The United States had prepared scenarios for dealing with every conceivable threat, but it had no contingency plan for dealing with September 11. Even on December 7, 1941, War Plan Orange had gamed out a war with Japan. As of September 11, 2001, the U.S. was in unknown territory.

CHAPTER 6

September 11

IN WARFARE, success requires that strategy be combined with meticulous tactical planning and execution. September 11 was not only a strategic conception. It was also a carefully planned and superbly executed special operation. There is a tendency in the United States to dismiss Al Qaeda, arguing that anyone prepared to die could have carried out the operation. In fact, while the willingness to die was important, the professional planning and execution of the operation was the key to everything. Al Qaeda cannot be understood without understanding its mastery of the art of covert planning and operation. Understanding the operational complexity of September 11 provides a look into Al Qaeda's soul.

Osama bin Laden wanted to coax just the right response out of the United States by creating a situation in which the United States could not ignore him. His goal was to cross a threshold that Americans would deem intolerable (something bin Laden had failed to do with his previous attacks on the U.S. embassies in Africa or the USS *Cole* in Yemen), causing a massive attack to be launched on the Islamic world that used the most advanced and sophisticated methods available. Bin Laden was confident that if the U.S. plunged into the Islamic world, he would get the uprising he wanted. He had studied the Afghan war against the Soviets carefully. He felt he knew how to survive the initial American attack and, over time, defeat the Americans. But first, he needed the Americans to attack.

Commercial Airliners as Strategic Weapons

September 11 didn't initially register as a major scenario with U.S. intelligence, because it broke the paradigm that framed all thinking on terrorism—save that it used the classic terrorist instrument, commercial airliners.

Aircraft are essentially long tubes attached to giant explosives— jet-grade fuel. Commercial airliners and their passengers were once referred to as prepackaged hostages. They sit in a long, metal tube, strapped into seats without space to move, and when it is airborne, there are no usable exits. Normally there are only two or three people on board who know how to fly the plane, and if they are killed, everyone dies.

A small number of hijackers (as few as one) can take control of an aircraft and force it to go where they want, kill as many of the passengers as they want, and, if they are prepared to die themselves, kill everyone aboard. The passengers normally include women and children and are therefore highly sensitive politically. Factoring in that all those passengers have families on the ground, a hijacker can create extraordinary political chaos. Aircraft hijackings are the easiest way to kidnap hundreds of innocent people. And, on an international level, the threat to hostages frequently generates demands for capitulation on key issues, drawing public attention to hijacker grievances. Hijackings create situations in which very powerful states are rendered temporarily helpless by normally weak players.

All sides in the terrorism game have spent decades studying the hijacking problem. Hijackers have focused on the issue of organizing without being detected, getting on board an aircraft with weapons, seizing and controlling the aircraft, and managing the political process of the post-hijacking negotiations. Counterterrorism experts have focused on the issues of penetrating terrorist groups, screening passengers for weapons, retaking hijacked aircraft with minimal loss of life among the passengers, and, like the terrorists, managing the negotiations. From the first hijacking of planes to Cuba in the 1960s, to the events of September 11, the hijacking of aircraft has been professionalized on both sides.

Al Qaeda had carefully studied the Palestinian movement. It understood the function of airline hijackings and their limits. It understood that kidnapping a few hundred people had its uses, but also that a hijacking—or a string of hijackings—would not generate the response that was needed from the United States. Hijackings were irritating and troublesome, but they did not represent a strategic threat. The U.S. was not going to change its Middle East policy over hijackings. Threatening the lives of a few hundred people wasn't going to get Al Qaeda what it wanted.

However, Al Qaeda looked at commercial aircraft in a totally novel way—not as prepackaged hostages but as enormous explosive devices. A large commercial jet, carrying fuel for long distances, is a flying bomb, guaranteed to explode on impact. Moreover, it can cause extraordinary secondary damage as the remaining fuel burns at extremely high temperatures until consumed.

The reason that no one had looked at commercial aircraft this way before was the guidance problem. An aircraft requires a pilot to take off and hit a particular target. As the Japanese realized late in World War II, an aircraft can be a useful weapon if the pilot is prepared to go to his certain death. Pilots prepared to do that are rare.

This was Al Qaeda's breakthrough and insight. Al Qaeda had people who were prepared to die. As a religious rather than a secular group, Al Qaeda sincerely believes that physical death, properly undertaken, is the entry into eternal life. Given the sincerity of belief, it is possible to find men who are prepared, not to risk their lives, but to go to their certain deaths. With that single innovation, Al Qaeda could turn an aircraft into a devastating, offensive weapon. More important, they could carry out attacks that would transcend by sheer magnitude any prior terrorist attack and force the United States to respond. Al Qaeda could effectively set in motion the process it wanted.

Planning the Seizure

Al Qaeda, a group that lacked an air force, realized it could carry out air attacks on the American homeland using precision-guided munitions. To carry out the operations, a number of steps were necessary: assembling and training the team, penetrating airport security, seizing control of the aircraft, and flying the aircraft into the target. The size of the immediate assault team was determined by the nature of the aircraft. There had to be at least one person trained to fly the aircraft. There had to be enough people to take control of the aircraft and defend the Al Qaeda pilot from passengers during the final attack phase.

Commercial aircraft have a pilot and copilot on domestic flights. To take control of the flight (without a warning being transmitted), both pilots need to be killed or disabled with near simultaneity and without warning. This means that the cockpit must be penetrated before flight attendants or other passengers can spread a warning. The problem, owing to the narrowness of the doorway into the cockpit, is that two people cannot easily enter simultaneously. Thus, the attackers must either have a weapon that disables very quickly, or two men must maneuver into the cockpit.

Two sets of skills were needed to carry out the mission effectively. Someone had to know how to fly the plane (ideally, two people would have that skill, so the death or injury of one pilot would not abort the mission). Second, all involved had to be trained to kill very quickly, and with weapons that would have a high probability of getting on board a plane. So for each aircraft that was to be seized, five people would have to be deployed into the United States prior to the operation.

The attack sequence requires that the hijackers be as close to the front of the aircraft as possible, minimizing warning time and potential interference from the passengers. The flight attendants in front of the aircraft must be killed very quickly, along with any resistant passengers in first class. The other passengers must be quickly herded back into the main cabin, while a blocking team takes position near the entry to first class. At that point, the assault on the cockpit begins. Once that is successful and the aircraft is being flown by members of the assault team, the rest of the team must concentrate on preventing passengers from mounting an attack on the hijackers.

There were two competing requirements. On one hand, it was best to hijack the largest plane possible, since that would carry the most fuel and create the greatest explosion. On the other hand, the larger the plane, the more passengers there might be—and the more difficult it would be to control them. The ideal situation would be a large airliner with few passengers, which is not easy to find and even less easy to plan for.

There was an intersecting requirement. Different planes have different controls. There are at least seven types of aircraft flying transcontinental routes. On the transcontinental runs, an extremely common type were 757s and 767s. Luckily for Al Qaeda, these aircraft were not only common but also were identically rated. In other words, if you were trained to fly one, you could fly both, thus substantially increasing the number of flights that would be available for hijacking.

It also created a problem. The Boeing 757 is a narrow-body, single-aisle aircraft. The 767 is a wide-bodied, double-aisle aircraft that requires more hijackers to control. There are two aisles in which counterattackers could advance, along with movement over the seats on three axes. If only 757s were seized, smaller teams were possible. The 767, however, was larger and more common on transcontinental runs and packed a bigger punch. Since it was impossible to know what aircraft would be available when planning for the operation began, Al Qaeda trained on the 757/767 family of aircraft exclusively.

The various requirements dictated the size of the team, with an optimal number being five people. The pilot could serve as part of the assault team but could not be risked excessively, as the operation would fail entirely without him. There were three possible scenarios for seizing the plane:

1. Bursting into the cockpit, killing the pilots, and replacing them with hijackers.
2. Bursting into the cockpit and inducing the pilots to vacate their seats by making them think that this was a normal hijacking. Pilots were under orders to cooperate with hijackers (suicide pilots were not considered a factor).
3. Using attendants or passengers as hostages to force the pilots out of the cockpit.

Deploying and Preparing

Al Qaeda faced the problem of pilot training. There are not many facilities around the world that offer training in flying commercial aircraft—and the trainees could not afford to be noticed. Outside of the U.S., where many of the airline training facilities are government owned, purchasing pilot training would quickly come to the notice of government officials simply because self-motivated trainees are rare. In other words, ambitious young men in Pakistan do not simply go and write a check for training in a Boeing 757 without calling attention to themselves.

This does happen in the United States, and it happens frequently enough not to be noteworthy. In fact, a fairly significant number of those purchasing pilot training are foreigners. Some training was obtained in Malaysia, but Al Qaeda determined early in their planning that the most secure way of obtaining flight training for their operatives was to do it inside the United States. It was evident, then, that the operation inside the United States would be enormously complex and would have to begin well in advance of the actual attack (which greatly increased the risk of discovery). The operatives had to penetrate the United States, receive needed financial support—as well as documents and other material—receive their training, receive their orders, and assemble to execute those orders. And they had to do all of this without being detected. This was the hard part.

An extended covert operation inside enemy territory is risky under even the best of circumstances. This operation was made all the more difficult in that American intelligence and security services had designated Al Qaeda a top-priority target. U.S. intelligence knew enough about Al Qaeda that Al Qaeda could not be certain which of their operatives were blown and which were unknown. This meant that each person added to the operation increased the probability of detection.

There was another challenge as well—Al Qaeda had to send operatives capable of getting through flight school. Two things were needed for this. First, the student had to have a fairly good mastery of the English language. Second, the student had to have enough education to be able to master the complexities of the system.

These requirements excluded most of the people Al Qaeda had trained. Mastery of English alone screened out many operatives. Illiterate peasants, no matter how well motivated, could not constitute the bulk of the operational staff. The pilots had to be both multilingual and fairly well educated, which increased the likelihood that they would be known to the CIA and FBI, because it was precisely these people who were the most visible.

The problem was not only the detection of the operatives. The extended deployment of Al Qaeda personnel meant that they would periodically have to be "touched" in order to sustain them. They would need to get money, documents, and orders. There was another well-known factor in covert operations: They had to have their temperatures taken.

The psychological pressure on an operative deployed covertly is enormous. He is operating in a dangerous environment, always afraid of betrayal and discovery. He works under false identities, and very often the pressure is enough to make him crack. The process of adapting to new identities sometimes causes operatives to "go native"—go over to the other side psychologically and, at times, even operationally. Moreover, if an operative is captured, his captors are going to do everything they can to turn him. During World War II, the entire German espionage network in Great Britain had been turned, unbeknownst to German intelligence.

The bottom line is that operatives cannot be left in the field without periodically taking their temperature. This is not done by e-mail or telephone—in fact, both methods are not only ineffective but dangerous. Therefore, field personnel either have to be visited by their controllers or extracted to a safe haven for R&R—and careful inspection. Moving Al Qaeda personnel to the United States to receive pilot training solved the training problem but increased the security problem. There would have to be periodic movement of Al Qaeda personnel in and out of the United States. Many of the strange movements that were reported concerning Al Qaeda personnel undoubtedly had more to do with taking their temperatures than any other cause.

One solution to this problem was to have operatives living together, maintaining one another's morale and keeping an eye on one another. But having large numbers of operatives living together in enemy territory is bound to draw attention. Also, this violates another principle of covert operations—don't put all your eggs in one basket. With everyone living together, a single breach of security would not only compromise the entire operation, it would neutralize all of the operatives permanently. They therefore were separated into smaller groups.

By dispersing them in small groups for the duration of pre-operational deployment, Al Qaeda still had the difficult problem of managing them. Although these were clearly high-morale units, self-motivated and unlikely to go rogue, they still needed to be touched periodically. If, on the other hand, each team was served by a dedicated two-man team, it would increase those with a need-to-know of the general operation by 40 percent. As a result, for each five-man team, at least two others had to know their identities. If a single two-man team moved around touching all teams, that two-man team was the weak link that could destroy the entire operation.

Size is the perennial problem of covert operations. More is better from an efficiency standpoint, but fewer is better from a security standpoint. All of this posed a particular problem for Al Qaeda, whose advantage is stealth. The smaller Al Qaeda is, the more secure it is, as it has a smaller probability of betrayal. There is a second, equally important factor: The fewer recruits Al Qaeda takes in, the more secure it is, as there will be a lower probability of penetration by enemy intelligence services. Therefore, Al Qaeda must not only be small, but it cannot increase the size of its core operating units quickly. Indeed, from a security standpoint, it shouldn't increase its size at all. Moreover, Al Qaeda's personnel were a wasting asset. They tended to be used up when conducting a suicide mission and, given security constraints, were difficult to replace.

The reality was that each aircraft required five men, with four as a minimum. Each man had to be deployed to the United States, housed and fed, trained where needed, financed, and finally ordered into action. In addition, each cell needed to include at least one and probably two men (in case something happened to one of them) who knew about the team and probably something about their mission, in order to provide support. That meant seven men per aircraft with some knowledge of the mission. Also, there had to be a support team who didn't know about the mission but did know at least something about what was going on. That means that for each aircraft involved, seven would be directly involved, and another three would have some supporting role.

If the two-man support team were to service all deployed units, then a security breach in the support team would compromise the entire operation. It would become the weak link. Therefore, using a dedicated support team for each attack team is more secure, in spite of the fact that it increases the number involved in the operation. An additional general support team of three or more, handling finance, documents, housing, liaison, and so on, could support more than one attack unit with less risk. So, with four attack teams, there would be at least another eleven men—in the United States alone—and probably more. That did not include links in Europe back to Al Qaeda itself. Supporting covert operations can create a rapidly growing network.

Intelligence shows that there were thoughts given initially to a massive day of terror, in which up to ten aircraft would be hijacked.

That was an obvious impossibility, as it would require the involvement of approximately one hundred operatives and support personnel. No conspiracy with that many people involved could have survived undetected for as long as was necessary to conduct the training and acclimate the teams to their environments—even if suitable personnel were available, which is a dubious assumption. The operation clearly had to be limited to a manageable number of people.

Selecting the Aircraft

Another factor entered into the equation—the peculiar structure of the U.S. air transport system. The aircraft used would have to be loaded with aviation fuel, so they had to be at the beginning of their trips. It also meant the aircraft would have to be going the longest possible distance in order to have the greatest fuel load. Since aircraft traveling on over-ocean trips receive special scrutiny and require passports for boarding, intercontinental aircraft were out of the question. That meant that transcontinental aircraft would have to be used.

This generated an inescapable conclusion. Any attack had to involve East Coast targets—Washington and New York could not be left out of the attack—so the aircraft chosen must take off from East Coast cities. Transcontinental flights take off from Boston, New York, Philadelphia, and Washington airports. Other eastern cities reach the West Coast through airline hub cities like Houston.

There was a second limiting factor. The attacks had to be carried out with near simultaneity. A single hijacking would be noted by the air traffic controllers and immediately passed on to all pilots. These pilots might or might not increase their alertness, but two hijackings noted by air traffic control would galvanize the system. Everyone would become extremely alert. The weapons that the operatives used were effective but ultimately could be defended against. If the pilots realized that a hijacking wave was under way, and certainly if they realized that a wave of suicide attacks was under way, they might be able to resist the hijackers. Therefore, the hijackings needed to take place nearly at the same time, the impacts ought to occur nearly at the same time, and, if possible, air traffic control should not know that hijackings were under way until as late as possible.

Aircraft targeting New York and Washington would have to take off from one of the four northeastern cities. Transcontinental flights begin departing at about 6:30 A.M., but the airports are not very crowded then. The bulk of flights to the West Coast start taking off at about 8 A.M., which is also when airports are jammed and security is the weakest. Also, the goal was clearly to cause the maximum number of casualties possible, and most offices in the United States become fully staffed between 8:30 and 9:00 A.M., particularly in the financial sector.

This meant that selected aircraft should take off no earlier than 8 A.M. Also, the aircraft could not be hijacked until it had reached a cruising altitude. Assaulting the cockpit on a severe up-angle would increase the difficulty unnecessarily. It was also necessary for the aircraft to be as stable as possible and out of the control of the airport tower in order to minimize the chance of sudden instructions from the tower—and early detection of the hijack. In other words, the hijackers needed about fifteen minutes of flight before beginning aircraft seizure. To seize aircraft taking off at 8 A.M. meant boarding by 7:45 and passing through security at about 7:30—a time when airports in the Northeast are particularly crowded with passengers. This fit in with the other variables and set the time frame of the assault.

There was another variable—air traffic control delays caused by weather. The U.S. air traffic control system revolves around hubs, many located in a band down the center of the United States. As the day goes on, some of these cities are likely to experience delays caused by weather or mechanical problems on the ground. These delays back up traffic throughout the system, sometimes causing ground delays. The ground delays affect not only aircraft heading to those hub cities but other aircraft lining up behind them.

The situation can become a mess, and the later in the day you travel, the more likely you are to encounter delays—having already started, they can persist for hours, particularly during weekdays. It was necessary to disperse the attack teams through multiple airports—Boston's Logan Airport was the only one used by two teams—in order to minimize the chance that all four teams would be knocked out. The likelihood that one of the airports would experience delays later in the day was substantial. That meant that putting off the attacks until later in the day in order to coordinate with West Coast operations risked having some of the teams trapped on runways in the East, which was clearly unacceptable.

All of this came together logically. The attack had to take place early in the day but not before the workday began. It had to occur when violent weather was at a minimum. It had to be confined to the Northeast corridor. It had to be a weekday that had no unusual characteristics that might trigger security alerts. That meant an attack in late summer or early fall, on an ordinary weekday morning.

It was critical that the attacks be as closely coordinated as possible. Five men (or four in one case) could not control the passengers on an aircraft who knew they were going to die. Three or four operatives, no matter how well armed, could not resist an assault by determined passengers. The best that would happen, from the hijacker's point of view, would be crashing the plane ineffectively. The worst would be losing control of the aircraft altogether. Moreover, seizing a plane from an alerted crew would be much more difficult than taking it from an unaware crew.

An advantage that the hijackers had was that hijackings are well understood in popular culture. While dangerous, the best course is to cooperate with the hijackers, not offer resistance, and allow authorities on the ground either to negotiate release or assault the aircraft once landed. Given that perception, the probability of resistance was low—as long as the passengers were unaware that this was not a traditional hijacking.

The last challenge would be the times when aircraft hit their targets—which had to be bunched as closely as possible. The hijackers were aware that with cell phones and onboard telephones it was possible for passengers to hear news from outside the aircraft. That meant that once the first target was struck, passengers in other aircraft might know that this was no ordinary hijacking and shift their behavior from passive to aggressive. In addition, in order to maximize uncertainty, ground contact—including transponders—would have to be shut off. It followed from all of this that the period between the seizure of the aircraft and impact would have to be as short as possible. It also meant that there had to be an abort code, if one or more of the teams were compromised, using cell phones. That is why teams notified one another as they took off, as later cell phone records indicate.

What the hijackers could not control was the actual time of take-off. While they purchased their tickets in late August using credit cards, they were choosing a period where air traffic delays due to weather were at a minimum statistically. There was a hurricane out in the Atlantic and some bad weather over the Northwest, but the North-east was crystal clear and had been forecast to be that way for days.

Four planes were selected for hijacking. American Airlines Flight 11 was a 767 out of Logan International Airport in Boston heading for Los Angeles. United Flight 175, also out of Logan and also a 767, was headed for Los Angeles as well. American Airlines Flight 77 out of Dulles was a 757 headed for Los Angeles. United Airlines Flight 93 out of Newark was a 757 headed for San Francisco. All were heading for the West Coast. All were 757/767s. And all shared another char-acteristic: They had relatively few passengers. All four aircraft could carry more than 200 passengers. American 11 had 92 passengers, United 175 had 65; American 77 had 64 on board; United 93 had only 44. It is interesting to note that with online ticketing services, it is possible, while purchasing tickets, to select a seat. It is therefore possible to see how heavily booked a particular flight is.

The Assault

The planes were all supposed to take off at about the same time, shortly after 8 A.M. Three of them took off within 17 minutes of one another: American 11 at 8:02; United 175 at 8:16; American 77 at 8:19. United 93 was delayed in taking off from Newark and didn't get off the ground until 8:43, just three minutes before American 11 hit the south tower of the World Trade Center. United 93 was also the only aircraft with only four hijackers on board.

The hijackers waited until the aircraft was at or near cruising altitude. Aboard American 11, Mohamed Atta, an Egyptian who served as pilot, was in command of the team. As his plane started its takeoff roll, he called Marwan al-Shehhi, from the United Emirates, to tell him the operation was a go. Also on board American 11 were the Saudi Arabians Abdulaziz Alomari, Wail Alshehri, Waleed Alshehri, and Satam al-Suqami from the United Arab Emirates.

Fourteen minutes later, United 175 took off, commanded by al-Shehhi and four Saudis: Fayez Ahmed, Ahmed Alghamdi, Hamza Alghamdi, and Mohand Alshehri. At about the same time, American 11 approached cruising altitude and the assault by Atta's team was under way. Four minutes after United 175 took off, at 8:20, American 11 was under the control of the hijackers, which we know because its transponder was switched off. One minute before that happened, American 77 took off from Dulles. This was an all-Saudi team commanded by Hani Hanjour. Under his command were Khalid al-Midhar, Nawak Alhazmi, Majed Moqed, and Salem Alhazmi.

American 77 behaved differently than the first two flights. American 11 was seized by 8:20, turned south toward New York, and crashed into the World Trade Center at 8:46, an elapsed time from takeoff of 44 minutes. United 175 hit the north tower of the World Trade Center at 9:02, elapsed time of 46 minutes. American 77 took off from Dulles at 8:19. Its transponder did not go off until 9:09, and it took an additional 26 minutes to hit the Pentagon at 9:35. Its passengers clearly knew—from cell phone calls—that this was no ordinary hijacking but apparently didn't organize an assault on the cockpit. By then, it was only a few minutes ahead of F-16 fighters out of Langley Air Force Base that were streaking northward at supersonic speeds.

United 93 went completely awry from the hijackers' point of view. Commanded by a Lebanese named Ziad Jarrahi, it had only three Saudi operatives: Ahmed Alhaznawi, Ahmed Alnami, and Saeed Alghamdi. Delayed on the ground about 45 minutes after scheduled takeoff, the hijackers waited until after breakfast was served to start their assault. The first intrusion did not take place until 9:30, 47 minutes after takeoff and after both attacks on the World Trade Center were complete. The pilots were alerted about cockpit intrusions by ground control and probably knew other details from listening to pilot chatter. It took a full ten minutes to take control of the plane, switch off the transponder, and turn the aircraft. At this point, the passengers, who were fully aware of what was going on because of cell phones and seat phones, organized an attempt to retake the plane. It crashed at 10:03, ending the day's assault.

Mysteries

There are any number of things that are unknown and ultimately unknowable. One team traveled to Maine by car, then boarded an aircraft bound for Boston. Perhaps they were meeting with liaisons there. Perhaps they felt that by not having two teams pass into Logan Airport the same way it would increase the chances of success. It is just unknown.

It is also not clear what weapons were used. It has always been assumed that box cutters were the only weapon the hijackers used, but that has not been proved. They may well have had other weapons— although probably not guns—in addition. The hijackers nearly had a fight over a parking space in the parking garage at Logan Airport. Was this simply a case of nerves, poor judgment, or a deliberate attempt to draw attention to the car, which was loaded with suggestive intelligence, most of which pointed nowhere and wasted a huge amount of investigative resources?

The unknowns are ultimately not important. What is important is to note the sophistication and planning involved in the attack, and the accuracy of Al Qaeda in forecasting the American response. On September 11, the United States went to war, which is precisely what Al Qaeda wanted, and which the United States, under the circumstances, could not have avoided.

CHAPTER 7

Defending the Homeland: Crisis and Irrelevance

WHEN IT FINALLY BECAME CLEAR that the plane crash in Pennsylvania on the morning of September 11 marked the end of this wave of attacks, all thoughts within the National Command Authority turned to a single question: What next? From the beginning, the assumption was that the attack had been carried out by Al Qaeda. The United States had been dealing with Al Qaeda for years and knew there was no other terrorist group with the capabilities and ambition to carry out an operation like September 11. Thus, from the beginning, the "who" was assumed; it was the "what next" that frightened everyone.

The attacks of September 11 were of a magnitude never before seen, and the immediate fear was that the tempo of Al Qaeda operations would be stepped up as well. The intelligence and security agencies of the United States were ordered to present their assessment of the threat. The answer that came back boiled down to this: "We do not know the extent of Al Qaeda's capabilities in the United States, but we have reason to believe that there are additional cells deployed in the United States and no reason to doubt their capabilities."

With even the limited information available, it is clear that the operatives planned the operation meticulously. They thought through all of the variables and, while unable to control all of them, were careful to control as many as possible. They sized the operation carefully, to achieve a balance between effectiveness and security, and they timed the operation carefully, increasing the probability of maximum damage. They were both patient and cautious, key characteristics of covert operations. The operation was carried out by disciplined and capable men, able to analyze the situation carefully and execute based on that analysis. And that was the real problem for the United States.

The President and his advisors now had to come up with a plan for defending the homeland from another September 11–type attack. The immediate response—grounding the American civilian air traffic fleet—could not be continued indefinitely, nor was it a real solution. Aircraft were only one way to attack the United States. The fear haunting everyone was that Al Qaeda had acquired nuclear weapons—or, at the very least, chemical and biological weapons. The anthrax attacks that followed September 11 increased the already deep fear and suspicion regardless of their origin: The United States was facing a sophisticated enemy with substantial resources. Worst of all, it was an enemy about which the United States did not really know very much.

The United States was not prepared for a covert war on its own soil. It had neither the intelligence nor covert operations capabilities to carry this out. Neither did it have a legal system that would facilitate it. There was no domestic intelligence organization. The Central Intelligence Agency was barred by law from conducting intelligence operations in the United States, and it had been fairly scrupulous in following that law since the 1970s. The FBI was not really an intelligence organization. FBI agents were focused on solving crimes that had already happened, not on forecasting the future.

As a result, there was no one who could give a definitive answer to the question "what next?" In fact, there was no one who could give even a general answer. What was known about Al Qaeda in the United States was contained in the files of individual FBI agents and in the regional offices. No one had systematically compiled what little intelligence there was. September 11 was off of everyone's road map.

Just as the public was shocked, so too was the National Command Authority. The situation was worse than on December 7, 1941. In that case, there was some understanding of the enemy's intentions and capabilities. Here there was none. Nor did the FBI and CIA have any reason to think they would develop intelligence in the coming days or weeks that would solve the problem. The U.S. was flying blind.

As a fallback position, the U.S. resurrected the warfighting plans that had existed during the Cold War. In a sense, there was a similarity. Assuming the worst-case scenario—as was necessary—the danger was that Al Qaeda would launch an unconventional (nuclear, biological, or chemical) attack on the United States. Washington had worried about such attacks constantly during the Cold War, and they had contingency plans for dealing with them. It didn't matter whether the weapons were delivered by missiles or Ryder trucks. The effect was the same.

Therefore, the focus on the afternoon of September 11 was on the survival of the government. As soon as the planes began hitting their targets, the President was moved around the country according to preset plans for nuclear war, following a predetermined path that led eventually to Omaha, Nebraska. That was no accident. Omaha was the location of Offutt Air Force Base, and Offutt was the headquarters of what used to be called the Strategic Air Command, now called Strategic Command. Offutt had a hardened command center from which nuclear war was to be waged. It was the place the President should be—not in Washington, nor in the command aircraft popularly called Looking Glass. In the old nuclear war plans, the goal was to get the President to Offutt, where he could take direct control of SAC. It was always assumed that the President wouldn't be able to get to Offutt in the event of a Soviet first strike, but that's where he was supposed to go, and on September 11, that is where he went.

The rest of the government went through its dispersal procedures. Scattered around the Virginia, West Virginia, Maryland, and Pennsylvania countryside are backup command-and-control centers where the senior leadership of the government, military, and intelligence organizations, along with key support staff, are supposed to go in the event of war. To be more precise, the government is supposed to split.

One part is supposed to remain in Washington, while a small subset relocates to these dispersed, hardened sites. As the President returned to Washington on the evening of September 11, the government executed its dispersal plan—with the disappearance of Vice President Dick Cheney symbolizing the dramatic relocation of the leadership.

By Tuesday night, the government was in a position to survive a direct attack on Washington. Now it was necessary to devise a plan to defend the rest of the United States against an enemy that could not be identified, about whom minimal intelligence was available, and whose intentions were utterly unknown. The simplest solution—to find and kill members of Al Qaeda—was easier said than done. Its senior leadership was in Afghanistan. Its operational layers—commanders, financial support, and so on—seemed to be somewhere in Europe. Its operatives in the U.S. could be everywhere, somewhere, or nowhere. Killing Al Qaeda was not an option on September 11. Instead, the government's full attention had to be shifted to something Americans were not used to hearing: defending the homeland.

Homeland Defense, the Soviet Union, and McCarthyism

In warfare, the concept of defending the homeland is tinged with defeat. The point of warfare is to make the other side defend its homeland. A purely defensive posture gives the attacker tremendous advantages. He can choose where and when he will attack. Above all, he can hide his intentions, retaining the most important element in warfare: the element of surprise. The defender will be attacked at the most vulnerable time and place. The defender will lose unless he is able to absorb the first attack and then shift to the offensive.

The United States has historically had little conventional experience with defending the homeland. The last major foreign invasion of the United States took place during the War of 1812, when the British occupied Washington and attacked New Orleans. In the modern era, foreign threats to the homeland have been scarce.

This does not mean the United States was not afraid of threats to the homeland. To the contrary, the twentieth century was filled with exaggerated fears of attack. During World War I, there were indications that Mexico might ally with Germany and invade the United States. After World War I, the United States developed a scenario called War Plan Red that was intended to counter a British invasion of the U.S. Before and during World War II, the United States had an irrational fear that the Japanese intended—and were able—to attack and occupy the West Coast. There were fantasies of a German fifth column serving as a spearhead for a German invasion. None of these threats materialized, and in fact, it is noteworthy that no serious plans were ever made for dealing with the threats.

The primary reference point for America's serious concern for homeland defense was the Cold War and the threat posed by the Soviet Union. It is reasonable to say that the threat and fear of nuclear war—and the potential annihilation of the United States or even the world—defined the American psyche from the time the Soviets exploded their first atomic bomb to the end of the Cold War. There was deep-seated understanding during the Cold War that the American homeland was not only vulnerable but that it constituted the front line of nuclear war.

The mind-set of the Cold War is relevant here since during those years the American public learned to live with the understanding that their lives were in the hands of a small group of men—both Soviet and American—whose political and military calculations could lead to both personal and national catastrophes. Several generations of Americans had grown up and lived with a sense of vulnerability to nuclear war and of a threat to the homeland.

It was understood that nothing could stop an intercontinental ballistic missile—no defense was possible, at least not until it was claimed a missile defense was possible under Ronald Reagan. What was possible was deterrence. The Soviets would not strike if they knew that the consequence would be their own annihilation. Mutual Assured Destruction—an offense substituting for a defense—became the foundation of national and personal security. The American treasury was opened wide for any plan that would guarantee that the American nuclear force would survive a Soviet first strike. What made the Cold War bearable was the understanding that the leadership of both countries was rational, and that neither side would risk its own annihilation.

It was not the threat to the homeland that stunned the American public on September 11, but the fact that the attackers came out of nowhere and could not be deterred. Death was not an unacceptable outcome for Al Qaeda. In fact, they seemed to welcome it. Moreover, there was no Moscow and no Kremlin. There was no seat of power, no decision makers on the other side to negotiate with or even to threaten. What made Al Qaeda so frightening is that it appeared to be both implacable and beyond negotiation.

There was also the potent fear that the enemy was already here among us. The idea that the attackers had lived and trained in the United States was startling, not only because it demonstrated American vulnerability but also because there was every reason to believe that there were other cells of Al Qaeda operatives already in place in the United States. "Sleeper cell" went from being a term of espionage novels to an ominous term used in everyday life. The immediate questions after September 11 were simple: How many operatives were in the U.S., what were their plans, and when would they strike next?

The problem of homeland defense presented itself in these terms—finding the sleeper cells and preventing other Al Qaeda members from entering the country. It posed a problem that the United States was ill-suited to deal with. The U.S. already had experience in dealing with the possibility that covert Soviet operatives had penetrated the United States during the Cold War and had handled it so poorly that it traumatized an entire generation and caused U.S. intelligence and security services to shy away from anything that reminded them of that period. The ultimate legacy of Joseph McCarthy is that he left the United States institutionally and intellectually incapable of coming to grips with Al Qaeda on a domestic level without reviving a deep national nightmare.

In order to grasp the full complexities facing the government regarding homeland defense, it is necessary to examine the impact a very different era—the 1950s—had on the ability of the United States to deal with Al Qaeda. This period in American history was dominated by McCarthyism, which defined what was impermissible in dealing with conspiracies. McCarthy became the negative standard against which all counterconspiratorial actions were judged. Al Qaeda was certainly a conspiracy. Fighting Al Qaeda became hopelessly entangled in the collective memory of McCarthyite excesses.

The Soviet Union, like any great power, conducted extensive espionage against all powers—enemy, allied, and neutral. Its espionage efforts differed somewhat from those of other countries because it had an organized apparatus of individuals to draw on—the Leninist parties that were organized after World War I. The existence of these Communist parties gave Soviet espionage two dimensions where most countries had only one. First, it conducted conventional political, economic, and military espionage for straightforward national security reasons. Second, the wide network of Communist parties allowed the Soviets to wage a much more public campaign for revolution in the countries in which they were working.

There was an inherent incompatibility in these two goals. The essence of national espionage is utter secrecy. The essence of revolution is publicity. The contradiction in Soviet goals created conceptual chaos on both sides. The Soviets recruited agents, particularly in the pre–World War II period, whose primary goal was to participate in a political revolution. They engaged in espionage against the United States in order to strengthen the Soviet Union, thereby increasing the likelihood of global revolution and revolution in the United States. In the 1940s and '50s, however, Joseph Stalin had little faith in a revolution in the United States. He regarded the Communist Party of the United States as a propaganda tool and as a recruiting ground for espionage agents. This created massive confusion among Communists as to whether their primary goal was revolution in the United States or serving the state interests of the Soviet Union.

This confusion was compounded on the American side. The U.S. was conceptually trapped between two principles. On one side was the constitutional right to dissent. On the other side was the constitutional prohibition against treason. This was compounded to some extent by the issue of whether calling for a violent revolution constituted treason—an issue made moot to some extent by the fact that everyone knew that talking about revolution was simply hot air. The real issue was that believing in communism—even Stalin's communism—was a constitutional right. Engaging in espionage was not.

Not all Communists were engaged in espionage, even if all of them, as a matter of moral principle, were engaged in subversion. Nor were all of the Soviet Union's espionage agents Communists, secret or otherwise—although prior to the collapse of the Communist Party in the mid-1950s, a majority of them had begun their espionage careers as Party members. The overlap was not trivial.

It posed a massive dilemma for the United States, which was engaged in a dangerous confrontation with the Soviet Union. The Soviets had constructed a substantial network of espionage agents in the United States. In the event of war, which seemed quite likely, many of them would be ordered to engage in covert operations within the United States. The U.S. government had a constitutional obligation to destroy this espionage network, even though it had a great deal of difficulty distinguishing between the espionage network and the legal Communist Party. The difficulty was compounded by the Soviet strategy of having members of the Party who were espionage agents cut all ties with it and, if possible, completely hide any past connection to the Party.

What was required was a surgical tool to distinguish between members of the Communist Party who were simply engaged in political agitation from members who were agents of the Soviet Union. Another tool was needed to distinguish between former members who simply changed their mind about communism and former members who had been ordered to go covert. Unfortunately, no such tools existed.

What happened instead was pure chaos, the issue being seized upon by political opportunists on both sides. On one side, the difficulty of distinguishing between those who were political advocates and those who were engaged in espionage was solved by arguing that anyone who had ever been linked to the Communist Party had to be destroyed. On the other side, the espionage issue was treated as a complete fabrication being used to justify the suppression of the American left and the destruction of civil liberties. The search for espionage agents among those who had joined the Party in the 1930s and then left was treated as a witch hunt.

Both sides conspired to create an intellectual, moral, and security circus. Joseph McCarthy, J. Edgar Hoover, founder of the FBI, and their allies used the search for Soviet agents to increase their own political power, and by the time both sides were done, there was no institution with enough moral legitimacy to systematically protect against espionage. By the time it was done the FBI and CIA were allowed to hunt for infiltrators in their own ranks, but accusing a congressional aide or State Department official or anyone else of being part of the Communist conspiracy was not something that could be done without severe political repercussions. Because of McCarthyism, the U.S. became increasingly incapable in dealing with deliberate covert conspiracies that arose in subsequent decades.

An anticonspiratorial mind-set took hold in U.S. society, and the term "conspiracy" frequently was followed by the word "nut." In a remarkable sequence, the assassinations or attempted assassinations of John F. Kennedy, Martin Luther King, Robert Kennedy, George Wallace, and Ronald Reagan were all carried out by lone gunmen. Not one involved even two conspirators, and in no case did anyone but the gunman know what was happening. The point is not whether or not there was a conspiracy in any of these cases, but rather, that American police and security officials badly wanted there not to be a conspiracy. The American experience with conspiracies had become too painful. There was abhorrence within the intelligence and security agencies of explanations that involved deliberate planning by multiple individuals, especially individuals with an ideological mind-set or linked to a foreign government. No one wanted another McCarthyite witch hunt.

The problem with September 11 was that it was indeed a conspiracy. Even worse, it had to be assumed to be an ongoing conspiracy. Somewhere in the United States, there were men planning additional acts of mass murder. Moreover, this was not a randomly selected group of Americans. It was a group of Muslims. Not all Muslims were in Al Qaeda, but all members of Al Qaeda were Muslims. With some exceptions, Muslims can be recognized as Muslims, in the sense that in the United States, most have ethnic characteristics as well as religious beliefs.

The administration and some lawmakers immediately clashed. On one side was a reasonable, deep fear of Al Qaeda, generating a demand that the government secure the country from this clear menace, regardless of what it took. The first civil right was, after all, the right to live. On the other side, there was not only an institutional commitment to civil rights but also a deep revulsion against conspiracy theories. Even more, there was a deep distrust of government conducting a search for a conspiracy. Fear of Al Qaeda collided with fear of another witch hunt in which innocent people were harmed.

Indeed, because of both the Constitution and McCarthyism, the United States had an extraordinarily weak national security apparatus. Remarkably, the CIA respected its own limitation of being unable to operate domestically. The FBI was a law-enforcement institution, not an intelligence service, meaning the same agency responsible for searching for Al Qaeda was also responsible for stopping the interstate transport of stolen car parts. FBI agents hated assignments for monitoring political groups, since they had frequently ended careers. State and local police were similarly poorly equipped. The Immigration and Naturalization Service was overwhelmed and poorly organized, while the Border Patrol was focused on capturing Mexicans coming across the Rio Grande. Customs was looking for drugs.

No one was focused on Al Qaeda in the United States, because no one wanted the responsibility. It was a nightmare assignment, and neither the executive branch nor Congress wanted to hunt for people who would, once again, have two identities—agents of a foreign power, albeit a nonstate power, and members of legitimate religious and political groups. The United States was rendered incapable of a rational homeland security policy by the calamity of the Red Hunts. Everyone knew that the homeland needed to be defended, but no one could articulate a defensive plan that could satisfy the contradictory and inconsistent demands of the American polity.

War or Crime?

The United States had fought wars against foreign countries and understood the rules of war and how they applied. The United States had also prosecuted criminals and was familiar with those rules as well. The problem following September 11 was that the United States couldn't figure out—from day one—whether Al Qaeda consisted of criminals or warriors and therefore could not determine whether the Constitution or the rules of war applied.

In war, the death of innocents is an inevitable by-product. It is expected that, during a bombing raid or a guerrilla attack, bystanders will be killed. It is in the nature of war. In the United States, the purpose of law is to protect the innocent. There was no way to extract Al Qaeda from the Islamic community in the United States without harming innocents. If this was war, that was acceptable. If this was a criminal investigation, it was not. In the aftermath of September 11, no one thought this out. Bush simultaneously spoke of the country being at war and of bringing Al Qaeda to justice, without grasping that these were very different things. As the shock wore off, an underlying tension emerged: Homeland defense was to be carried out in the riptide of the two concepts. It could satisfy neither camp.

Consider this analogy from December 7, 1941. Assume that after December 7, FDR had announced that the United States would hunt down and bring to justice every Japanese pilot who had attacked the United States, placing criminal responsibility on them, rather than acting as if a state of war existed between the United States and Japan. It would follow from this that the United States, apart from having to capture the pilots, would also have to carry out a judicial proceeding to determine whether and to what degree each individual pilot was responsible.

That would obviously be madness. The pilots were not guilty of a crime. There were no legal protections available to Japanese soldiers and sailors, apart from the rules of war contained in the Geneva Convention. No finding of guilt was necessary or relevant, nor was punishment the central theme. It was a matter of defending the United States and defeating Japan. The question about any individual was not whether he had done anything against the United States, but simply whether his death would serve the goal of defeating Japan. If a soldier was taken prisoner, his treatment was governed by the Geneva Convention, and he remained a prisoner as long as the war went on—regardless of what he did or didn't do against the United States.

When Timothy McVeigh was captured following the attack on the Murrah Federal Building in Oklahoma, the essential question was his guilt or innocence—had he done it or not? The determination of his guilt or innocence took place through a procedure that was defined by the Constitution and the various criminal codes. The procedures were focused on protecting his rights—including the assumption of innocence—and following the rules of evidence. Terry Nichols was also found guilty, based on evidence that he had materially aided Timothy McVeigh in the attack. McVeigh was not a prisoner of war and was therefore put to death based on his actions, not his membership in an army.

What is Al Qaeda? If we treated a member of Al Qaeda as if he were a terrorist like Timothy McVeigh, his prosecution would fall within the criminal code. He would be presumed innocent and the rules of probable cause and evidence would apply. Therefore, defeating Al Qaeda would require proof in court as to the precise illegal actions taken by individual operatives. It also meant that stopping an Al Qaeda operative *before* he carried out an action would be extraordinarily difficult. Prior restraint is not a major feature of the American legal system. Fighting a war against covert operatives using the criminal code as the primary vehicle would be nearly impossible.

At the heart of homeland defense there is this question: Is this a war or a criminal investigation? The answer is crucial. In a war, the primary goal is the destruction of the enemy army before it can strike. In a criminal investigation, the primary goal is to identify those who have already committed a crime and bring them to justice. The latter is a matter of evidence and process. The former is a matter of locating and destroying enemy forces. No coherent answer was available after September 11. From the beginning of the war, the United States slipped among three completely distinct notions of what was going on—criminal prosecution, war under the Geneva Convention, and war under extraordinary circumstances.

The Geneva Convention clearly didn't apply to Al Qaeda. The Geneva Convention of 1949 states in Article 2 that fighters will be considered combatants so long as the following conditions apply:

(a) That of being commanded by a person responsible for his subordinates;
(b) That of having a fixed distinctive sign recognizable at a distance;
(c) That of carrying arms openly;
(d) That of conducting their operations in accordance with the laws and customs of war.

The Geneva Convention deliberately intended to exclude soldiers in disguise with hidden weapons from its protections because the framers of the Convention regarded such behavior as outside the bounds of civilized warfare. The "franc tireurs" who had carried out terrorist actions against uniformed soldiers were regarded as engaged in illegal actions under the rules of law. The phrase had originated in the Franco-Prussian War of 1871 and was specifically used by the framers of the Geneva Convention to distinguish those protected by the Convention from those who weren't. Al Qaeda did not qualify for protection under the Geneva Convention—except for those fighting openly in places like Afghanistan.

Obviously, the U.S. criminal system does not apply to people captured by the Army in Afghanistan. That would be like prosecuting Japanese captured at Guadalcanal for federal crimes. Even if the Japanese were out of uniform and hiding his weapons, no one would think that a grand-jury investigation was required to deal with him. If the Japanese had invaded California, U.S. criminal law would not apply to soldiers in uniform regardless of the harm they did. As for Japanese soldiers on covert missions, even ones carried out in the United States, another legal system applied.

During World War II, enemies caught out of uniform were turned over to military tribunals. During most of World War II—on all sides—the usual outcome was execution. That was accepted practice for anyone out of uniform—spies, partisans, or soldiers switching uniforms. The military tribunals do not have to mete out the death penalty—although this was the custom during World War II to discourage such behavior as outside the bounds of civilized warfare. They can provide other justice. However, by precedent, this has been the way in which people who do not fit under criminal law or the law of war are dealt with. This is where the notion of military tribunals came from after September 11.

There were a number of advantages to this system. The United States was not required to act only after an attack was carried out, nor was it required to hold only those who had aided and abetted the specific attack. The United States was allowed to define Al Qaeda as a corporate entity—not a nation-state but a resistance movement as defined by the Geneva Convention, albeit one that was in violation of the Convention in its practices. It allowed the United States to treat members of Al Qaeda as enemies, without having to justify it through the judicial system.

The problem was that this war was being waged inside the United States. The practice of capturing people in the United States—including American citizens—and treating them as military captives not covered by the Geneva Convention raised hackles everywhere. The critics of military tribunals were reasonably concerned that the federal government would use its authority under this practice recklessly or against people other than Al Qaeda. This was not a trivial concern, but it left open the question What is to be done? Some advocated criminal prosecution—leaving open the question of how you stop someone before he commits a crime or who is skilled at hiding his intentions. Others wanted the use of the Geneva Convention, until they realized that it either did not apply or, if it did, that it would allow the U.S. to hold prisoners until the war was over—in effect, indefinitely.

There was no coherent legal doctrine under which to treat Al Qaeda because the law had never anticipated this. If a foreign nation had attacked the United States, the Geneva Convention would apply to its soldiers. If Timothy McVeigh, a U.S. citizen, blew up a building, the judicial system applied. What do you do with a foreign conspiracy waging war on U.S. soil? Are they criminals, soldiers, or something else? A vast, complex, and fairly incoherent debate raged, carefully avoiding the obvious: The U.S. legal system was not equipped to handle this kind of threat.

Organizing for Homeland Defense

The normal reaction when someone is hit hard is to cover up, to defend against the next blow. It is impossible to completely cover a human body, and the more extreme the defensive posture, the less of a threat you are to your attacker. This makes him freer to hit you again, and since it is impossible to completely protect your body, he will continue to pound you. The only limits on the damage he can cause you are his own patience and stamina.

What is true for individuals is equally true for nations. The first instinct after Pearl Harbor was fear that an invasion of the West

Coast was imminent and a demand that defensive steps be taken. Of course, if the Japanese had been able to send an invasion force to the West Coast, they could not have been stopped. The coast was much too long to defend. If all the forces that were built up in the next two years were deployed along the coasts of the United States, it would still not have been enough to protect the coasts from invasion.

After September 11, the instinct for defense dominated the nation's response. As the towers fell and the last aircraft crashed in Pennsylvania, the immediate question was simple: How do we prevent further attacks? The first step was simple, brilliant, and unsustainable. Secretary of Transportation Norman Mineta, working out of the White House, ordered the Federal Aviation Administration to ground all aircraft in the sky at the nearest airport, regardless of final destination, and to halt any further takeoff of aircraft.

The action worked. If there were any further plans for hijacking that day, Mineta shut them down. Given the constraints on the hijackers, we suspect that there were no further plans for that day— or at least not more than one or two additional planes. The problem was, of course, that he had also shut down the U.S. air traffic system. This pointed out a key dilemma of defense. It is possible to deny an enemy the use of your own systems if you are willing to shut those systems down. However, if the system is shut down, you may do as much damage to yourself as the enemy would have if he had destroyed the system. It was impossible to keep the system shut, but it was also equally difficult to defend it.

In 2002, there were 8,789,123 commercial airline departures in the United States. On average, 24,085 commercial departures take place in a single day. In 2002, a total of 539,811,008 passengers checked into U.S. commercial airports, which means that on average, 1,479,380 passengers check into airports daily. Given the size and structure of the U.S. commercial air system, it is impossible to prevent the penetration of today's perimeter defenses. It is almost impossible to imagine any system that would work and simultaneously allow the current volume of air traffic.

The vulnerability of the air transport system is a microcosm of the vulnerability of the United States as a whole. An advanced industrial country is dependent on systems that are extraordinarily vulnerable to explosives. It is difficult to blow up a farm. It is relatively easy to blow up a power plant or a bridge or a ship. The more advanced a country is industrially, the more vulnerable it is to an attack that can cripple its economy.

Consider the following examples:

- The United States is divided by the Mississippi River, which runs from the Gulf of Mexico north to Minnesota. There are numerous bridges crossing it, but the bulk of rail and road traffic uses perhaps two dozen high-volume bridges. If those bridges were destroyed, east-west auto, truck, and train transportation would experience massive disruptions and delays. The U.S. economy, which is highly integrated and depends on that transport net for just-in-time deliveries, would be paralyzed. All the major bridges would not have to be destroyed. If only half of them were simply damaged, the delays in transport would be devastating.

- Approximately 25 percent of all American petroleum is refined in the greater Houston area, with the bulk of this production concentrated in the suburb of Pasadena. The oil that feeds those refineries is brought in from the Gulf of Mexico via the Houston Ship Channel, a narrow waterway dredged regularly and maintained by the Coast Guard. If a supertanker were to sink in the Houston Ship Channel, the waterway could be blocked for weeks or months. The effect would be a devastating oil shortage in the United States.

- Manhattan, on an average workday, has about 3 million souls on the island. There are six bridges and four tunnels off the island, not counting railroad and subway tunnels. An attack using any chemical or biological agent would—regardless of the potency of the attack—generate an enormous panic. With chaos in Manhattan, U.S. financial and broadcast systems would likely fail.

These were some of the major targets. There were lesser, still-devastating targets, ranging from shopping malls to professional football games, but the fact was that defending all of these targets was physically impossible. Defending the commercial airline system was impossible. If Al Qaeda wanted to strike, if it had the resources to strike, it could not be stopped.

The Bush administration was caught in the classic political bind of warfare. The best military solution is sometimes to ignore the threat, absorb the attack, and focus all resources on the offensive. Politically, it was impossible to announce that there were no genuinely effective measures (and that those few that could be taken would not be used). With the country on the verge of panic, the President had a tightrope to walk.

President Bush tried to walk the tightrope publicly by combining warnings of an impending Al Qaeda attack with ordering administrative shifts and asking for legislation to deal with needed measures. In reality, the administration had little hope that these actions would succeed in blocking an Al Qaeda attack. At least for political and morale purposes, the administration's efforts were crafted to make it appear that something substantial was being done when in actuality that was not the case.

The administration began by focusing on the things it could do without congressional approval, such as appointing a "homeland security czar." The person selected, Tom Ridge, had no background in the field and therefore had absolutely no idea what he was doing, but that was not a problem since, in fact, he would have nothing really to do. His job was simply to appear to be in control of an apparatus that did not yet exist, exercising authority he didn't yet have. Ridge was an amiable and relaxed man, which was the essential definition for a job that would have driven more intense people insane. But the appointment was not trivial. The President had few chips to play, and a symbolic move had value.

Second, the military was reorganized. Prior to September 11, there was no unified military command that was responsible for the United

States. There were commands for every other region in the world, but not for the homeland. The reason had to do with *posse comitatus*, and a deep aversion to anything that smelled of military control of the United States. The result was that the people watching the skies—the North American Air Defense Command of the Air Force—were part of U.S. Space Command, while the people watching the coasts—the U.S. Coast Guard—reported to the Department of Transportation. There was no integrating of military assets for a period of time.

A command was set up to protect the United States. Its logical name would have been U.S. Command, but that name was simply too controversial, with many claiming that the military had no authority over U.S. soil and should not in any way be given command author-ity. The name selected made no sense—Northern Command—but it was the best that anyone could come up with. Northern Command took over a wide range of Air Force and Army assets that were designed to protect the United States, such as North American Air Defense Command, which controlled all fighters in the U.S., and many Reserve and National Guard units in the United States that would be called up in the event of another September 11. It achieved very little—the homeland was not better defended after NorthCom was established—but little harm was done, either, except that valu-able time and effort were spent on reshuffling the deck.

The intelligence community was left essentially unchanged. The same people who had the watch on September 11 kept their jobs. After December 7, 1941, Roosevelt had fired Commander in Chief, Pacific Command, Admiral Husband Kimmel not so much because he was responsible for it, but because the President knew that he had to be seen as cleaning house—moving from peacetime to wartime. Roo-sevelt brought in younger commanders, like Chester Nimitz and Dwight Eisenhower, promoting them over much more senior com-manders. He not only brought in urgently needed fresh blood but drove home the fact that the world had changed completely. Bush did nothing like that in the intelligence community. No heads rolled. No fresh blood was promoted. It was business as usual.

The most important shift that occured was that a Joint Terrorism Task Force (JTTF) was set up nationally and in many metropolitan areas, integrating FBI, CIA, Customs, INS, and the endless other intelligence services under federal control with state and local police. This did not make collaboration much easier, but it created a clearly defined arena for conflict.

Finally, the Homeland Defense portfolio was transformed into a cabinet-level department called the Department of Homeland Security (DHS, not to be confused with the DIA's humint service—Defense Human Services, or DHS), integrating a wide range of feuding agencies under one umbrella and creating some new agencies within Homeland Security. Coast Guard reported to DHS now—but the FBI did not, continuing to report to the Justice Department, and to hunt for stolen-car rings at the same time that they hunted Al Qaeda.

Ultimately, most of this didn't matter. Al Qaeda was a global organization, and most of its apparatus was outside the United States. Defeating Al Qaeda in the United States was going to occur overseas. Even if a particular cell in the U.S. was broken, it would be replaced by another as long as Al Qaeda, the base, continued to operate. Homeland Defense, therefore, was a hopeless enterprise to begin with. Apart from the inherent defect of a defensive posture, it was almost impossible to create an effective apparatus for homeland defense in the United States. From a legal, moral, and political standpoint, it just wasn't going to happen.

The United States was going to remain vulnerable. It was not economically feasible to close the U.S.–Mexican border. This meant the Islamists would travel to Latin America, where large Muslim communities existed, then move into Central America, where they made contact with one of several rings specializing in smuggling highly sensitive individuals—at a cost of $5,000 to $20,000 a head, depending on the head—into the United States. Once in the U.S., they would travel unimpeded anywhere they wanted to go.

The only defense was to play offense. Al Qaeda had to be defeated globally in order to defend the United States. That was not going to be easy to accomplish: It is a vast world, and there are very few members of Al Qaeda. At the same time the U.S. was fumbling with a homeland defense strategy, an offensive strategy was beginning to take shape. It was directed at a country in which the U.S. had decades of experience. The first target would be the base itself—Afghanistan.

CHAPTER 8

Preparing for a Counterattack

THE UNITED STATES HAD TO STRIKE, and strike hard. During the first twenty-four hours after the attacks on September 11, a consensus was reached in the Bush administration that the United States had to take offensive action as quickly as possible. By taking the battle to Al Qaeda, it could be destroyed or, at the very least, sufficiently disrupted to undermine its ability to carry out attacks against the United States.

The urgency had to do with psychology and politics as well as with military considerations. The American public was experiencing emotional riptides after September 11. People were in a state of shock, they were enraged, and they felt helpless and vulnerable. They were ready to be led into war, but without some decisive action, the likely outcome was a moral crisis—a deep uncertainty about the ability of American institutions to protect them. And that could turn ugly very quickly. Al Qaeda was counting on that.

The United States had faced this problem once before. After Pearl Harbor, there were no significant military options available. The Japanese were rolling up one victory after another. There was a sense of fear and a sense of impotence, and the danger was that this mindset could quickly turn into defeatism. Roosevelt knew that the United States could defeat Japan in the long run, and so did the Japanese. Apart from imposing military reality on the United States, the Japanese needed to use temporary American inactivity to convince Asia and the Americans that the U.S. was permanently incapable of resisting Japan.

Roosevelt urgently needed to strike back against Japan to shore up public confidence in the government's long-term ability to wage war and to let Asia know that Japan was vulnerable. Roosevelt's solution was a dangerous stunt—the Doolittle raid on Tokyo—in which he risked a scarce U.S. carrier to launch army bombers against Tokyo. Militarily, the net impact was negligible, but its overall value was enormous. The Doolittle raid signaled to everyone that the United States was prepared to take risks, that it could be successful, and that Japan was going to suffer for Pearl Harbor. The Doolittle raid bought Roosevelt time to organize more effective action by buying him credibility.

The other side of the Doolittle raid was the effect it had on the Japanese public. Having had an uninterrupted diet of rapid military successes, the Japanese people were giddy with self-confidence. The Doolittle raid, in which U.S. bombers struck Tokyo, not only shook the self-confidence of the Japanese, but it caused a crisis of confidence between the public and the military as well as within the military itself. Japan no longer took its own security for granted and, on a small scale, diverted forces from offensive to defensive operations.

Following a successful surprise attack, the only option for the attacked nation is to move rapidly to the offensive. That shift can have significant benefits even if the attack itself is militarily insignificant (which doesn't mean the response has to be insignificant). Either way, the response must come quickly—and in the case of Afghanistan, that meant very quickly indeed.

The northern part of Afghanistan consisted of the Hindu Kush, a western extension of the Himalayas that had peaks well over 10,000 feet. Winter came quickly in the Hindu Kush, and it came hard. It was some of the toughest terrain the United States would ever fight on, and while U.S. military leaders thought they could maintain military operations in the winter, no one was certain of it. They did not want to *have* to be fighting in late November and December. They wanted the war over by mid-November if possible, which meant it had to start quickly—certainly by early October—if it had any chance of achieving even its extremely modest goals. And that further limited how ambitious the war could be.

Afghanistan was a much more substantial operation than the Doolittle raid, but it shared with it a core characteristic. It had to start sooner than anyone really liked and had to be over more quickly than some thought possible. That meant it had to involve a much smaller force than many planners thought prudent. Afghanistan shared this with the Doolittle raid: Political considerations meant that the United States had to take greater risks and pursue more modest goals than were ideal from a strictly military standpoint.

First Thoughts on Afghanistan

Psychology aside, there was an important military mission involved in Afghanistan: destroying Al Qaeda's sanctuary. Enough was known about Al Qaeda's structure to conclude that simply killing bin Laden or his lieutenants would not be enough. The organization had been built to survive that. However, by disrupting the command-and-control system and breaking up the training centers, it might destabilize Al Qaeda sufficiently to delay new operations—and that delay might give U.S. intelligence an opportunity to map out Al Qaeda more effectively and plan some surgical operations.

On the most general level, the purpose of attacking Afghanistan could not be simply finding and dealing with Osama bin Laden or Al Qaeda's command structure. That would turn a military offensive into a police investigation that in all likelihood would also fail to reach its objective. It would probably not destroy Al Qaeda. The initial impulse—to deal with bin Laden—gave way to a broader objective: to destabilize Al Qaeda by unseating Afghanistan's Taliban government, destroying Al Qaeda's facilities in Afghanistan, and forcing Al Qaeda's leadership into abandoning its command facilities without devolving command onto the next layer of leaders.

Generations of Afghans have defended Afghanistan from foreigners. Their military advantage was an intimate knowledge of an extraordinarily difficult terrain, coupled with a superb tactical intelligence network built around relatives and clansmen. They knew where they were and where the invader was, while the enemy did not know where the Afghan fighters were (and frequently were themselves totally lost). Understandably, this resulted in the Afghans choosing the time and place of combat. If the enemy approached and Afghans needed to decline combat, they could disperse and regroup as and when they wanted. If the enemy approached and were vulnerable, the Afghans would attack, annihilate, withdraw, and disperse. In Afghanistan, the enemy was always at a disadvantage.

The U.S., however, never had a plan or any intention of occupying Afghanistan or pacifying it. It would take many months to build up a force that would have any hope of doing that, if it could be done at all. The British had failed to take Afghanistan during the ninteenth century, and the Soviets had failed in the twentieth. The United States was not even going to try. Operation Enduring Freedom—as it was to be called—was much more modest than "liberating" Afghanistan. It was intended to drive the Taliban out of the major cities and create American bases in Afghanistan from which to hunt Al Qaeda.

Capturing or killing Osama bin Laden was a crapshoot at best. Afghanistan is a large country, and capturing any one man was uncertain. In fact, there was a bit of debate over whether the United States actually wanted him dead or even captured. If he was known to be out of action, succession might neatly devolve according to a prescribed plan. On the other hand, if bin Laden was on the run, or if his death could not be confirmed, command devolution might become sticky. Taking command and giving orders and then discovering that bin Laden was still alive could prove awkward. His subordinates would hesitate, and that hesitation would be valuable to the U.S.

Right from the start, this situation provided built-in tension in U.S. planning. As the U.S. military began moving toward a war whose public goal was "bin Laden dead or alive," U.S. intelligence was raising the question of whether "bin Laden in limbo" might not be the best outcome. This raised an issue that would come up time and again. The mission, from a military standpoint, had to be crisp and clear. The mission, from an intelligence operations standpoint, had to be subtle and complex. From the beginning, the distinct cultures of the military and intelligence communities raised issues that would haunt the Afghan campaign and the war in general. This placed the Bush administration in a quandary. This was primarily a covert war run by intelligence organizations. It had to have complex and unstated goals. It was also in part a military operation, which had to have very clear goals. The administration's public presentation of this war was trapped by this dilemma.

Planning the Afghan War

On September 11, the Commander in Chief of Central Command, General Tommy Franks, was on a plane heading for Pakistan to talk about terrorism and other matters with Pakistani president Pervez Musharraf. He was ordered to return immediately to Central Command Headquarters in Tampa, Florida. On September 12, he received orders from the Secretary of Defense to begin planning for operations in Afghanistan.

For the next nine days, Central Command would work around the clock to develop a plan whose basic outline was presented to the President on September 21. The plan called for the destruction of Al Qaeda in Afghanistan and the Taliban regime that was protecting it. The final decision to implement the plan was made on October 2, and the war began on October 7, just twenty-six days after September 11. Even though there were contingency plans and studies to draw on, the ability to implement a war plan in under thirty days at intercontinental distances was an extraordinary achievement.

The United States maintains contingency plans for an amazing range of military possibilities. Every once in a while, the media reports that "the Pentagon had planned a war with ——— (fill in the blank)." These reports are absolutely true and have almost no practical meaning. The Joint Staff's J-5 Division (designated Plans) exists primarily to develop a plan for virtually any contingency. Some of these plans are sketchy, some detailed but updated only every few years, and some are kept current, depending entirely on the perceived likelihood of such an operation.

The U.S. always maintained a plan for invading Afghanistan, but until the middle of the 1990s, the plans were vague at best. Starting in 1997, when the Taliban took over Afghanistan, more attention was paid, but it was not until after the attack on the U.S. embassies in Kenya and Tanzania that serious attention was paid to planning. And even that serious planning didn't amount to much, because it was the general view that invading Afghanistan was extremely difficult and probably not worth the effort. One of the reasons Bill Clinton responded only with a few cruise missile attacks during the 1990s is that no one wanted to get into Afghanistan. The plan was never scrutinized because, given the difficulty, no one ever thought a president would authorize it.

The U.S. Army, in particular, was extremely concerned about the mission. The Army, more than any other service, bore the scars of Vietnam—and an intense dislike of large-scale counterinsurgency operations. The Army particularly disliked wars in which there was no clear-cut goal, or where the goal of complete victory could not be reached because of a lack of resources. Desert Storm was their kind of war.

The Army took one look at the Afghan operation and did not so much balk as wonder how it could be carried out. Having suffered most of the casualties in the Pentagon attack, the Army wanted payback as much as anyone else. Unlike Haiti or Kosovo, it was not going to try to get out of the mission, but it had serious questions on how it was going to carry out the operation.

The U.S. had carefully studied the Soviet experience in Afghanistan, partly because the U.S. had helped organize the mujahideen and partly out of pure *schadenfreude*—pleasure at someone else's pain. After Vietnam, it had been a pleasure to watch the

Soviets get the same treatment. But the U.S. had never expected to have to fight a war in Afghanistan with American troops. This was not a case in which the military was being sent to fight in a place it didn't know. This was the military being sent to fight in a place it did indeed know, and it didn't like what it knew. The Soviets, with 300,000 men and few scruples, never came close to pacifying Afghanistan. They managed to take and hold the major cities, and they controlled certain areas of the country more than others, but they never came close to winning the war. The United States Army didn't have 300,000 combat troops—at least not without using up all available reserves. The drawdown of the military after the end of the Cold War had reduced the Army's combat capability. And even so, the Soviet experience had demonstrated that 300,000 troops weren't enough.

A bigger problem was how to get a large number of troops into Afghanistan. The United States had never in its history fought a war in such an inaccessible place. Afghanistan was on the other side of the world, was completely landlocked and had no ports of its own. Sending troops and equipment into the country was almost impossible, as was supporting those troops once they were there.

The U.S. Army was primarily an armored force, designed to fight the Soviets in central Europe. Its doctrine and training all revolved around bringing Armored Fighting Vehicles, Infantry Fighting Vehicles, Self-Propelled Artillery, and huge amounts of petroleum, oil, and lubricants (POL) and munitions into a theater of operations, getting close to the enemy, and destroying it. To get that equipment into a country, the U.S. Army needs a large port and a lot of time. During Desert Storm, it had Saudi ports at its disposal and still required six months to bring its forces into position to begin fighting. The nearest sizable port to Afghanistan is Karachi, in Pakistan. It was not clear that the Pakistanis would allow the Americans to use that port, but even if they did, Karachi is—as the crow flies—nearly 400 miles from the Afghan border.

There was no way that the Army could mount a Desert Storm–like offensive in Afghanistan. Apart from everything else, there was no time.

The United States did not have months to launch an offensive into Afghanistan; it had only weeks. During the first days of deliberation, due to weather and political considerations, it was decided that the attack on Afghanistan had to begin within one month of September 11. Thus, a conventional attack by the Army was out of the question.

There was also the element of strategic surprise to consider. Following the Desert Storm model, the United States would need several months to build up its forces. Staging a major offensive into Afghanistan at any time was tough; doing it during winter was impossible. Al Qaeda did not think the United States had time to stage an attack before the snows came. If there was to be any strategic surprise, the attack had to come before the winter. But that also meant that the campaign had to be over before winter set in, which meant a short campaign with very few American troops. The problem was simple: How could the U.S. start an invasion of Afghanistan so quickly and maximize its element of surprise?

A concept had been developed during the 1990s that attempted to solve the problem of rapid deployment so the United States could begin waging war in weeks rather than months. The doctrine—partially tested in Kosovo—was, in theory, the precise solution needed in Afghanistan. It was a theory of airpower, rapidly deploying to the theater, working with a small number of special operations troops on the ground.

The sequence of any air campaign had been fixed in Air Force thinking since the mid-1980s:

1. Suppression of enemy air defenses, called SEAD.
2. Attack the enemy command, control, communications, and intelligence system, making it impossible for the national command authority to command its military.
3. Attack enemy troop concentrations and facilities to shatter ground forces.

The idea was to shatter the enemy's ability to see, think, talk, and command his troops, allowing the U.S. Army to roll in with little or no opposition to its forces. The underpinning of this theory was that technology had evolved to a point where it would work even in as difficult a case as Afghanistan.

However, Afghanistan posed serious complications. There really weren't a lot of air defenses to worry about, and those that did exist were man-portable, shoulder-fired missiles, not massive SAM installations or swarms of fighter aircraft. In addition, there was not a great deal of what was called Command, Control, Communications and Intelligence, or C^3I, to destroy. Military forces in Afghanistan were controlled by local leaders—warlords. They did not require orders from Kabul; nor, for that matter, did their units require orders from the warlords. Command devolved to very low levels—the equivalent of company and platoon level. Finally, there were rarely troop concentrations worthy of the name, which made the attrition of ground forces difficult. In other words, U.S. military doctrine did not appear to be congruent with Afghan military reality.

Airpower by itself could not defeat the Afghans. Its primary advantage—advanced space and aerial intelligence systems—was made almost useless by the nature of the Afghan military, the terrain, and the weather. The Air Force could hit anything it could see, but the problem in Afghanistan was that there was not a whole lot that the Air Force could see, and not a lot that was worth hitting. If the new doctrine was going to work, airpower had to take on smaller targets and smaller ground units—targets that could not easily be seen by reconnaissance aircraft or satellites.

The Air Force needed eyes on the ground to do its work. This is where U.S. Special Operations Command (SOCOM) became essential. SOCOM comprised units from all armed services: Special Forces from the Army, SEALs from the Navy, Air Force Special Operations teams, and Marines. Also included were specialized units like Delta Force. SOCOM worked very closely with the Central Intelligence Agency's Directorate of Operations/Special Activities Division, which ran paramilitary forces around the world. These units could work by themselves or be forged into composite units when their specialized skill had to be combined.

In Afghanistan, however, the Army Special Forces teams had the most important mission. Special Forces are highly trained and capable in the art of special operations, but their most important use is political. Their task is to work with, train, and advise indigenous forces. During the Vietnam War, they worked with native troops throughout Indochina. They were also trained to work with clandestine groups in Eastern Europe and the Soviet Union and virtually anywhere else they were needed. Their most important work in Afghanistan would be to collaborate with native forces—and to work closely with the CIA.

SOCOM therefore had two complex missions to carry out. First, it had to provide targeting for U.S. airpower. Second, it had to support an indigenous ground force to engage and defeat the Taliban. And it had to do so in under one month. This was by far the most difficult part of the mission. The United States could not possibly get a winning ground force into Afghanistan in time to launch operations within the one-month framework laid down by the President (or even within the six months it had taken in Kuwait for Desert Storm). In fact, the United States most likely couldn't get a winning ground force into Afghanistan at all—that had been learned from the Russians.

To stage troops, stockpile supplies, and, if necessary, launch air strikes, the United States had to have operational bases near Afghanistan. If Special Forces were to get into Afghanistan, they would have to come from somewhere. The Navy could put carriers in the Arabian Sea for tactical air strikes, and strategic bombers could fly missions from Diego Garcia or Saudi Arabia, but the helicopters bringing the supplies and troops had to take off from somewhere closer.

The obvious choice was Pakistan, which had been an ally of the United States for decades. The U.S. had run its operations in the Afghan war against the Soviets from Pakistan. Moreover, a deal had to be made with Pakistan under any circumstance, since U.S. naval strike aircraft would have to fly over Pakistani territory on their way to Afghanistan. Pakistan's northwestern frontier had to be blocked to control Al Qaeda fighters.

But Pakistan was the major backer of the Taliban, and President Pervez Musharraf had been sympathetic to the Islamist forces. In many ways, the Pakistani intelligence services had created the Taliban government. Therefore, it would have been nearly unthinkable for Pakistan to throw itself open to the United States so the U.S. could wage war on the Taliban. If Musharraf were to agree to it, he would likely not last very long in office—or stay alive.

Musharraf understood that the United States was bent on war and that he could find himself sandwiched between a hostile United States and India, Pakistan's traditional enemy. He could not afford to be isolated in this way. Nor could he afford to allow the United States to use Pakistan openly as its main base of operations. He simply had not had sufficient time to consider his best political moves, and he certainly could not allow Karachi to become the main port from which war matériel flowed.

Still, as long as it was done quietly, Pakistan could safely offer several things the United States needed. The key was to do it as secretly as possible. First, and most essential, it could permit U.S. overflights of its territory, which would allow carrier strikes to take place against Afghanistan. Second, the Pakistanis could allow the U.S. to establish secret bases along Afghanistan's southern border with Pakistan, enabling the United States to try to recruit Pashtuns into its coalition. Politically, Musharraf could handle this so long as he had deniability. And these were not trivial offerings. They were not enough on which to base the war, but they were a start for events that would come later. That left the Russians—and the Iranians.

Recruiting the Russians

If the United States was going to wage war in Afghanistan, it had to rent an existing army. Fortunately for the United States, Afghanistan had never been a single nation, and the Taliban did not control all of the military in the country, particularly in the northern areas that bordered the former Soviet Union.

The Taliban had conquered most of the country, but its conquest depended less on its own military power than on a fragile coalition of autonomous warlords that it had put together. Even so, there were forces in Afghanistan that still resisted the Taliban, the most important of which were called the Northern Alliance, a coalition of Uzbeks and Tajik groups that resisted the Pashtun Taliban. The Northern Alliance was motivated to fight the Taliban and was available for rent or lease. They were also trained and, to a reasonable extent, armed. Combined with U.S. airpower, in theory, they could destroy the Taliban and get rid of Al Qaeda in Afghanistan.

The U.S. had abandoned the Uzbeks and Tajiks after the war with the Soviets, but the Russians had picked up their option, albeit for a much smaller sum and lower commitment. After the breakup of the Soviet Union, the northern border of Afghanistan was shared by three newly independent Soviet republics: Turkmenistan, Uzbekistan, and Tajikistan. Independence is, of course, a relative term. The Russians had political, military, and economic interests in all three countries. They did not want the Taliban pushing up to the frontier of these countries, in large part because they did not want radical Islam increasing its strength in these countries. Keeping the Northern Alliance alive as a buffer made a great deal of sense.

The Russians, of course, had a much more serious Islamist problem: Chechnya. In the Russian view, the main problem in Chechnya was "Wahabi outsiders," shorthand for Islamist Saudis. The Russians also regarded the Wahabis as behind the Taliban regime. They viewed Osama bin Laden as a Saudi agent with multiple motives, including keeping Central Asian energy and pipelines off the market, thereby improving the competitive position of the Saudis. The Russians had been warning the United States for several years about the threat. The United States downplayed the threat, preferring instead to focus on human-rights violations by the Russians in Chechnya, where the Russians claimed the Wahabis were operating.

After the Taliban victory in 1996, the Russians began to return to Afghanistan, covertly this time. The Russians, who were comfortable in a world of changing alliances, entered into a deal with their former enemies. One was Ahmed Shah Massoud, leader of the Tajik Jamiat-I-Islami. The other was Abdul Rashid Dostum, leader of the Uzbek Jumbesh-I-Milli. They pumped arms to both men through supply centers set up at a former Soviet air base in Tajikistan. They also supplied Dostum, on a somewhat lesser scale, through Uzbekistan. By 2001, the Northern Alliance was, to a great extent, owned and operated by Russia.

For the Russians in particular, there would be a particular satisfaction in the Americans coming to them and asking for help. Not only did they have bitter memories of American support for Afghan guerrillas during the eighties, but the Russians had warned the Americans about both the Taliban regime and Al Qaeda. In November 2000, for example, the Russians were circulating a report generated by former Afghan president Rabbani that claimed Osama bin Laden himself was overseeing operations by Taliban troops against the Northern Alliance. Similar reports were being provided to the United States by the Iranians. Russia wanted American support for a major push by the Northern Alliance to try to force the Taliban to stop supporting Chechen rebels. The Clinton administration did not deny the Russian claims but remained opposed to an intensification of Russian operations in Chechnya and a Northern Alliance operation against Afghanistan.

Part of the reason is that the Clinton administration did not believe the Northern Alliance had a chance in Afghanistan. But another part of the decision rested on Clinton's core strategy toward the Islamist threat. Clinton recognized that there was a threat from Al Qaeda, but he did not want to put the United States in the position of being in broad opposition to Islamist movements. The U.S. intervention in the Balkans was on the side of Muslim communities, and it was hoped that this would buy the United States some velvet among the Islamists. Siding with the Russians on Chechnya and renewing the Afghan civil war did not fit with this strategy.

Thus, it was a satisfying moment for the Russians when Richard Armitage, U.S. Deputy Secretary of State, flew to Moscow a week after September 11 to meet secretly with Vyacheslav Trubnikov, a deputy foreign minister who was a former head of Russia's foreign intelligence service. The topic was access to Russian intelligence on Afghanistan and, above all else, access to the Northern Alliance.

Also on the table was a more sensitive issue. If the United States was going to wage a war in Afghanistan, it would have to have bases in Uzbekistan and Tajikistan. The Iranians would not allow bases in Iran. For political and other reasons, Pakistan could not provide large enough bases quickly enough and with enough security. If the United States was going to invade Afghanistan, it would need Russian approval to use and expand bases in the two former Soviet republics, which were independent but in the Russian sphere of influence.

Russia was not eager to see the expansion of the U.S. military in those countries. U.S. military expansion was a highly sensitive issue for the Russians. NATO expansion had already brought U.S. military influence to the frontiers of the former Soviet Union. Vladimir Putin, who had come to power partly as a result of Boris Yeltsin's inability to restrain the Americans in Kosovo, was a creature of the Russian national security complex and relied on it as a political base. Russian generals vigorously opposed—to put it mildly—letting U.S. bases spring up in Uzbekistan and Tajikistan. Their view was that once there, the Americans would never leave. They pointed out that American domination of these countries would inevitably freeze Russia out of the natural gas pipeline schemes that had been developing over the years.

Both Uzbekistan and Tajikistan had been flirting with the United States since the mid-1990s, participating in various U.S.-led military exercises and working to attract Western businesses. The United States already had some troops and helicopters in Uzbekistan on September 11, the result of a joint NATO–Uzbek exercise. They would remain. The U.S. military was quite familiar with Uzbekistan and surrounding countries, having conducted military exercises there since 1998. Nevertheless, to use Uzbekistan for bases now, the United States would have to get the Russians' approval.

The Russians had a fundamental strategic decision to make. That decision would be part of the basis of any American attack on Afghanistan. Since the 1980s, the Soviet Union had sought closer economic relations with the West. They wanted trade and Western investment. This policy had been created not by Mikhail Gorbachev, as most thought, but by Yuri Andropov, while he was head of the KGB. Andropov knew (he was one of the few in the Soviet Union privy to the facts) that the Soviet economy was collapsing. The cost of the arms race coupled with the inefficiency of the Soviet economic model was bringing the Soviet Union to catastrophe. He knew that the Soviet Union's only hope was to trade geopolitical interests for economic interests—reduce the threat to the West in exchange for economic benefits.

Andropov hoped that the Soviet Union could buy enough time to institute economic reforms so that the political structure of the Soviet Union—the dominance of the Communist Party—could be preserved. He became Chairman of the Soviet Communist Party to pursue these goals, but he fell ill and died within months. Ultimately, Gorbachev became Chairman and carried out the twin policies of *perestroika* (restructuring) and *glasnost* (openness), also ending the Cold War. It didn't work, and the Soviet Union collapsed anyway. But Gorbachev's basic policy remained in place under Boris Yeltsin: seek accommodation with the West at all costs in order to improve the Russian economy. Essentially, the problem was that the West in general, and the Americans specifically, didn't need anything from Russia—at least not from the end of the Cold War until post–September 11. In mid-September 2001, the United States needed Russia badly, and the number-two man in the U.S. State Department had rushed to Moscow asking for help. Putin had to make a critically important decision. Would he help the United States, and if so, what would be his price?

The simple answer was to exchange territory for economic benefits. But the Soviet Union and Russia had been pursuing this policy for a generation, and it no longer had any credibility. Russia's problems were so vast, so deeply cultural and structural, that any amount of aid or investment was simply irrelevant. The simple answer didn't work, and Putin had come to power because he knew it better than anyone else. The Russians didn't want to refuse the Americans, but what the U.S. was asking for was enormous. They were asking to station troops in the former Soviet Union to invade Afghanistan, a country Russian troops had bled for. The equivalent was the Russians asking for bases in Guam in order to invade Vietnam.

Armitage's visit in mid-September was followed by an intense week of discussion within the Russian leadership. On September 22, a few days after Armitage's trip, Putin gathered his national security team at his dacha in Sochi, on the Black Sea. About a dozen men pondered a fundamental question: not whether to condemn Al Qaeda or support the United States, but whether to allow the United States to move its armed forces deep into Russia's sphere of influence—using Russian resources to do so.

The Americans perceived it differently. Obsessed with Al Qaeda, they had no interest in dominating the countries north of Afghanistan or the routes that vital oil pipelines would traverse. But the Russians knew that as the war ended and the passions subsided, the Americans would become aware of the strategic position they held. Getting the Americans out would not be easy. This war was not going to be over anytime soon—that alone would keep the Americans there for years. And when the Americans build bases, the Russians were aware, they build big bases, with American companies, businessmen, wives, and children. Americans come big, the Russians knew, and they tend to stay.

The Russians could not afford to think about this as a temporary arrangement. If the United States came and decided not to leave, nothing short of war would get them out—and the Russians were in no position to wage war. They had to look at this arrangement as ceding the region to the Americans. They did have a choice: Unless the Russians granted them an air corridor through FSU airspace, it would be difficult for the Americans to get to Uzbekistan and Tajikistan. The only other route in was through Iran, and the Americans were not going to get air transit privileges there anytime soon. China was another alternative, but that was also unlikely—and a very long way around. The Americans needed the Russians. The Russians could say no and make it stick.

There was a strong argument for keeping the Americans out, and the Russian military strategists made it. But the same people who were most sensitive to a growing American presence were even more worried about a much more important issue: the threat to the disintegration of the Russian Federation. The fabric of Russia was already being torn apart by the Chechens. The Russians knew that support for the Chechens came from Al Qaeda. But they thought there was more to it than that.

The Russians believed that the United States was backing the Chechen rebels in order to get a lock on regional oil supplies. The United States had extremely close relations with Eduard Shevardnadze, President of Georgia. The U.S. knew that arms were being smuggled into Chechnya from Georgia and that this was one of the main supply routes to the Chechen rebels. The Russians also believed that the Americans knew this and supported it because the Americans wanted an independent Chechnya. This seemed the only explanation for the Clinton administration's bizarre policy of opposing Al Qaeda everywhere except in Chechnya. The Russian leaders had already undergone the disintegration of the Soviet Union. They did not want to go through it again with Russia. Chechnya was a core issue for Putin.

This defined the Russian response: They wanted to align the American struggle against Al Qaeda with the Russian struggle. Specifically, they wanted the United States to halt its public criticism of Soviet actions in Chechnya. While the Americans were pounding Afghanistan, Russia didn't want to hear State Department condemnation of them pounding Chechnya. Even more important—and this was nonnegotiable—they wanted a guarantee from the United States that it would shut down the arms-smuggling route from Georgia into Chechnya. In broader terms, they wanted the United States to commit to not supporting secessionist forces in Russia.

While Putin was meeting with his advisors in Sochi, Bush was meeting with his national security team at Camp David in Maryland. Bush, knowing the Sochi meeting was going on and needing an answer quickly since the Russian decision would define American planning, called Putin. They talked for almost an hour. At the end of that conversation, a deal was cut. The Russians would permit the Americans bases in Uzbekistan and Tajikistan, would provide the Americans with their top-tier intelligence on Afghanistan and Al Qaeda, and would provide immediate logistical support for U.S. intelligence teams moving into Afghanistan. Piecemeal cooperation that had already taken place after September 11 was turned into systematic cooperation. Most important, Russia would allow the Americans access to the Northern Alliance.

In return, the United States would agree to limit its presence in Central Asia in terms of size and length of stay and would agree to force Georgia to shut down arms smuggling. The U.S. would also give the Russians a free hand in Chechnya and take no steps to facilitate the disintegration of Russia. Later, on February 21, 2002, after the main fighting in Afghanistan was over, forty American Special Forces troops dressed in civilian clothes landed in Tbilisi, Georgia, to begin the process of closing off the flow of arms, payment on the U.S. end of the bargain. Right or wrong, the Russians believe the Americans were behind the arms flow to Chechen rebels. Right or wrong, the Americans went to Georgia to show their commitment to Russia.

Chechnya was not at all unimportant to Russia, and its potential loss was viewed as a catastrophe. But there was a deeper and more complex layer in Russian reasoning. The Russians understood the American mood, and they understood that for the Americans, the behavior of nations in the days and weeks following September 11 would define relations for a generation. The United States was locking in its relations with the world as profoundly as it had on December 7, 1941. No ambiguity would be permitted.

Vladimir Putin was a protégé of Yuri Andropov. He had been raised in the belief that the future of Russia rested in an accommodation with the West. Putin certainly had his doubts about that strategy by 2001, but he also understood that the Russians were in no position to engage in a geopolitical competition with the United States, especially in its current economic and military position. The Russians and Americans had had a good deal of friction since President George W. Bush had come to office. One of Bush's early decisions was the expulsion of a significant portion of the intelligence section in the Russian Embassy in Washington, something the Clinton administration had let slide. Putin was prepared to chill his relations with Washington over those issues. But refusing to cooperate with the United States over its punitive operations against Al Qaeda in Afghanistan would represent a break by Russia with the United States over an issue so fundamental that it would end any hope of collaboration between the two nations on any level. It would end the Andropov strategy once and for all, at a time when the Russians couldn't compete with the United States.

The Americans were coming into Central Asia to go after Al Qaeda, and they were going to use the Northern Alliance to do it. The only thing the Russians could achieve by not collaborating was to delay the United States—and to permanently sour relationships. Potentially, there was something to be gained from collaboration and a great deal to be lost from resistance. On September 22, 2001, eleven days after Al Qaeda's attack, the United States had its answer from the Russians: They would help.

CHAPTER 9

The War in Afghanistan

Renting an Army: Russia

U.S. intelligence teams began to move into Afghanistan days after the agreement with the Russians. The U.S. had few intelligence assets on the ground in Afghanistan and had broken contact with many of the groups it had supported during their war against the Soviet Union. There was more than a little bitterness on the part of former Afghan allies at the way the U.S. had turned away from them after their war against the Russians. There was also a great deal of distrust of the United States and its motives. The United States had not been impressive in its military actions since Desert Storm. Potential Afghan allies were concerned that the U.S. would not only be ineffective but would abandon them to the tender mercies of the Taliban.

The Russian agreement gave the United States a hunting license among the Northern Alliance, nothing more. The U.S. would have to negotiate deals directly with all Afghan factions it intended to recruit. In the north, there were two key factions and two key leaders. One was Jamiat-I-Islami, which was predominantly Tajik and was led by Ahmad Shah Massoud. A remarkably popular and charismatic figure, Massoud had been one of the most effective commanders fighting the Russians. He had had extremely close relations with the CIA and had been one of those who felt betrayed when the Clinton administration imposed a policy of strict neutrality on the struggle between the Taliban and its enemies. But Massoud was the key.

The problem was that Massoud was dead, murdered on September 9 in a suicide bombing carried out by Al Qaeda. Two men claiming to be journalists had arrived at Massoud's headquarters in Khoja Bahauddin in northeastern Afghanistan. They identified themselves as representing the Islamic Observation Center in London and carried a letter of identification from its director. The men had traveled from Pakistan and were able to get through Pakistani lines and, more amazingly, Taliban lines to get to Massoud's headquarters.

There were some suspicions about them, and they were not granted an interview. However, the day before September 9, they became increasingly insistent. They were permitted access to Massoud in the late morning of September 9. A translator was present who was a friend of Massoud's, since the journalists spoke Arabic and the interview was being conducted in Dari. As the first question was being asked, the camera exploded. It had been loaded with explosives. The two "journalists" were killed, as was Massoud.

There is little question that Al Qaeda was behind the attack. The method of attack, the timing, and the capture of several operatives in Belgium who supplied false documents to the two attackers all indicate the link. The organizer, a Tunisian called Tarek Maaroufi, is being held by the Belgians for attempting to bomb the United States Consulate in Milan. Moreover, publications and Web sites close to Al Qaeda, such as "The Voice of Jihad," have claimed a link. The question is, Why did Al Qaeda do it?

One explanation that has been widely circulated, based on some released Defense Intelligence Agency documents, is that Massoud was killed because he had knowledge of the September 11 attacks and Al Qaeda wanted to shut him up. That explanation makes little sense. The attackers arrived at Khoja Bahauddin weeks before. They traveled a circuitous route that took several weeks. Prior to that, the operation had to be planned and organized. Therefore, the assassination had to have been planned more than a month before September 9. Even if Massoud had gotten some information about the attack on the U.S., he would have had weeks to pass it on to his Russian intelli-

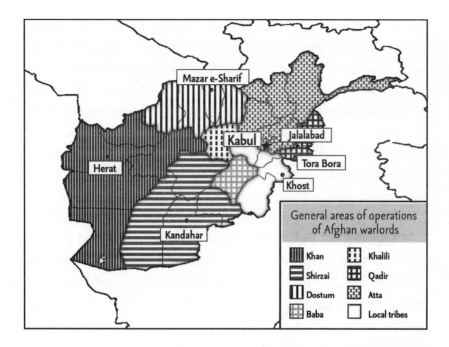

General areas of operations of Afghan warlords

Khan, Khalili, Shirzai, Qadir, Dostum, Atta, Baba, Local tribes

gence contacts or to other intelligence agencies. This was a pretty ineffective way to silence him.

A better explanation has to do with what was going on in the battlefield. The Jamiat-I-Islami held an area in northeastern Afghanistan, near Tajikistan. Taliban forces had been pressing Massoud's forces, which had given way but had not broken. Just before the assassination, Taliban forces began to mass but didn't attack. The night of September 9, after Massoud was killed but while Jamiat-I-Islami was still claiming publicly that he had been only wounded, the Taliban attacked. At the same time, Kabul radio began broadcasting in Dari the news that Massoud was dead. Less than forty-eight hours later, the World Trade Center came down.

Al Qaeda fully understood that the United States would attack Afghanistan after September 11. They also understood that the Northern Alliance was the best ground option the United States would have, and that Jamiat-I-Islami constituted the most reliable force in the Northern Alliance. Moreover, they understood that Massoud was not only the leader of Jamiat-I-Islami but a potential leader of national standing. If he was dead, there would be no national leader, Jamiat-I-Islami might fragment or become ineffective on the battlefield, and the Northern Alliance might become much less useful to the United States.

This, in microcosm, gives us a sense of the complexity of Al Qaeda planning. Having planned the strikes on the United States, they carefully gamed out the probable American response and examined the resources the Americans had available. Then they acted to deny the Americans their resources. However, it also reflects the weakness of Al Qaeda. They analyzed the situation with extreme care, yet they were ultimately incapable of reshaping it. Massoud was dead, but neither Jamiat-I-Islami nor the Northern Alliance was broken. Whereas Massoud was the military leader, Jamiat-I-Islami had a political leader as well, former Afghan president Burhannudin Rabbani. (Rabbani was actually still officially recognized as Afghanistan's legitimate president by the United Nations.) He was able to hold Jamiat-I-Islami together after the assassination, while the United States continued its work of buying off individual Northern Alliance field commanders.

Another crucial individual for the U.S. to court was the commander of the Uzbeks, Abdul Rashid Dostum, leader of the Jumbesh-I-Milli. Dostum was legendary even in Afghanistan as a brutal and utterly unprincipled figure. Feared by his enemies and his followers, Dostum had managed to double-cross just about everyone he came into contact with at one time or another, switching sides numerous times. The only reason Dostum stayed with the Northern Alliance was his well-founded belief that the Taliban, having no trust in him whatsoever, would execute him if captured. His troops were nicknamed "Carpet Robbers," a tribute to their tendency to loot anything and everything. Dostum was one of the reasons—albeit not the main one—that U.S. plans to fight the Taliban had always been put on hold.

The only thing to be said for Dostum was that he was better than his main rival among the Uzbeks, Abdul Malik. Malik had been allied with the Taliban until a battle at Mazar e-Sharif in 1997. Malik double-crossed the Taliban in the middle of the battle, switching sides without warning. He took about two thousand prisoners whom he then executed.

After September 11, Dostum was measured against different criteria. First, any U.S. scruples about working with him were destroyed along with the World Trade Center. Second, post–September 11 plans envisioned an attack on Afghanistan by the Northern Alliance without the direct involvement of American troops. That meant that Dostum would be free to wreak his usual havoc without fear of consequences. After September 11, that changed. Not only would there be U.S. covert and SOCOM forces on the ground, but the plan called for the occupation of key Afghan cities and territory by conventional U.S. forces after the main battle ended. Dostum's freedom of action would be severely limited. The U.S. could trust Dostum because they could outgun him.

Renting an Army: Iran

The Russians were the necessary piece because they gave access to the Northern Alliance, but they were not sufficient. Another piece was needed, and the keys to that piece lay in Iran. Like the Russians, the Iranians were bitter enemies of the Taliban for a number of reasons, including religious and cultural differences. There were, more importantly, strategic issues. The Iranians saw the Taliban as a creature of Pakistani intelligence, the ISI, and they did not want to see a strong Pakistani presence on their eastern frontier.

They did not regard the conservative Wahabi presence in Iran as benign. The Saudis, who were among the few to recognize the Taliban, were Iran's rival in the Persian Gulf. From Iran's point of view, the Taliban represented the interest of two countries, Pakistan and Saudi Arabia, both of which were Iranian rivals. Iranian intelligence had been deeply involved in Afghanistan for years, particularly working with—and to protect the interests of—the Shiite minority in Afghanistan.

For that moment Hezb-i-Wahdat, led by Karim Kalili, was the most important Shiite faction. The Shiite Hazara tribe held the strategic town of Bamian northwest of Kabul in the Hindu Kush. They blocked the advance of the Taliban toward Mazar e-Sharif and were a base from which to attack Kabul. Ishmael Khan was a more important Shiite warlord, but it was Kalili who had the keys to the north at the moment, and the United States needed his cooperation. Kalili and Khan's only real support came from across the border in Iran. Their participation in any U.S. war in Afghanistan required two things—a go-ahead from Teheran and cash.

Iran saw September 11 as an important opportunity to rid itself of the Taliban. Its goal was to bring down the Taliban and then see the United States withdraw. The Iranians did not think that this was going to be a very difficult goal to reach. They knew that the Americans were not going to be in any position to occupy Afghanistan after they brought down the Taliban, regardless of what they might think. The Iranians wanted the Americans to get bogged down, and would do everything possible to encourage the Americans to invade Afghanistan.

From the U.S. perspective, dealing with Iran would be tricky. After all, the United States and the Islamic Republic of Iran had had terrible relations since 1979. The United States was the Great Satan, and although George W. Bush had not yet made his speech on the "Axis of Evil," memories of the Iran hostage crisis still reverberated in American culture. There may have been deeper geopolitical issues between the United States and Russia, but the atmospherics between Iran and the United States were far more poisonous. As an Islamic country, Iran needed a cover before it could publicly collaborate with the United States against an Islamic regime. So, for that matter, did the United States.

Iran made some early signals of its intentions. First, it sent official condolences to the mayor of New York after September 11, the first time any such gesture had been made since the 1979 revolution. Second—and even more strikingly—it offered itself as a place where damaged American aircraft could land during missions over Afghanistan. It was not a militarily critical offer, but it was a public gesture that Iran was prepared to collaborate in an American war in Afghanistan, and Iran's willingness to make such a gesture was significant. It had not changed its basic view of the United States, but it desperately wanted the United States to take out the Taliban.

The two countries slid into collaboration. In fact, the Iranians had been meeting regularly—and fairly publicly—with the United States on Afghanistan prior to the war. An international group had been set up after the Taliban victory called the "6+2." It consisted of the six countries neighboring Afghanistan—Iran, Turkmenistan, Uzbekistan, Tajikistan, Pakistan, and China—plus the United States and Russia. This group met in Geneva occasionally, the only forum in which the United States and Iran met officially in any capacity.

On a second level, there were meetings in which American allies went to Iran to speak on behalf of the United States. For example, on September 25, British foreign minister Jack Straw traveled to Teheran to discuss Afghanistan—obviously carrying messages from U.S. officials. Japan's Prime Minister Koizumi sent a delegation to Iran offering financial support for various economic projects, implicitly in return for cooperation on Afghanistan. Another non-administration entity—the United States Senate—also sent a delegation to talk with the Iranians.

But the most important talks were taking place off the record. U.S. officials had been having quiet conversations with Iranian officials in a number of countries, most notably Germany. Some had taken place before September 11, but they intensified afterward.

The decisive meeting on the war took place in Geneva on September 25. The meeting was officially secret, with envoys being flown in from the U.S. and Teheran, and with German and Italian envoys present as honest brokers and to provide the Iranians with domestic cover: Iran could say that they were not meeting with Americans alone. The content of the meeting—and names of the envoys—were kept secret to minimize exposure, but the topic was the future of

Afghanistan after the Taliban was unseated. This was Iran's crucial question, and it wanted two assurances for cooperation. First, the United States would not try to govern directly but would create an Afghan government. Second, the interests of the Shiites would not only be respected but their leaders, Karim Kalili and Ismail Khan, would have control over their provinces.

In other words, what the Iranians wanted officially was a formal Afghan national government. What they actually wanted was regional autonomy. They did not want the Afghan government controlled by Pakistan. Nor did they want their Shiite allies swamped. They wanted Shiite provinces to be controlled by Shiites effectively independent of the national government. These provinces would serve as effective buffers along Iran's eastern frontier. One idea that came out of the meeting was to send Francesco Vendrell, a United Nations official, off to Rome to meet with the ex–king of Afghanistan, Mohammad Zahir.

Zahir would have been the perfect Afghan ruler from Iran's point of view. He formally represented a strong Afghan state, but was so old and weak that he could not possibly govern—nor could his successors, because the institution of the monarchy had been totally discredited. The Americans didn't care what kind of government Afghanistan had, as long as it wasn't controlled by the Taliban and as long as the United States would have bases from which to prosecute the war against Al Qaeda. The United States had no plans for rebuilding Afghanistan—they had neither the resources nor the will.

The Zahir idea never got off the ground. Too many people distrusted him and the people around him. Nevertheless, it established the basic framework of postwar Afghanistan—a strong-sounding central government that was actually weak, and the U.S. doing nothing to undermine practical Shiite autonomy. With the basic future—or nonfuture—of Afghanistan established, the next step was to have these things confirmed at a high level, but without making it appear publicly that the two sides were collaborating. That was Jack Straw's job.

Straw met with President Khatami on September 25. There had been two phone calls with Tony Blair prior to the meeting, but nothing had been settled. The Iranians preferred dealing with the British, since they felt they could achieve the same ends without the political fallout of talking publicly to the Americans. They knew that Straw was carrying messages from the White House and that their replies would be carried back. They knew that the British could speak authoritatively for the Americans.

The American view on the Iranians was that they were already in the game, with forces on the ground supporting the Shiites, and that Iran would welcome any change in Kabul that drove out the Taliban and the Pakistanis. They couldn't achieve that alone or with the Russians. Therefore, the Iranians needed the United States to do their heavy lifting. They had no choice but to cooperate, and therefore, the thinking went, being overly generous was unnecessary. The issue was how to escalate demands on the Iranians.

Straw carried the American requests. First, they wanted the Iranians to close off the Afghan–Iranian border to guarantee that Al Qaeda didn't get through. Second, they wanted Iranian intelligence to provide support for U.S. intelligence in hunting for Al Qaeda. Third, they wanted the Iranians to cut off aid to Hezbollah and any other group the U.S. identified as terrorist. Finally, they wanted the Iranians to make certain that no financial support was coming through to Al Qaeda from Iran. Straw was diplomatic, but the Iranians clearly heard the voice of the Americans upping the ante from a request for help on Afghanistan to a commitment to complete collaboration.

The Iranians looked at the American situation the same way the Americans looked at the Iranians—the Americans were locked in. The United States was going to invade Afghanistan. That was a given. The United States needed cooperation from forces on the ground, and the Iranians controlled two of the most important ones, particularly of those up north. Without that collaboration, the U.S. assault would become much more difficult. Regardless of what Iran said, the United States would take whatever terms were offered.

President Khatami responded by agreeing to work on the ground in Afghanistan with the United States as long as autonomy was respected. He agreed that Al Qaeda was a threat to both countries and promised to control the borders. Khatami made no guarantee on intelligence collaboration and rejected outright the request for halting aid to anti-Israeli groups. Straw never expected any other response. He knew that Iran couldn't guarantee its border controls—and that would become a major issue in December as Al Qaeda moved into Iran—but for now, he had the basic issue settled. Iran would work with the United States on the ground, and the United States would respect the autonomy of the Shiites. Khatami left the meeting with Straw for an urgent meeting of the Iranian national security council—to report and get a commitment on the plan. Straw left to report to London and Washington.

The agreement came almost immediately. By September 26, the Russians and Iranians were both on board. The war could move forward. However, there were now only fifteen days until October 11. The situation wasn't quite as bad as it seemed, since the war would begin with strategic bombing that didn't require any forces on the ground, but it still wasn't good. The war would begin in two weeks, and the diplomatic groundwork had only now been completed. The U.S. had only a couple of weeks to get into Afghanistan, make contact with the various groups, persuade them to cooperate, and get them any weapons and equipment they would need.

Making Contact

The Northern Alliance and the Shiites were going to be the mainstays of American strategy, but they were not and could not be the whole thing. There were others the U.S. would court as well. Among them was Gulbuddin Hekhmatyar, leader of the Hezb-I-Islami. Hekhmatyar made Malik look like a man of integrity. He had worked for the CIA during the war against the Soviets. Then, when most of his faction—oriented toward Wahabiism—joined the Taliban, he went into exile in Iran in the city of Qom, the seat of the despised Shiites. During the civil war prior to the Taliban victory, Hekhmatyar basically destroyed Kabul with a constant rocket barrage.

The United States had files on Afghan leaders who had worked with the U.S. in the past, but the files were valuable only if those leaders could be found and persuaded to join the United States in a war on the Taliban. Almost all of the CIA operatives and Special Forces troops that had worked with the Afghan mujahideen over a decade before had gone on to other things. Most were no longer in government service; others had gone on to important administrative positions. All of them were at least ten years older than when they were in Afghanistan and Pakistan. The most effective operatives, who had the closest relations with crucial Afghan leaders, had been there during the early 1980s. But that was almost twenty years before. All were now in their forties, and the ones who had been majors or lieutenant colonels or their equivalents—the ones who were senior enough then to have carried weight with the Afghan leaders—were in their late fifties at best.

Those were exactly the ones who were needed—and they were needed in Afghanistan within days of September 11. There was no time for training or conditioning. In scenes resembling a bad Rambo movie, men who had done yeoman's service fifteen or twenty years earlier were now approached and asked to undertake one more op.

Old relationships had withered. Old contacts had died. There was deep distrust of the Americans, but it was not as hopeless as it seemed. A fundamentally important characteristic of Afghan society was that money repaired old relationships, created trust, and could almost resurrect the dead. Loyalty was for sale in Afghanistan—and Americans arrived carrying money.

The old Afghan hands who were sent into Afghanistan in late September and early October carried with them huge amounts of money. Individual agents parachuted into the country with several million dollars in American cash strapped on their backs. Unlike in previous operations, the CIA agents were authorized to spend the money as they saw fit. There was no bureaucratic process in place to slow things down. It was understood that some of the money would be inevitably squandered or misspent. But if the U.S. was going to go to war in Afghanistan a month after September 11, there was no choice. The CIA returned to a model it had used in World War II—picking good people and trusting them.

The problem was that they did not have many good people or much time. Air strikes were to begin before October 11, and CIA agents began moving into Afghanistan around September 27. That was the fastest they could get there. They had to collect their gear and money in Washington, then fly to a former Soviet air base in Uzbekistan. From there, they were ferried into Afghanistan in Russian helicopters and started to do business. It took five precious days to get them where they needed to be. Then they had a little over two weeks to get the cooperation of indigenous Afghan forces.

They were headed to three places: the headquarters of Mohammed Fahim, Massoud's successor; the headquarters of Dostum at Darra-e Suf, south of Mazar e-Sharif; and Banyan, where Karim Khalili, the Shiite Hazari commander, was based. But these were only the starting points. Fahim, Dostum, and Kalili were commanders only in the loosest sense of the word. Their subordinate commanders were themselves autonomous operatives who could and sometimes did go their own way. And the next level of commanders also had options, and so on down the line. Families and clans were the basic social unit. These clans were linked together by business and marriage, but they were also sometimes torn apart by these things. If the Northern Alliance was a tense coalition of mutually mistrustful leaders, their own organizations were no more tightly bound.

Therefore, the handful of aging CIA operatives who had been assembled to build the American alliance had to do more than persuade three men to collaborate. They had also to persuade their key lieutenants in a complex and virtually endless process. It was less coalition building than herding cats. Two local commanders who were engaged in a blood feud with each other would each insist on more money than the other as a matter of honor. It was not a simple business. This was why getting the Russian and Iranian go-ahead was more like receiving a hunting license than a coalition. Without their consent, nothing would have been possible. With it, the work would actually start.

The CIA operatives went in with a huge amount of money. The standard number that is thrown around is $70 million, although the correct number was probably higher. That figure was likely the amount spent in direct payments inside Afghanistan, but it did not cover payments into secret bank accounts around the world for senior leaders such as those in the Pashtun tribe who later turned on Mullah Omar and the Taliban. Seventy million dollars was what might be called walking-around money. However, for a country as poor as Afghanistan, $70 million was a lot of cash. Whoever received a piece of it would have the ability to spread it around among his own followers, increasing his power. If, on the other hand, he refused the money, one of his rivals might take it and undercut his authority.

The United States had two advantages in spending money this way. First, it was very difficult for the Afghans to refuse. Refusal could cost one his power or life. Whoever took the money had huge instant leverage within the clan or province, and very few could afford to pass on such a windfall. Second, the three targeted groups were bitter enemies of the Taliban. The Russians had saved them from a very unpleasant end by supplying them with weapons and other supplies, but had never given them any hope of defeating the Taliban. For the Russians, this was just a holding action.

The Americans, on the other hand, were not there to create a buffer zone. They were there to take down the Taliban regime. From Fahim, Dostum, and Kalili's point of view, and that of their followers, this was a dream come true. The Americans not only needed them to defeat the Taliban, they needed them to run Afghanistan afterward. At all levels, these people were highly motivated to cooperate with the Americans.

That is why the amount of time available wasn't much of a concern to U.S. planners. With Russian and Iranian buy-in and a huge amount of money being passed around, securing cooperation would not be hard. And it has to be remembered that these were already experienced fighters. They might need supplies and coordination, but they were ready to go to war fairly quickly. With the Russians moving supplies into Afghanistan and the U.S. paying cash for the supplies, the Northern Alliance was in the game by the first days of October. They were not yet ready to engage the Taliban, but they were ready to be positioned.

The next step, on the ground, was to move in U.S. Special Forces and CIA operatives in the Special Activities Division (SAD) of the Directorate of Operations (DO). With all the covert units moving into place—in spite of the fact that there were actually a small number of individuals involved—the opportunity for chaos was substantial. U.S. covert operations had historically been marked by intense friction, lack of coordination, and rivalry among the various uniformed organizations (as well as the ages-old struggle between the uniformed personnel and Agency SAD personnel, known inside of Langley as the knuckle-draggers).

This was nothing compared to the tension between mainstream American military forces and special operations. Culturally, there was a tremendous difference between the two sides. The regular military operated through a clear chain of command and had clear areas of responsibility. The special ops teams were built to be, as the saying went, "high-speed and low-drag" units, with minimum formality and maximum efficiency. They also operated with minimal accountability, sometimes leaving chaos in their trail that the regular military forces had to clean up.

From the regular military's point of view, these special operations teams brought chaos to the table. They were unpredictable and uncontrollable on the battlefield, and when they had to work parallel to regular forces, they would cause more problems than they solved. From the point of view of special operatives, the regular army was too slow and too bureaucratic and just slowed down the special operations types. All of this was doubled for the Directorate of Operations/Special

Activities Divison operations. Add to this the rivalries between individual special operations forces (Navy SEALS, Army Special Forces, and so on), and you had a prescription for chaos. Ever since Vietnam, it was well known that putting all of these players together in one mix was an invitation for failure.

In an extraordinary and atypical show of common sense, everyone, including the CIA, decided that the regional CINC, Tommy Franks, should have overall command of the operation. In a further show of intelligence, Franks permitted the local commanders of the Special Forces teams to take responsibility for their own operations. September 11 had stunned everyone so completely that the usual games were completely suspended. He sought to solve the tension between the need for collaboration and the need to support initiative in the field.

The Buildup

The buildup for ground operations began as soon as the Russian go-ahead was given. Within a week, a former Soviet Air Force base in Uzbekistan—Chirchik—was taken over by the United States Air Force as a logistical hub for the Afghan operation. Another air base, Khanabad, near Karshi, south of Tashkent (called K2 by U.S. personnel) and therefore more secure, quickly became an even more important base. Supplies started pouring into Khanabad and Chirchik, carried by a variety of American transport aircraft flying in over Russian and Central Asian airspace.

Chirchik was the logistical hub that reached out to smaller bases near the Afghan border. From these bases, Special Forces men and supplies would be ferried by helicopter and, later, by C-130s into Afghanistan proper. What was particularly good about these bases was that they had been built by the Soviets. Unlike American military facilities, which have a limited buffer, Soviet air bases were vast areas where it was impossible to see what was going on inside. The Taliban and Al Qaeda agents that were all over Uzbekistan may have known that the Americans were there, but they could not have known how many were there, or where, or when they were moving out. Soviet-style security helped the United States retain an element of surprise.

Moving the Special Forces teams into Afghanistan took time. For example, Team 595 didn't move into Dostum's headquarters at Darra-e Suf until October 19. CIA/SAD teams had already moved in, setting up the political bases for cooperation during the last week of September, but the Special Forces teams, there to establish military liaison, needed another couple of weeks to move from Fort Bragg, North Carolina, to staging areas and from there into Afghanistan.

One of the major holdups was airlift. The CIA teams were using Russian helicopters to move in. SOCOM's helicopters, meanwhile, loaded with communications gear, intelligence equipment, and weapons support systems, had to move from Europe and Hurlburt Field in the Florida panhandle to Chirchik, and then to forward bases. They had to be loaded on fixed-wing aircraft, flown in, off-loaded, and prepped. It took time. Other aircraft, the MC-130, loaded with special intelligence gear, had to be brought in. Even a light, fast force like Special Forces had to be assembled.

There was, therefore, a gap between the covert political arrangements and the arrival of Special Forces, which pushed the start of the war over the thirty-day mark. That mark was not hard and fast, but the President and his advisors wanted speedy action. They did not want it to appear that the United States was not responding swiftly. However, there was a solution: The air strikes could start early. The Air Force's strategic force was ready.

Air Force doctrine required a three-stage approach. First, the air defenses had to be taken down. Second, the command, control, and communications capability had to be destroyed. Only when that was done would the Air Force turn its attention to destroying the Taliban with strategic strikes and close air support for the Northern Alliance. Even if Special Forces couldn't be on the ground until mid-October, the air strikes could begin earlier. The Air Force had a mission to carry out and its early air strikes, even if less than essential, could provide a symbolic start for the war.

On September 19, the first aircraft left the United States, to join those already deployed in the Persian Gulf. Additional aircraft deployed to Kuwait, Saudi Arabia, Oman, and Diego Garcia. The United States was constrained as to where they could send the aircraft. The problem wasn't so much political as logistical. Getting aircraft to a base was easy. Getting supplies—from jet fuel to spare parts to munitions—to the base was the hard part. Aircraft could be in position to operate in a day, but it would take several weeks to get enough supplies into position so that the aircraft could operate. This assumed there were suitable storage facilities at the site.

The roughly 175 aircraft in theater were joined by about 150 additional aircraft. Long-range bombers would be flying air strikes from as far away as Fairford Air Force Base in England and Diego Garcia, while tactical fighters would have to fly out of bases in the Persian Gulf after extensive refueling, as well as from carriers in the Arabian Sea. In fact, the critical aircraft in the theater were not the attack aircraft but the refueling aircraft that made it possible for the fighters to strike into Afghanistan. It was the lack of refueling aircraft, rather than lack of fighter aircraft, that limited the number of sorties that could be flown. It also meant that each mission had to be synchronized, lest the tactical fighters run out of fuel during the mission. For this reason, the Iranian offer to allow U.S. aircraft to land in Iran in an emergency turned out to be valuable—a failure in the refueling mission could make such a landing imperative.

The planning for the war was nightmarish. The movement of forces, equipment, and supplies into multiple countries in so short a period of time was a monumental feat, mitigated only by the fact that the actual numbers were relatively small. Compared to Desert Storm, the forces being employed were minuscule. Desert Storm focused on getting forces into one country—Saudi Arabia—in order to seize a specific entity—Kuwait—controlled by a single, integrated military force—Iraq. Afghanistan involved getting forces into as many as a dozen countries to achieve a political end other than seizing territory, which was controlled by a complex and diverse group of military forces. And none of this could truly be preplanned. It was all being done on the fly, with the clock ticking down to October 11—one month from the attack on the United States.

War

The decision to launch air strikes on October 7, 2001, was made five days earlier, at a meeting of the National Security Council. That was the day on which the senior leadership became confident that all the pieces were in place. There was enough airpower to begin the war, political arrangements had been made in the region, and there was confidence that the ground elements would be in place by the time they were needed. In a sense, this was a "just-in-time" war.

Another assessment was held in the White House situation room on Friday, October 5, when all preparations were examined. A final review was held at Camp David on Saturday, when Donald Rumsfeld reported back on a trip he had just completed to the front-line states. Bush polled every member of the national security team, asking each of them if it was ready. Then he asked the Chairman of the Joint Chiefs of Staff, General Richard Myers, whether Tommy Franks was ready to go. Myers said that he was, and Bush ordered that air attacks begin on Sunday, October 7, 2001, Washington time.

The first bombs fell on Afghanistan at about 9:30 P.M. local time, not too long after dark. U.S. technology allowed aircraft to see in the dark, so the U.S. preferred to start air wars at night. The Afghans were still blind. Thirty targets were attacked, including command centers, surface-to-air missiles, radar sites, and suspected Al Qaeda camps. A good part of the Afghan Air Force, a handful of obsolete aircraft, were destroyed. The attacks continued throughout the night with additional waves of F-16s from bases in the Persian Gulf, and with strikes flown from carriers and by British jets. All of this was controlled from the air-warfare command-and-control center the United States maintained at Prince Sultan Air Force Base, fifty miles south of Riyadh, Saudi Arabia.

A command-and-control center in Kandahar, the true capital of the Taliban government, was destroyed as well as the Presidential Palace and main military base in Kabul. Herat, Jalalabad, Mazar e-Sharif, Konduz, Bagran, and Halmand were struck. Air strikes hit and destroyed targets at every point of the country.

Not a single U.S. aircraft was lost. It was a superbly planned and executed operation, truly global in scope. The problem was that it was fundamentally irrelevant to the war. It was a case of doctrine driving operations. U.S. doctrine said that wars begin with the United States seizing air supremacy, which means that it can carry out attacks without danger to the aircraft. Then command-and-control facilities must be attacked in order to paralyze the enemy's forces, followed by attacks on ground troops. Operation Enduring Freedom opened with a textbook display of this doctrine.

The problem was that the United States enjoyed air supremacy before the first sortie was flown. The fixed SAM positions had to be taken down, but that required no more than a half-dozen sorties at most. The Afghan Air Force wasn't taking off to challenge U.S. aircraft, so the F-14 air-to-air fighters were not needed. Most important, the Afghans did not have a centralized command-and-control system either from a political or a technical standpoint. Knocking out a command bunker in Kandahar did not materially affect the ability of the Taliban to resist, nor did the number of sorties the United States flew have a chance of really hurting the Taliban forces.

The United States had to strike on October 7 for political reasons rather than military reasons. And in this case, the political problem was in Afghanistan, not the United States. American operatives were approaching various Afghan leaders to join the United States in a war against the Taliban. Making even a verbal commitment could get back to the Taliban. Massoud had just been killed; other Afghan leaders didn't want to join him. The question on the minds of the key leaders like Kalili and Dostum, men whose lives were literally over if they bet wrong, was whether the United States was actually coming in or whether it was just another plot to get them to bleed on behalf of the United States while the Americans stayed safe. The Afghans, while being bribed by the CIA, knew perfectly well that without a serious American military commitment they wouldn't live long enough to enjoy the money they were being given.

The CIA was very busy assuring local leaders that it meant what it said, but thus far the U.S. hadn't actually done anything except send in CIA agents—not a group with very high credibility in Afghanistan. The CIA reported back to Langley—and Langley to the National Security Council and the President—that the Northern Alliance and the Shiites were eager to take on the Taliban, while some of the Pashtun leaders could be bought. However, none of them were prepared to make a move until they saw that the United States had skin in the game.

The U.S. knew that it couldn't get troops into Afghanistan in time. It also knew that if the Northern Alliance was to launch an attack before winter, it would have to start moving right away. The CIA reported that the Northern Alliance would not begin to forward-deploy simply on the word of the United States. The Northern Alliance was afraid of the Taliban. Taliban forces had beaten them badly during the civil war, and the Northern Alliance continued to take the short end of the stick when they engaged the Taliban. The only way that the Northern Alliance would forward-deploy was if the United States demonstrated (beyond a shadow of a doubt) that it was coming in, and showed that it could protect the Northern Alliance from a Taliban attack.

The Northern Alliance believed that the United States had no strike aircraft in Uzbekistan, Tajikistan, or Kyrgyzstan, and that the U.S. would not have any in place until November at the earliest. They also knew that the Russians were not going to intervene if they got into trouble. The Northern Alliance told the CIA operatives that they did not see any way in which the United States would be able to support them if the Taliban launched an offensive. They were in the northern tier of Afghanistan. The U.S. had aircraft to the west, but no permission to fly over Iran and no aircraft to the east. The view of the Northern Alliance was that they were again being sold a bill of goods by the CIA; they would forward-deploy when they saw that the United States could reach all the way to the north.

That's precisely what the United States did on October 7. Air strikes around the country were designed to demonstrate to the Northern Alliance—and other potential partners—that the U.S. could, quite easily, send B-52s and B-2s on carpet-bombing missions as far north as Mazar e-Sharif and Bagram, easily destroying Taliban forces massing to attack. They also demonstrated that the aircraft carriers offshore could, with midair refueling, provide tactical air support anywhere in Afghanistan. In other words, the Northern Alliance could deploy, be in position to begin offensive operations when they linked up with U.S. Special Forces later in October, and be protected by U.S. airpower while they did so. The air offensive also demonstrated that this was not a repeat of the Clinton retaliations, but a major and irreversible commitment by the U.S.—or at least as irreversible as anything could be at that time.

Military planners saw the October 7 attack as the doctrinally necessary preparation for a ground assault. The CIA wanted the attack so it could lock down Afghan commanders up and down the line by demonstrating U.S. capabilities and will. The fact that Air Force planners endorsed the operation helped in Washington, but the planners were looking at this both too narrowly and without a sufficient sense of irony. Carrying out counter-C^3I and counter-SEAD operations in Afghanistan was theater of the absurd.

There had to be a system for calling in air strikes. For this, close air controllers had to be deployed with the attacking Northern Alliance forces. To get the CACs in, U.S. Special Operations teams had to move into Afghanistan, with U.S. Army Special Forces being critical in establishing liaison with Afghan forces on the ground. However, as the air war began, the Special Operations/Special Forces teams had not yet been deployed.

Taliban Prepares for War

The Taliban knew how the United States fought wars and was prepared for it. The American attack was fully expected. In a sense, their strategy was indifferent to how the Americans attacked. If the U.S. launched another token cruise missile strike, Al Qaeda would only look stronger in the Islamic world. If the United States launched a conventional war on Afghanistan, the Taliban and Al Qaeda would revert to guerrilla tactics and bleed the Americans dry the same way they bled the Soviets. Either way, bin Laden and Omar would be getting the kind of results they wanted.

The Taliban was a light infantry force, optimized for operations in Afghanistan. The fighters could come together in larger formations or disperse into squad-level units. Drawn from various tribes, particularly the Pashtun in the south, the Taliban claimed to have about 300,000 fighters. The reality was that the Taliban had about 30,000 to 50,000 troops that it controlled directly or through extremely loyal warlords, and several hundred thousand more that were currently part of the Taliban's force but whose primary loyalty was to local tribal leaders whose loyalty to the Taliban varied with the political winds—and with CIA cash.

The Taliban did not expect the United States to move as quickly as it did. Osama bin Laden's thinking had been shaped by Desert Storm, and he thought the Americans would use that war as the model. That meant a buildup of forces somewhere outside of Afghanistan, a massive air campaign, followed by multidivisional maneuver forces. They were prepared for any number of variations on this theme. For example, there was the Soviet model, in which Soviet special forces moved in first to seize Kabul and other cities, and were followed by conventional forces.

All of these models assumed that the United States would depend primarily on its own conventional forces. The Taliban knew that the Northern Alliance would probably participate in the attack, but they did not believe that the Americans would rely entirely on the Northern Alliance for their ground forces. The Taliban had done everything possible to render the Northern Alliance impotent, battering them with attacks. And, most important, they had killed Massoud, the Northern Alliance's most important leader.

The Taliban was counting on the fact that the U.S. would need a country that would provide a base of operations. They knew that neither Iran nor Pakistan would allow the United States to base the hundreds of thousands of troops needed to invade Afghanistan. To do so, the Taliban believed, the United States would have to invade or occupy one of those countries. Not only would that take several years, but it would force the U.S. to do exactly what Al Qaeda had hoped for: make war on multiple Islamic countries simultaneously.

The other alternative was the northern route, through Turkmenistan, Uzbekistan, and Tajikistan. The Taliban knew two things about this attack plan. First, it would require Russian acquiescence. The Taliban knew that the Russians still regarded these three countries as part of their sphere of influence, because Taliban and Pakistani intelligence was constantly running up against Russian intelligence and security people in these countries. Russians were all over these countries and did not plan to leave.

Bin Laden had learned, from studying American strategy in Kuwait, that U.S. forces depended heavily on armored forces. Transporting heavy armored fighting vehicles and self-propelled artillery to a distant theater of operations was done by sea—and just as Afghanistan had no ocean ports, neither did Turkmenistan, Uzbekistan, or Tajikistan. Ships would have to bring the armor to Russian ports and the vehicles would have to be transported into these countries by rail. The Taliban knew that the Russian train system wouldn't allow that to happen very quickly.

Finally, the Taliban did not think that the United States had the necessary forces to carry out the operation under any circumstances. The Taliban was quite sophisticated about fighting wars against major powers. Not only had they fought the Russians, but Al Qaeda members had studied U.S. operations in the Persian Gulf, Israeli operations in Lebanon and in the occupied territories, Indian–Pakistani clashes, and, of course, the Iran-Iraq war. They may not have studied at West Point, but their collective knowledge of enemy capabilities and how wars are fought was substantial.

The Taliban knew that the United States had stretched itself close to the limit of its effective combat power in Desert Storm, and that in the decade since Desert Storm U.S. forces had been drawn down considerably. They also knew that Afghanistan had swallowed some 300,000 Soviet troops that never took control of anything but the cities and some major roads. The numbers didn't add up from the Taliban's point of view. The U.S. simply didn't have enough combat power to take Afghanistan, and if it marshaled all of its forces against Afghanistan, it would have no reserves available for action anywhere else.

Al Qaeda believed it had created the perfect situation. The United States couldn't ignore September 11, but it couldn't take Afghanistan. The most the U.S. could do was move insufficient forces into Afghanistan and then hopelessly bog down. And whichever option the United States chose, it would be apparent to the other factions in Afghanistan that, in the long run, the U.S. did not have the ability to impose a solution on Afghanistan. That would keep the pro-Taliban coalition in place. No one wanted to side with a loser.

The Pakistani government, the only one to formally recognize the Taliban, and the Saudis, who also had close ties to the Taliban, shared this evaluation. Both had extensive experience with American intelligence and the U.S. military, and neither believed that the United States could launch a regime-threatening attack at all, and certainly not until the summer. It was simply not possible.

This was one reason why the Pakistanis held a fairly rigid position on the basing of any U.S. assets in September and most of October. They shared the Taliban's read of the situation and expected U.S. military action to be ineffective. The Pakistanis, along with the Taliban, therefore engaged in a series of symbolic gestures and consultations. Offers of turning over bin Laden to third parties for Islamic trial were simply gestures designed to confuse the situation. Neither the Taliban nor Al Qaeda thought they were facing a serious military threat, even though they were certain they would be attacked.

When the bombing started, the war seemed to be taking the expected course. The United States was hitting Afghanistan fairly lightly with strategic airpower and naval air, plus the inevitable cruise missiles. They were following the standard American war plan of taking out strategic targets. They were also hitting Al Qaeda training camps and incidentally killing some personnel, but the camps were hardly concentrated, populated targets. The Taliban's intelligence in Uzbekistan told them that the Americans were only beginning to fly in troops and matériel. The Taliban knew that the Russians were bringing in supplies for the Northern Alliance, that their traditional enemies among the Shiites were engaging with the Americans, and even that there was unrest among their own Pashtun tribe. They also knew they had defeated these elements before, and that nothing the Russians or Americans were bringing in was going to change that equation.

What the Taliban and its Pakistani and Saudi friends had failed to take into account was that U.S. airpower had evolved dramatically since Desert Storm. It assumed, because it didn't see U.S. fighter and attack aircraft in Uzbekistan, that it would face only naval airpower, which was limited in strength and reach. The Taliban also assumed that naval airpower, as in Desert Storm, did not have the advanced precision-munitions capabilities that the Air Force had. They were wrong on both counts. The Air Force could conduct intense precision strikes on Afghanistan without having bases nearby, and the Navy had dramatically improved its capabilities.

Boots on the Ground

The United States fully shared the Taliban analysis, and understood the fundamental obstacles in attacking Afghanistan. The United States also knew that it had to act and didn't have enough time. It knew that it had to depend on the Northern Alliance and that the Northern Alliance could not defeat the Taliban alone. It knew that imprecise bombardment would not achieve anything. The United States knew it had a serious problem.

The solution to the problem was the Special Forces that began arriving in Uzbekistan shortly after the bombing began on October 6.

The United States had the ability to destroy anything it chose. But aircraft, flying at 15,000 feet, couldn't possibly see the targets that needed to be destroyed in Afghanistan. The U.S. needed eyes on the ground to achieve that. The eyes belonged to combat air controllers.

Combat air controllers were the critical military specialty for the United States in Afghanistan. In a very real sense, the entire campaign rested on a handful of men drawn from the Air Force and Naval Aviation whose specialty was calling in air strikes. There were never more than a few dozen of these men deployed in Afghanistan, but they were the ones who enabled airpower to be effective. Calling in an air strike consists of more than simply designating the target. It also requires a selection of munitions appropriate to the target, a vector of attack to minimize the chance of friendly casualties, rapid damage assessment, and so on. Sometimes a laser designator is used to pinpoint the target for laser-guided munitions. Sometimes when he lases the target, the target shoots back. The combat air controller not only has to be skilled at his own trade, he also has to be able to operate as an infantryman. He walks to his target.

In order for him to be effective, he has to get close. U.S. Navy SEAL teams and British, Australian, and New Zealand SAS served in many cases on long-range reconnaissance that culminated in calling in air strikes on targets—particularly in the first two weeks of war, after the air strikes began but before Special Forces were on the ground. However, for the CAC to be effective, he had to be delivered to his observation point and then had to be protected while he did his work.

The air strikes were not stand-alone attacks but were linked to assaults from Northern Alliance forces. Therefore, if the CACs were to do their jobs and the Northern Alliance was to exploit the damage being done by the air strikes, someone had to tie these two together. The mission of carrying out this kind of warfare falls to the U.S. Army's Special Forces. They had gathered in Uzbekistan, some coming in from their bases in the United States, others from Jordan where they were completing a training exercise. These forces would later be inserted in the south, around Kandahar, in support of the future president, Hamid Karzai.

Special Forces teams began moving toward Uzbekistan as the first bombs started to drop and prepared to move into Afghanistan by the middle of October. Team 555 was sent in, just after midnight on October 19, by MH-53 J Pave Low helicopters flown by Air Force Special Operations pilots that landed just north of Bagram Air Force Base in the town of Taqhma. There they linked up with CIA personnel who had made the necessary arrangements with General Mohammed Fahim, the defense minister of the Jamiat-I-Islami, the Tajik forces of the Northern Alliance. They would work with General Bismullah Khan and his subordinate commanders.

A second Special Forces unit—Team 595—was flown into Afghanistan, meeting up with their CIA liaison at Darra-e Suf in the mountains south of Mazar e-Sharif. Their assignment was Abdul Rashid Dostum, who commanded the Uzbek Jumbesh-I-Milli. Team 595 became legendary during the war through photos showing them riding horses in the first American cavalry charge of the twenty-first century.

Teams 555 and 595 were joined by two other teams: Team 553, which went into Bamian, setting up liaison with the Shiites, and 585, which went into Kunduz. For eighteen days, these four teams represented the sum total of American presence on the ground in Afghanistan, save for CIA and some other isolated Special Operations teams that were primarily hunting for Osama bin Laden and his lieutenants.

A Special Forces group consists of three layers of command. The basic operating unit of a Special Forces group is the "A Team." The A Team has twelve men and is usually commanded by a captain—someone in his late twenties or early thirties. The second in command is a warrant officer, an experienced enlisted man. There is a master sergeant and nine other noncommissioned or enlisted men. Each of them has one or more of these specialties: demolitions, intelligence, weapons, communications, and engineering. The A Team has sufficient redundancy built in that it can operate as two separate teams and can, if necessary, break down into four- or three-man units. Since they were also accompanied by a CAC, these were thirteen-man teams. They were supported by two B Teams, battalion-level groups that are primarily logistical support teams designed to facilitate the work of the A Teams. These B Teams each consist of about fifteen people. Eighty-two Americans were on the ground in Afghanistan.

The job of the Special Forces was to make certain that the Northern Alliance moved forward into contact with the Taliban and that air strikes smashed the Taliban's front line. This created serious tension. The Air Force did not see its greatest contribution as attacking extremely small-value targets. The problem was that there were only small-value targets in Afghanistan—men, weapons, and some huts. A second problem was to determine who and how the air forces were tasked. There really weren't all that many aircraft in theater, and there were a lot of targets—who would get them was a real issue. CENT-COM tried to set up a system for allocating strike aircraft. No one was particularly happy with the system.

The initial phases of bombing (between October 7 and October 19) had left the Northern Alliance fairly unimpressed; the Air Force's SEAD and Counter-C^3I strategy seemed to them simply random bombing. If this was the level of support they were going to receive from the United States, they were not going to attack. Attacking and failing would mean the destruction of their military—and themselves. Nothing they had seen prior to October 19 convinced them that they were going to win any battles.

Starting on October 19, however, their perception of U.S. air-power began to shift. The Taliban was holding lines near enough to the Northern Alliance's that the effect could be seen. They were holding those lines because they had profoundly miscalculated the effectiveness of the U.S. air attack. Their positions were hammered by a wide variety of precision-guided munitions and by carpet bombing from B-52s. The effect was not devastating, but it was sufficiently damaging that the Taliban realized its positions would eventually be destroyed. Moreover, by the end of October, the attacks were being followed by advances by the Northern Alliance, designed to take advantage of the shock and disorganization that inevitably followed air attacks.

By early November, Central Command had decided to move on Mazar e-Sharif. There were a number of reasons for this decision. Mazar e-Sharif was the most isolated from the Taliban, and it was cut off from reinforcements. Also, no one really trusted Dostum. In order to take Mazar e-Sharif, Dostum would have to cooperate with two other commanders, Attah Mohammed and Mohammed Mohaqiq. Dostum had pledged that he would cooperate, but Mazar e-Sharif would be a litmus test. The U.S. had to know more about Dostum before they went deeper into Afghanistan.

With the 595 A Team in place, a battalion commander from the 5th Group, Lt. Col. Max Bowers, led a team to Dostum's headquarters. His job was to coordinate the assault on Mazar e-Sharif. The plan was simple: encircle the city and bombard the forces. Under no circumstances was anyone prepared to engage in urban warfare. The U.S. had no troops on the ground and none of the Northern Alliance commanders wanted to risk their forces. So the question was simple: When the attack began, what would the Taliban do?

The answer came quickly. The assault on the city began on November 9. At dawn, as the Special Forces called in heavy air strikes, the commanders and the Special Forces could see the Taliban withdrawing from the city. By the night of November 9, the Taliban positions had essentially disappeared. Mazar e-Sharif was an open city, and the Northern Alliance could move in at will, mopping up as required. The United States and Northern Alliance appeared to have won a stunning victory.

The Taliban had completely miscalculated the effectiveness of U.S. airpower and had probably underestimated the ability of the United States to buy cohesiveness in the Northern Alliance. But by early November the reality was clear to them, and they knew that they would have to recalculate their strategy. They would not have until spring. Indeed, if they held their positions around the cities, they wouldn't survive until the winter.

The Taliban did not grasp that the United States understood the core weakness of its alliance system: The alliance depended on interest, not ideology. And on the level of interest, the United States could defeat the Taliban. Once the U.S. had demonstrated its commitment to the war, the dollars being passed around by CIA agents would corrode the Taliban's alliance system with dizzying speed. Once massive resupply reached the Northern Alliance, and Special Forces helped lead them, Northern Alliance offensive power, multiplied by airpower, would prove irresistible. And once SOCOM brought in its teams dedicated to locating targets for air strikes, any unit larger than a squad was liable to attack as long as it remained close to cities.

It took the Taliban until November to absorb these lessons. Between the start of the war and early November, when the Taliban went to its dispersal strategy, the goal of the United States was to create the foundations of the Taliban's collapse—without the Taliban's realizing it was collapsing. The Americans did not want a massive retreat. They wanted the Taliban to stand and fight for as long as possible, because the longer they stood, the more the U.S. could kill. In November there were accusations in the U.S. media and among politicians that the war was going too slowly. That was precisely what Central Command wanted.

The Taliban had been surprised by the speed of the American air campaign, but it had not panicked. They knew that the Americans had not brought major forces into the region. They knew that a Marine Expeditionary Unit was offshore, but they also knew that it had not even 2,000 Marines on board. In other words, the bombers had come, but the U.S. Army was nowhere to be seen. Nor would the Army have frightened them.

In Afghanistan, the cities are the prizes to be won after the war. They are not the means for winning a war. Wars are won and lost in the countryside, the mountains and deserts. Unlike advanced industrial societies, in which cities function as economic and political hubs,

Afghanistan's cities were preindustrial. They did not push wealth out into the countryside, nor did they project power. Wealth was pushed into the cities, and political power arose in the countryside. Holding the cities would not win a war. Holding the countryside would.

This was the strategic mistake made by the Soviets, who seized Afghanistan's cities only to discover that the ability of the Afghans to fight had not been eroded at all. Indeed, they discovered that they were trapped in the cities with a population that had to be fed. Their enemy, the mujahideen, could survive indefinitely outside the cities and slowly bleed the Soviets to death. Only after defeating the Soviets and winning the civil wars did the Taliban take the prizes—the cities.

From the Taliban's point of view, they could not hold the cities. At most, they could force the enemy into urban warfare, draining them at the cost of the annihilation of Taliban forces trapped inside the city. Holding the city would not help them win a war against the Americans anyway. The key was controlling the countryside, through a strong Taliban military capability and a strong system of alliances with other groups in the country.

The Taliban therefore made a strategic decision not to stand and fight in front of Mazar e-Sharif. They held until it was clear that an assault was in the offing. They then gave the order to abandon positions, disperse in the countryside, and plan to begin regrouping in the winter. The Taliban recognized its mistake in underestimating both the effectiveness of U.S. long-range bombing and underestimating the willingness of the Northern Alliance to hang together in order to defeat the Taliban. They recovered rapidly from their mistake and proceeded to a new strategy: withdraw, regroup, and launch, over time, a new guerrilla war designed to drain the Americans as they had drained the Soviets.

The withdrawal from Mazar e-Sharif was repeated over and over in the other cities. On November 11, Taliqan fell; on November 13, it was Kabul. The Taliban did not intend to hold and was not defeated. Facing an impossible military situation, it executed a difficult and complex military maneuver: withdraw, disperse, and regroup. Obviously, many fighters would be killed, would surrender, or would simply disappear. But the Taliban had no choice. At the same time, the Taliban thought it had, in the long run, a winning strategy.

The United States understood the strategy. Whatever headlines the media were flashing—that the Afghan cities were falling to the U.S. like dominoes—Central Command knew that it had not yet defeated the Taliban. Apart from the failure to kill or capture most of the troops (the Northern Alliance was not inclined to hunt them down as they filtered southward, since it would disperse troops needed to defend against other rivals), the heartland of the Taliban, in the Pashtun country around Kandahar, remained untouched. The war would not be over until Kandahar fell. And Kandahar would fall only if a Pashtun was prepared to rise up against his own tribal brethren.

The United States had recruited the Northern Alliance. They now needed to recruit a renegade Pashtun leader. None of those approached would consider allying with the United States while the Taliban remained undefeated in the north. As with the Northern Alliance, the Pashtuns wanted a demonstration of the ability of the United States to bring their power to bear and defeat the Taliban— indeed, that proof was even more urgent in the Pashtun south. By November 9, as Mazar e-Sharif was falling, the military framework for a political shift was emerging.

Karzai

The Americans discovered their Pashtun in Hamid Karzai. Karzai had anti-Taliban credentials. He had gone into opposition to them in 1998 and had moved across the border to Quetta in Pakistan. He had good relations with a network of Pashtun leaders who were unhappy with the Taliban. In retaliation, the Taliban murdered Karzai's father, Abdul Ahmad Karzai, in 1999. The elder Karzai had been the chief of the Popalzai tribe who had had strong support among the Popalzai and other southern tribes.

Hamid Karzai was made the new Popalzai chief, even though he had older brothers—all of whom lived in the United States. It is at this point that Karzai took a step that bought him credibility with the Americans. Working from Quetta, Karzai assembled a 300-vehicle convoy of mourners and, in opposition to both the Taliban and the Pakistani government, took his father's body from Quetta to their hometown of Kandahar. The Taliban, afraid of a massive split among the Pashtun, did not intervene. Karzai came out of the incident not only as the leader of the Popalzai but also as a significant figure among the Pashtun.

Immediately after September 11, Karzai began to mobilize against the Taliban. He knew that the United States would be attacking, and he moved to position himself to be an asset for the United States. His plans, drawn up in Quetta, were to create a tribal militia that would operate in the Pashtun regions against the Taliban. Karzai approached both the Americans and the British, with whom he had better relations, for support.

The United States was not at all certain about how to proceed in the Pashtun regions. It understood that as long as the Taliban retained their power base in the Pashtun belt of Afghanistan, they couldn't be rooted out. However, the Pashtuns were not simply an Afghan phenomenon. They were an ethnic group that stretched over the Afghan–Pakistani border. The fate of the Pashtuns interested the Pakistanis as well.

Even after September 11, the immediate view of the United States was that the foundations of the U.S.–Pakistani relationship remained intact. The U.S. Ambassador to Pakistan, Wendy Chamberlain, refused to open relations with Hamid Karzai because it was U.S. policy that the primary responsibility for managing the Pashtuns rested with Pakistani intelligence. The ISI had been telling its American counterparts at the CIA that it would be able to split the Taliban, creating a moderate wing that would dominate it. The ISI told the CIA that they did not want Karzai involved in this, because he was considered too anti-Taliban. Therefore, in the weeks after September 11, the U.S. policy toward Pakistan remained unchanged—the Pashtun strategy remained a subset of U.S.–Pakistani relations.

The British were more favorably inclined toward Karzai, particularly because they didn't trust the ISI. The British view of the situation was that without an anti-Taliban rising in the Pashtun regions, there was no hope of any meaningful success in Afghanistan. Unlike the American State Department, the British saw the Pakistanis as part of the problem, not the solution, believing the ISI was inventing the notion of a moderate wing of the Taliban in order to buy time for its faction. There was not only no possibility of such a wing emerging, but also no real desire for one, according to the British.

A tremendous political battle broke out over Karzai in Washington. But ultimately it was not Karzai who was at stake—it was the Pakistanis. It was a debate that would define the strategy in the war, and the question was both remarkable and simple: Was Pakistan an American ally in this war or one of the main enemies? The fate of Hamid Karzai turned on the outcome of this dispute.

From the standpoint of the State Department, which values its ability to maintain good relations with other countries, U.S.–Pakistani relations remained the cornerstone of the U.S. strategy in South and Southwest Asia. India remained an ambivalent player, and Iran was hopelessly anti-American. U.S. relations with China were at an unpredictable stage, while the situation in Central Asia was chaotic at best. Pakistan may have been tending toward the Islamist position, and pro-American elements inside Pakistan may have been on the defensive, but in the end, Pakistan was the only game in town. If keeping relations with Pakistan meant following its lead on the Taliban, that was a price that would have to be paid.

Interestingly, the Central Intelligence Agency was also generally pro-Pakistan. The CIA's Pakistani hands had worked closely with the ISI during the 1980s, and the people who had been field operatives then were holding senior positions in 2001. These people had developed close working relationships with the ISI, relationships that went beyond Afghanistan to collaboration on sharing intelligence throughout the region. They understood that some of the ISI officers were profoundly Islamist, but they had been profoundly Islamist in the

1980s. That is what had endeared them to the CIA—their Islamism had made them committed anti-Communists and anti-Soviets. These were men who had risked everything and shed blood side by side with their Agency counterparts. The CIA knew that these agents supported the Taliban, but this policy, which had emerged gradually over the years in Pakistan, did not seem to represent a radical shift—merely the logical evolution of things.

The senior leaders of the Department of Defense had a very different view of the Pakistani situation. The Defense Department had close ties to the Pakistanis going back to the 1950s. However, people like Paul Wolfowitz argued that the Pakistani ISI could have disrupted Al Qaeda but didn't. Nevertheless, there was a deep institutional bias toward Pakistan even in the Pentagon. Rather than taking the view that the ISI had simply become Islamist, its defenders argued that it had become paralyzed by politics. Add to this the State Department's concerns about Pakistani sensibilities and the CIA's concerns about maintaining long-standing lines of communication into the ISI and we can begin to see the dynamic. Whatever Pakistan had been in the past, it was not that any longer, but institutional inertia in Defense, State, and the CIA placed a conceptual straitjacket on the United States. A battle broke out between the senior leadership of DoD and Washington's national security bureaucracy over Pakistan.

Pakistan's response during the first week after September 11 strengthened the Defense Department leaders' position. To put it simply, the Pakistani government equivocated. Superficially, President Pervez Musharraf condemned the attacks on the United States and promised support, but the United States had concrete requests. First, it wanted access to Pakistani territory in order to carry out special operations in Afghanistan. Second, it wanted access to Pakistani air bases for air strikes and logistical support. Third, it wanted access to Pakistani intelligence sources who could provide information on the location of Al Qaeda members. Finally, the United States was hoping that the Pakistani military would participate in operations in Afghanistan alongside American troops.

These proposals were completely logical in terms of the relationship the United States thought it had with Pakistan, but Musharraf's reply was ambiguous. On one hand, both privately and publicly he condemned Al Qaeda and said that he stood with the United States. At the same time, he publicly called on the United States not to attack Afghanistan but offered instead to serve as an intermediary in talks with the Taliban. On September 17, Musharraf sent a team of ranking military officers to Kabul to speak with the Taliban leadership, asking that the Taliban turn over Al Qaeda—although whom they should turn them over to was unclear. The Taliban made some gestures that it would investigate the charges or turn Osama bin Laden over to an Islamic tribunal. However, it was clear that the Taliban had neither the intention nor the ability to destroy Al Qaeda infrastructure on its soil.

The debate over Pakistan's intentions intensified. It was not clear to anyone whether the September 16 mission was a serious effort or was simply an attempt by the Pakistanis to cover themselves. What was clear was that Musharraf was having difficulty delivering the things that were asked for. Very quickly it became obvious that Musharraf either did not want to give the U.S. bases in Pakistan publicly, or he felt that he could not survive if he did. Moreover, it was clear that Musharraf could not generate the flow of accurate and timely intelligence the U.S. was convinced the ISI had. Musharraf was either reluctant himself, or trapped by political forces.

It became clear that the U.S. was not going to get formal military assistance from Pakistan, nor would it be permitted to base large numbers of troops there. What the Pakistanis agreed to was three things: First, the United States would be allowed to set up special operations bases secretly in the area of the Afghan–Pakistani border. These bases would not be formally acknowledged. In the event of war, the United States would be permitted to use Pakistani airspace to transit into Afghanistan. President Musharraf ordered the Pakistani military to increase patrols along the full length of the Afghan-Pakistani border in order to keep Al Qaeda from crossing into

Pakistan. The ISI would cooperate with the CIA on at least these levels.

From the American point of view, all that the Pakistanis had really given were some small, secret bases in Pakistan. The very secrecy of these bases convinced the United States that regardless of Musharraf's personal intentions—and that was hotly debated—the United States could not rely on the Pakistanis. There was a growing realization that Pakistan was part of the problem, not the solution. Rumsfeld and Wolfowitz were winning the fight.

Therefore, leaving the Pashtun situation in the hands of the ISI was not acceptable. The United States needed badly to split the Pashtun community without the help of the ISI. The obvious—indeed only—choice was Hamid Karzai. As the ISI started to recognize the direction the United States was taking—and the long-term implications of this strategy—they started an anti-Karzai campaign designed to discredit Karzai in the eyes of Afghan leaders in order to devalue him to the United States. They claimed (wrongly) that Karzai had long worked for the CIA and that he had been on the payroll of Unicol, a U.S. oil company with traditionally edgy operating policies. They also pointed out that Karzai had been close to the Taliban prior to 1994—something that was true—and, interestingly, that he had worked for the ISI, which was an interesting maneuver designed to soil Karzai in the minds of those in the Defense Department who deeply distrusted the ISI.

The United States had two basic choices in Afghanistan. One was restoring the monarchy, which was generally a nonstarter. The other was Karzai. The U.S. did not make the decision to support Karzai until the first week of November. It was a tough decision, and the U.S. didn't want to make it until and unless they were certain that things in the north would work out. On November 14, Team 574, under the command of Captain Jason Amerine, linked up with Karzai. Karzai did not have much of an army. Unlike the Northern Alliance, which had substantial forces standing by, Karzai had managed to raise a force of a few dozen, who were poorly armed. His strategy was going to be different—based more on negotiation and diplomacy than military might.

Karzai's view was that the key to defeating the Taliban was taking Kandahar, and that the key to Kandahar was the town of Tirin-e-Kot, about seventy miles northwest of Kandahar and a major center of Taliban activity. If Tirin-e-Kot could be taken, it would demonstrate to the rest of the Pashtuns that the Taliban was finished nationally. Karzai intended to use a traditional Afghan strategy—he planned to negotiate his way to power. He did that by making deals with various tribes that had had relations with his tribe and his father.

Karzai went after Tirin-e-Kot with only sixty men of his own, plus air strikes. He banked on the widespread sense that the Taliban was going to withdraw anyway, and that, if only in the short run, Tirin-e-Kot and the rest of the Pashtun region was on its own. Karzai negotiated the peaceful surrender of the city on November 16. The campaign continued in the Pashtun regions. Over the next three weeks there was progress, but it was not without setbacks (on December 4, for example, resistance was encountered in the town of Shawal-e-Kot with a friendly-fire incident involving a B-52, a JDAM, and a foul-up on the ground; Karzai was slightly wounded, and three Americans and numerous Afghans were killed).

Kandahar held out until December 7, when the Taliban abandoned the city and it was discovered that Mullah Omar, the leader of the Taliban, had disappeared. Indeed, during the period between the fall of Mazar e-Sharif on November 9 and the fall of Kandahar on December 7, the vast majority of Taliban and Al Qaeda fighters, including the leadership, vanished.

On December 7, 2001, three fundamental things were true:

1. The major Afghan cities were in the hands of American allies.
2. The bulk of the Taliban had either dispersed or, for those trapped in cities, had negotiated their way out, striking deals in Pashtun areas particularly.
3. The United States had lost track of Osama bin Laden.

The United States had achieved one of its Al Qaeda–related goals. It had completely disrupted Al Qaeda's command cell and had denied it its facilities in Afghanistan. It had also managed to kill a number of senior Al Qaeda personnel. On the other hand, the U.S. had failed in another mission: It had not destroyed Al Qaeda, nor did the U.S. know where it was.

In addition, the United States had not destroyed the Taliban. The Taliban had withdrawn—although certainly not in good order. It had suffered substantial casualties and desertions. Its network of supporting relationships had been disrupted, as the scrupulously realistic Afghans reoriented their loyalties toward the more powerful Americans and their allies. The Taliban government was gone, but the Taliban itself remained a force, clearly intending to regroup and begin guerrilla operations against the Americans and their allies after winter. Certainly, the United States had not occupied Afghanistan, but it had never intended to. It never had more than a few hundred special operations troops and CIA operatives on the ground. Occupation was neither a possibility nor a goal.

In short, as with many American military operations, the operation itself was extraordinarily well planned in an extremely short time frame, and executed with meticulous, professional acumen. The strategic goals of the operation, however, were only partially met. Al Qaeda was not fully destroyed. The Taliban had retreated to a likely position of sustained guerrilla warfare. And in addition, in the course of the operation, the United States won political responsibility for the fate of Afghanistan (and had to commit larger forces simply to hold the key cities and airports in order to continue prosecuting raids against Al Qaeda).

The United States could not abandon Afghanistan. The political repercussions would have been too great. Moreover, the return of the Taliban would have been inevitable, along with the return of Al Qaeda. Therefore, the United States had won the campaign, but the campaign was simply the preface to the rest of the war. Al Qaeda was loose in Afghanistan, in the region, and around the world. It still had to be destroyed.

CHAPTER 10

Tora Bora and Nuclear Nightmares

FROM THE BEGINNING, Al Qaeda was like a light breeze. You were never sure if it was the wind or your imagination. Intelligence services around the world strained every sensor, trying to detect Al Qaeda's movements, intuit its plans, and identify its centers. Only one thing was certain after September 11—the base was in Afghanistan. The Taliban was the one regime that shared Al Qaeda's global vision. It was the one place where Al Qaeda was at home. It was believed, therefore, to be the only place where they were sure to be found.

The Afghan campaign destroyed even that certitude. Its primary result was not the destruction, but the dislocation, of Al Qaeda. The dislocation was helpful, to be sure, because it disrupted the ability of the command-and-control system to operate. However, the fact was that as the cities of Afghanistan fell, the United States's knowledge of Osama bin Laden's location declined. Following Kandahar's fall, every day that passed decreased the certainty of the U.S. as to his whereabouts. For a brief time, the United States actually knew where bin Laden was and had a good idea of how to get him—but this quickly slipped away. The failure at Tora Bora was to be a definitive moment in the covert war against Al Qaeda.

The Battle of Tora Bora

The American mission in Afghanistan therefore evolved to one basic task: find bin Laden before he escaped from Afghanistan. The rest was all simply a means toward this end. Early in the war, a Ranger team had parachuted into Mullah Omar's compound in Kandahar, looking for Omar and bin Laden. Units of Delta Force were positioned in Pakistan—it was expected that bin Laden was in the Pashtun south, so sending the D-Boys into Uzbekistan would not put them in a proper position. They were assigned to conduct raids based on intelligence about the location of bin Laden and others. As the cities fell, Delta Force dispersed into Pakistan, teaming with SAD members whose job it was to provide them with intelligence in the hunt for bin Laden.

One would have thought that finding a six-foot, five-inch Arab in Afghanistan would not have been all that hard. Height and ethnicity would have made him stand out. And certainly there was a constant flow of intelligence, lubricated by massive amounts of cash and the promise of a huge payoff if bin Laden was found.

All of the leads, however, proved to be erroneous. Bin Laden had been on the run for a long time. He knew the rules. He traveled with a substantial bodyguard in multiple convoys. It was hard to tell which one actually contained him. He also kept away from the local population. Bin Laden did not trust the Afghans, assuming that they would turn him in for the cash. He therefore practiced outstanding discipline, keeping out of sight, moving in unexpected ways, and generally confounding the forces that were hunting for him.

It was reluctantly concluded that he was not to be found around Kandahar. The Pakistanis swore that he was not in Pakistan. However, the Pakistanis did not want any American incursions on their soil, and the one thing they were certain of was that if bin Laden was spotted in Pakistan, the Americans would be on top of him instantly. The Pakistanis therefore were making absolutely certain that no one in the ISI knew where he was either, and that if they did the Americans would never hear about it.

In late October, U.S. intelligence officers on the ground, and using radio intercepts, started to note that a growing number of Al Qaeda operatives, their families, and members of a group called al-Wafa (which claimed to be a humanitarian organization but actually served as Al Qaeda's logistical support system) were converging on the town of Jalalabad, east of Kabul. Jalalabad had been a hub of Al Qaeda activity before the war broke out and had substantial training and other facilities. There were reports that local Taliban leaders were moving Afghans out of their homes in order to house Al Qaeda fighters and their families. By November 1, the CIA had reached the conclusion that Osama bin Laden was not in Kandahar, as had been assumed, but was most likely in the Jalalabad region.

CIA asked Central Command to launch an operation against Jalalabad. Central Command didn't, for two reasons. First, the CIA had, in the past, not been particularly reliable in its intelligence; there appeared to be a lot of guesswork going on. Second, there just weren't that many forces available. The war in the north was reaching its climactic phase, with the Northern Alliance beginning to move on the Taliban around Mazar e-Sharif. Karzai was beginning his move in the south. It has to be remembered that at this point, even Tommy Franks wasn't in-theater. He was back at Central Command Headquarters at MacDill Air Force Base in Florida. And even though Delta Force (which would normally conduct such a body snatch) was available, there was no intelligence to act upon. The CIA wasn't providing specific locations for Osama bin Laden, just a general area.

By mid-November, as the Taliban's withdrawal from the north was being completed, more airpower, along with SOCOM troops, had become available. Air strikes on and around Jalalabad had intensified, particularly during the second week of November. On November 15, the CIA, which had focused its resources heavily on the Jalalabad region, reported to Central Command that Osama bin Laden had been sighted moving south from Jalalabad in a large convoy, one of several, heading toward a place called Tora Bora. As the Taliban prepared to move out of Jalalabad, the exodus toward Tora Bora intensified, with large numbers of fighters on the move—all heading toward Tora Bora.

Tora Bora was a nightmare dating back to the days of the Soviet occupation. It was a cave complex, located on the Pakistani border, southeast of Kabul. Its border location was critical as was its complex of caves and tunnels, many of which were dug under U.S. auspices during the Afghan–Soviet war. This was not simply a system of caves. These were artificially constructed and enhanced caves and tunnels, which were heated and ventilated. They were designed to withstand overpressure from explosions, and they had electrical generators. The Tora Bora cave complex occupies an area about five miles from north to south and seven miles from east to west. Each cave is 25 to 50 feet high, and the entrances are at various altitudes and at an inclination of 45 to 60 degrees, making attacks by troops and artillery difficult.

Tora Bora was physically inaccessible. It takes about 17 hours to trek from the caves to road level. The mountains are sheer, and passes are covered by dense forest. Many of the cave openings are high up in sheer cliffs, reachable only by strenuous climbing or, at times, with pack animals. The only way in is by horse or mule—or by heli-copter, although that is dangerous both because of the terrain and the danger of ground fire. It combines natural caves with man-made caves and is simply an awe-inspiring fortress. Conventional forces simply cannot close in on Tora Bora.

It is interesting to note that the Americans had fairly good intelli-gence on the fortifications, since they had helped design them. There has also been speculation that the company that was hired to build Tora Bora was the construction firm that Osama bin Laden's father founded—underwritten by Saudi money.

It was relatively easy to use the caves and tunnels in the Tora Bora complex to move across the border from Afghanistan into Pakistan. The United States was prepared to move across the border, and some smaller forces did, but it didn't want to push a major force across. The battle at Tora Bora posed diplomatic challenges continually for the United States. It was saved from the entire issue of moving into Pakistan with major forces by the fact that there really weren't major forces in the theater and—even more important—what force was available, such as the Marine force at Camp Rhino near Kandahar, was kept out of the battle.

The United States decided to continue the model that it had used previously. Indigenous forces were to provide the major force at Tora Bora. They were to be supported by U.S. airpower, coordinated by U.S. Special Operations troops drawn from all of SOCOM's components. This strategy had worked in the rest of the country, so it was expected to work here. The problem was threefold. First, they were fighting primarily Al Qaeda—foreign troops—not Taliban, who were inclined to make deals rather than fight. Second, Al Qaeda had a massive advantage in the terrain because they were defending, which meant that the attacking forces had to be prepared to take substantially more casualties than had previously been the case. Third, a lot of time had passed since the initial reports. Al Qaeda had had time to prepare. The Americans were still playing pickup games.

It was difficult, if not impossible, to use airpower to get into the tunnels. Even massive bunker-buster bombs could not penetrate the caves. The daisy cutter bombs—massive antipersonnel devices—were dropped primarily for psychological effect and the hope that someone might have been out in the open. The only weapons that had a chance of working were JDAMs that were guided three-dimensionally by GPS satellites. If you knew which cave you wanted to hit, and the target remained in place for several hours, you could order up a B-2 strike from Diego Garcia that could—with some enhancements that were made to the GPS system just for the battle of Tora Bora—hit the cave. All you needed was excellent intelligence, flawless weapons systems, the enemy remaining immobile for a few hours, and a lot of luck.

U.S. aircraft began hitting Tora Bora on November 30 and the United States began bringing Special Operations troops into the area.

But the key to the American warfighting effort was, as it had been in the north and around Kandahar, Afghan warlords who had been recruited by the CIA at a substantial expense and somewhat conflicting promises as to who would be the dominant force in the area after the war.

Three warlords made themselves available to the Americans. One was Zahir Qadir, twenty-eight years old and the son of a provincial governor. Another was Mohammed Zaman Ghun Sharreef, who had been in France for years and had returned to claim his place. The third was Hazrat Ali, an old warrior who had trained with the Americans during the war with the Soviets and who knew the Tora Bora complex intimately. It was Ali that the Americans relied on and backed most heavily.

The main offensive began on December 3. Ali's, Zaman's, and Zahir's troops, totaling about 2,500, were finally mustered along with about forty Special Forces troops. All advanced on Tora Bora. This much everyone agrees on. There is very little agreement as to what else happened over the next week or so. According to Zahir, he had not even heard that an attack was going to be launched until the morning of December 3. Zahir claimed that there was no plan and most U.S. advisers were with Ali. Ali in turn claimed that the U.S. had never really provided him with any real intelligence and hadn't given him an opportunity to build his own intelligence system, but that the Americans now—having waited for more than two weeks—wanted to go fast.

According to U.S. intelligence, Ali had told them that he knew where Osama bin Laden was and had made arrangements to have him delivered to the Americans in the village of Agam. According to Ali, he had said no such thing but he tried to make these arrangements after the offensive started. He claimed that the Americans were more interested in coordinating air attacks than in following up his intelligence leads.

The fighting was inconclusive, to understate the case. Tora Bora was a terrible objective to try to take. It was the kind of objective that multiplied the defender's capabilities many times over, while cutting the offensive capabilities of infantry troops to a fraction. It also undercut U.S. technology. Consider the fate of the JDAM, the golden child of the war.

A JDAM hits a particular coordinate on the map, defined three-dimensionally. It will do that perfectly, using GPS. However, it doesn't know anything about what is between it and the target. So in the mountains, the JDAM may be heading straight toward the target without realizing the coordinates are on the other side of the mountain. The U.S. had weapons that could handle terrain inputs—the Tomahawk cruise missile, for example—but they would be fired from ships, taking several hours to get to Tora Bora. The problem was that there wasn't any single system that could both get there fast and know the route. Airpower simply wasn't enough at Tora Bora.

None of the local commanders were prepared to have their troops chewed up in the meat grinder of Tora Bora. Their troops were their source of power; if they were decimated their power would evaporate, so they had no intention of carrying out a major offensive. Unlike the north, where U.S. airpower cleared the way for the attacking Afghan forces, the situation around Tora Bora could not be dealt with by airpower. This was an infantry fight—a brawl—and the Eastern Alliance, as they were called, had no interest in it.

Over the next week, the simmering tension that existed between the CIA and Central Command boiled over. This tension was not new. After Desert Storm, Norman Schwarzkopf had raged at the intelligence provided by the CIA, regarding it as insufficient and irrelevant. The CIA charged that Schwarzkopf and other senior Army commanders didn't know how to use intelligence. From the point of view of the CIA, the Army wanted simplistic absolutes and didn't want to deal with the complex situations they were facing. The Army argued that they needed fast, actionable intelligence, not hypotheses and subtlety.

This tension simply blew apart at Tora Bora. Tommy Franks wanted to know precisely where bin Laden was, where U.S. troops were deployed, and have a clear evaluation of the forces available to him. The CIA had a theory as to where bin Laden was but no real precision, and the Eastern Alliance troops available for the attack were a shifting kaleidoscope of brigands, fanatics, and opportunists, all with agendas and grievances going back generations.

The CIA argued that Franks should commit main U.S. forces— that the 10th Mountain Division forces deployed at Bagram Airport and in Uzbekistan, and the Marine Amphibious Unit available for deployment, should be rushed into combat. Franks took one look at the intelligence on Tora Bora and realized that these troops, not acclimated to the climate or altitude, would be cut to pieces if bin Laden's main force was actually in the mountains. Moreover, allied with the circus of Afghans the Agency had thrown together, these troops would be in more danger from their allies than their enemy.

The CIA knew that the forces it had rented were fairly unreliable. It also knew that Osama was only probably (or perhaps possibly) at Tora Bora. Nevertheless, they argued, adding U.S. troops into the mix was well worth it. The road to the south was open, which meant that bin Laden could slip across the border at will. That border had to be sealed with U.S. forces. It was, therefore, a strange case of the CIA arguing that the force it had thrown together could not do the job by itself, with Central Command arguing that the entire operation was so smoky that adding U.S. units to the battle could result in disaster.

By December 12, major U.S. formations had not entered into the battle, and the situation was coming apart. General Zaman suddenly announced that he had negotiated a cease-fire with Al Qaeda that would start at 0800 on December 13. Zaman added that Al Qaeda would surrender—but only to the United Nations. He had turned on the Americans. Rumoured to have been paid a large sum of money by Al Qaeda, they were engaged in the old Afghan game of trying to negotiate their way out of Tora Bora.

Ali was furious. He accused Zaman of betrayal and demanded that he call off the truce. The Americans were also furious. A meeting was called in Agam after first light, with all major commanders and subcommanders attending. While everyone watched, Americans called in a new round of air strikes on Tora Bora, letting Al Qaeda—and Zaman—know that the U.S. was not honoring any cease-fire. As important, they were letting Zaman know that the money he was rumoured to have collected from Al Qaeda for calling the cease-fire was his death warrant with bin Laden, who would now see him as having taken the payoff without having delivered. Zaman was now completely dependent on the United States.

The United States did something even more startling. A B-52 bomber flew over Tora Bora. It started releasing white smoke, and traced a figure eight in the air—representing 8 A.M., the time the cease-fire was to start. The bomber then traced two other letters: NO. A B-52 bomber had played skywriter over Tora Bora, letting Al Qaeda know that whatever deal they thought they had was null and void.

It was quite a gesture. The problem the United States had was that the continuation of the battle ultimately was not up to them. It was up to the Eastern Alliance, and they were clearly tired of the fight. Everyone was now conspiring with everyone and against everyone. Ali started talking to Al Qaeda through intermediaries whom he knew from his many years in the area. Tracing the patterns of treachery would be impossible. No one really knows what happened at Tora Bora on December 13 and 14.

What is certain is that the bulk of Al Qaeda, instead of being captured or killed at Tora Bora, escaped from the fortress. Over a thousand were seen going in. Only fifty-seven were captured. Some of them were exposed to the media on December 17 by General Zahir. That photo opportunity was the last shot fired at Tora Bora. If bin Laden was there—and intelligence released a few months later confirmed that he almost certainly was there—he had escaped. One of the fundamental goals of the Afghan campaign had not been achieved.

According to some reports by men who were with him when he moved south into Pakistan, bin Laden was deeply depressed by the events at Tora Bora. He had gone there with a thousand fighters, planning to make a historic stand—and knowing that U.S. troops could not force him out. He had not anticipated the chaotic conspiracies among the Afghan warlords—conspiracies that benefited him at Tora Bora but which he knew could turn and crush him with little warning—and had not anticipated the need to flee.

According to these reports, which were mostly consistent regarding bin Laden's tone, he basically told his fighters to try to make their way home and wait until they were either summoned or destroyed. He said the enemy's weapons were too powerful and could not, for now, be resisted. It is possible that he made such a speech while depressed. There is even some possibility that he meant it for a short time, but in spite of the fact that several witnesses reported the same thing, it seems unlikely as his long-term view. His long-term view in actuality was the same as the Taliban's, except on a global basis: disperse, regroup, and prepare to strike. The road took bin Laden to Pakistan. Some American intelligence analysts thought that bin Laden, who had been reported to have a kidney condition that required dialysis, would not survive his long trek. He did, meaning that he either had access to a portable dialysis machine that could be run off of a manual generator, or more reasonably, that analysts had inflated an illness as a life-threatening condition. It is extremely unlikely that bin Laden needed dialysis at this point to survive.

The Pakistani Crisis

Tora Bora borders on Pakistan's Federally Administered Tribal Areas—as untamed an area as there is in the world. The tribal areas were never occupied by the British, who could neither subdue them nor exploit them. It has always been an area just out of reach. Predominantly Pashtun, it is more an extension of Afghanistan than of Punjab-dominated Pakistan. One of the reasons that the Pakistanis became involved in Afghanistan in the first place was to have a degree of control over the Afghan government and decrease the possibility of a secessionist movement among the tribes. However, the tribes are too hostile to any government but their own to even bother to secede.

This is an area where no outside power has managed to exercise much authority.

It was the perfect place for Al Qaeda members to go. Some, mostly lower-ranking personnel, appear after Tora Bora to have taken a longer trek across the border of Iran. But according to all of the evidence available, Osama bin Laden's path led to Pakistan, to the tribal areas where Pashtuns (who shared his Sunni fundamentalism) would welcome him and protect him in regions that even the Pakistani Army hesitated to enter.

The end of the battle of Tora Bora marked the complete diaspora of Al Qaeda and created a new stage in the war. In this stage, the hunt for Al Qaeda focused first on Pakistan and then, to a somewhat lesser extent, on Iran. The burning issue was Pakistan's ability to control its frontiers and take responsibility for its territory, particularly the tribal areas. In order for that to happen, Musharraf had to commit himself to an alliance with the United States—and he had to be able to assert his control over both the ISI and the Army. Neither was going to be easy, even had Musharraf wanted to do it.

U.S. forces could and did poke across the Afghan–Pakistani frontier around Tora Bora. But the key to the situation was Musharraf, who had not been motivated to take the kinds of political risks that cooperating with the Americans would entail. However, in what would prove to be a massive miscalculation for the Islamist forces, an incident occurred that not only created a crisis but almost generated a nuclear war.

On December 13, as Tora Bora was lurching to a conclusion, Islamist guerrillas belonging to two groups based in the Pakistani-controlled portion of Kashmir— Jaish-e-Muhammad and Lashkar-e-Taiba—attacked India's parliament as part of an ongoing campaign in opposition to India's occupation of Kashmir. The Indians accused the Pakistani government of sponsoring the attacks and massed their conventional forces along Pakistan's eastern frontier. More important, perhaps, the Indians implicitly threatened Pakistan with a nuclear strike if the situation escalated any further. The December 13 attack was simply one of a series of attacks, and India's posture was that it was fed up with the situation. Tensions rose dramatically.

The crisis was a golden opportunity for the United States. Following Tora Bora, the United States knew that it would be impossible for it to pursue the war without the cooperation of Musharraf. They also knew that they had few levers to use on him. The crisis with India also created a massive crisis in Pakistan. There was serious doubt among the Pakistanis about the quality of their nuclear devices or delivery systems, although they bluffed well. Moreover, given the relative populations and their concentration, the Pakistanis would come out on the short end of any nuclear exchange. The Indians knew all of this, and Musharraf had reason to fear that the Pakistani nuclear force would not deter the Indians from attacking.

The Indians, of course, had no intention of starting any war, let alone a nuclear war. However, they were very sensitive to the strategic shifts that were taking place in the region. Ever since the 1950s, India's strategic orientation was toward the Soviet Union, while Pakistan was aligned with the United States. The fall of the Soviet Union did not dissolve the Indo–Russian relationship, but its value to the Indians was severely diminished. The Soviets had guaranteed Indian national security. Now they were gone. But the Chinese and Americans were still there, and that left the Indians badly isolated.

September 11 opened a new door for India. The Islamist movement had three enemies: Judaism, Christianity, and Hinduism. It regarded the land occupied by India as nearly as sacred as the land occupied by Israel. Recovering all lands that had been redeemed by Islam and then stolen by infidels was a core principle of the Islamists. As the United States was being drawn into confrontation with the Islamic world, a natural foundation for an Indo–American alliance had surfaced.

On a smaller scale, the Indians recognized the growing tension between the United States and Pakistan, India's historic enemy. It not only wanted to see this blossom, but India had every reason to want to make itself not only useful, but indispensable, to the United States.

India also knew that the United States wanted to limit the extent to which it was perceived as anti-Islamic. The U.S. did not want to move too hard against Pakistan or move too close to India. Indian intelligence realized quickly what the battle of Tora Bora meant. The United States would need the help of Pakistan, and Pakistan would not be in a position to give it. That gave the Indians an opening.

The jihadist attack on India's Parliament gave India a perfect opportunity. By responding to the attack with the threat of nuclear war, India put Pakistan in a terrible position. Unable to defeat India militarily and not certain that he could deter India's nuclear capability, Musharraf urgently needed someone to intercede on his behalf. Musharraf started shifting troops from the west to the east—away from the Afghan border the United States wanted guarded and east toward India, specifically saying that Pakistan did not have enough forces to protect both frontiers. He was telling the United States to get India off his back if it wanted Pakistani help.

Washington understood the message but also understood that merely shifting forces around was not the key. The United States needed Musharraf to fundamentally change his policy, taking risks with his personal future in order to stop Al Qaeda. Musharraf was trapped between the Indian threat, the American threat, and the threat of Pakistan's Islamists. He decided to publicly side with the Americans while doing as little as he could on behalf of the United States. It was a public affirmation with a knowing wink at the Islamists.

With India in the equation, and the genuine sense of impending disaster, Musharraf's calculation shifted. He was far less afraid of the Islamists than of the possibility that the United States would solve its Al Qaeda problem through an Indian attack on Pakistan. He needed to persuade the United States not to align itself with India, as well as to intervene actively to stop Indian threats.

The United States took its time, allowing the crisis to drag on. It was made clear that in return for any hope of alleviating the crisis, Musharraf would have to commit himself to crack down on anti-Indian operations in Pakistan-controlled territory and, much more important, commit himself to working with the United States to destroy Al Qaeda and its supporters in Pakistan. In other words, he had to commit himself to going to war with the ISI, his own intelligence service.

The United States did nothing to calm Musharraf's fears, nor did it move quickly. On March 19, three months after the attack on India's parliament, George Tenet, head of the U.S. Central Intelligence Agency, testified that the threat of nuclear war on the subcontinent was greater than ever. Everything the United States did—in tacit cooperation with India—was designed to increase the sense of isolation and desperation in Pakistan. However, by mid-January, Colin Powell was on his way to India and Pakistan to broker the deal. India would stand down and Musharraf would cooperate with the United States.

The U.S.–Indian routine would be repeated several times, applying pressure to Musharraf and providing a justification he could use with his own government. The bad cop—India—would respond to an Islamist provocation by threatening war. The good cop—the United States—would speak to the Indians and then tell the Pakistanis that they might be able to call off the Indian threat of war. In the meantime, Pakistan would have to make a gesture by increasing pressure on Islamists. Pakistan, not at all certain that the United States wouldn't permit India to launch a nuclear strike, had no choice but to back off.

As the United States saw the situation, Pakistan remained the center of gravity of the Al Qaeda problem. Until Pakistan turned on Al Qaeda—and its own ISI—Al Qaeda would survive and remain a fundamental threat to the United States. The United States also knew that it had limits on how far it could push Musharraf without toppling him or plunging Pakistan into unmanageable chaos—the perfect place for Al Qaeda to survive and flourish.

The crisis in Pakistan gave the United States the lever to get some control of the situation after Tora Bora. But the U.S. could not wait until the Pakistani situation came under control. In the course of using a nuclear nightmare against Pakistan, the United States, right after Tora Bora, found itself entangled in a nuclear nightmare of its own, as reports started filtering in that Al Qaeda might have acquired a nuclear device. This was the other dimension of the crisis, playing out in parallel and weaving itself into the fabric—the fear of Pakistan and its nuclear capability.

The Big Fear

The United States has been obsessed with nuclear weapons since the 1950s. In the minds of many, the Cold War was about nuclear weapons, and this fear had been seared into the souls of Americans. The idea that planes would be hijacked and driven into buildings was never a driving fear. On the other hand, the idea that someone would smuggle a nuclear weapon into the United States and detonate it was deeply embedded in all levels of the culture. As noted, when September 11 happened, the United States government activated government-survival plans that had been drawn up for nuclear war.

The connection was deep and visceral. That is why Vice President Cheney and President Bush were physically separated in the first months after September 11. The U.S. government was deeply afraid that Al Qaeda's next move would be a nuclear strike on the United States. There were serious fears that Americans would wake up one morning and find several of their major cities destroyed by nuclear devices.

There was a mystery. If Al Qaeda had nuclear devices, why wouldn't they have struck with them first? Why tip off your hand with September 11. One reason would be in order to have the campaign build to a psychological crescendo. That's a good argument, but it ignores a key problem. By staging September 11, Al Qaeda placed the United States on maximum alert. That meant that the risk to Al Qaeda had increased dramatically. If Al Qaeda had nuclear weapons, those weapons were the most precious things they possessed, and the chance that U.S. intelligence would locate those weapons increased dramatically after September 11. Losing the nukes would be a tragedy from Al Qaeda's point of view. If they had them and were planning to use them, using them as early as possible—as a first strike—made the most sense. Psychological crescendo or not, the logic was that Al Qaeda did not have nukes. In the absence of intelligence indicating otherwise, that was the only reasonable conclusion.

However, September 11 triggered an interesting process at the CIA—a very logical and reasonable process. Having missed September 11, every agency of the United States began asking a single question by the afternoon of September 11: What else did we miss? What other intelligence have we overlooked that might indicate Al Qaeda's next move? Analysts at the CIA were ordered to review their intelligence files and products on anything remotely related to Al Qaeda. Every bit of evidence was reexamined.

Evidence that seemed fairly routine prior to September 11 took on a completely different cast after September 11. The criteria shifted from having to prove the significance of intelligence to having to disprove its significance. Intelligence that was dismissed as having an insufficient basis six months ago was hauled out and reexamined and, barring clear refutation, increased dramatically in credibility.

Inevitably, the review process would paw through every bit of intelligence and elevate the significance and reliability of every source. The threat picture that existed on September 10 would dramatically change. CIA analysts were asked whether Al Qaeda had weapons of mass destruction before September 11 or if they were obtaining them now. The process was not a quick one. It took at least sixty days to gather the mountains of information that had been accumulated and another month to review it.

It is important to understand how the CIA, or any intelligence agency, evaluates intelligence. Every bit of intelligence has a source, and every source has a history. Whether the collection method is from a woman picking up a man in a bar in Beirut or a satellite intercepting cell phone calls, intelligence comes from someone. It doesn't matter if the source is on the payroll or if he doesn't even know he is being queried by an intelligence organization. The value of that information depends on two things: First, who the source is and where he is placed—is he a cabdriver or a government minister? Second, what is the source's track record? Has he been accurate in the past? He is evaluated on placement and on reliability. So a prime minister who has never once been wrong would—assuming a scale of 1–5, with five being the highest—be 5 by 5. You can have more variables and more numbers than 5, but in the end, it all comes down to this.

There is a standard game. Every case officer—the people who run sources—is evaluated according to the quality of his portfolio sources. Every quarter, his portfolio is reviewed for quantity and quality. Obviously, every case officer wants to maximize the value of his portfolio of sources. The CIA has all sorts of objective measures designed to keep the case officer from inflating the value of the source, plus analysts are always in the business of tearing down sources. Analysts are human, and they always want to claim that they are getting poor intelligence. Out of this constant struggle, every piece of intelligence is tagged to a source and carries with it the source's value.

The post–September 11 review generated a tendency to magnify information. No one wanted to be the analyst who passed over a report that might imply that New York was about to be destroyed. But there was another process at work as well. Prior to September 11, there was a class of sources that had proved to be fairly unreliable. There were Islamists around the world who had consistently forecast catastrophic doom for the United States in many unpleasant ways. Prior to September 11, these people had a low placement value and a lower reliability value. They were simply meaningless background noise.

In reevaluating these people after September 11, the inevitable happened. Those who had been sending e-mails predicting that New York would be attacked now had to be considered very reliable indeed. That they may have predicted this for the past five years did not detract from the fact that on August 15, for example, speaking in a mosque, they had said that the towers of New York would crumble. They had accurately forecast the event—and were now regarded as more reliable than before.

A huge swath of militant jihadist and anti-American sources suddenly had their reliability value increased. They tended to belong to groups that were suspected of being connected to Al Qaeda. So their placement value went up. On September 10, they were loudmouth lunatics. On September 12, they were well-placed reliable sources. They were suddenly driving the analysis. And there was no one who was going to disregard what they said—not after September 11.

Everything they said was monitored. After September 11, these sources were bragging about how they knew all about the attack, that their cousin was even now on his way to blow up the Sears Tower, and so on. U.S. intelligence suddenly looked at the world as filled with a huge number of well-placed individuals, all of whom were "chattering" about impending attacks. The entire system was having a spasm.

The highest tier of intelligence, naturally, concerned weapons of mass destruction, particularly nuclear weapons. The Islamist sources were being bugged, monitored, followed, scoped—everything possible. The fact was that those who knew about September 11 didn't talk, and those who talked didn't know—but then again, one couldn't be sure of that. Therefore, those with the loudest mouths and most vigorous imaginations were in the driver's seat. And as they vied with each other to forecast the most terrible disasters imaginable for the United States, they inevitably turned their attention to weapons of mass destruction, including nuclear weapons. By October, everyone in the world was speculating that the next strike would be WMD, and a profound concern began to develop in the government that Al Qaeda's next move would be nuclear.

All of this was intensely reinforced by the anthrax attacks in the United States. Just a few days after September 11, anthrax began to appear in letters mailed to a variety of public officials and media personalities. Anthrax bacilli were infecting the postal system. People were dying. It was logical to conclude that the anthrax attacks were part of an Al Qaeda campaign to completely destabilize the United States. The timing was right. No one was claiming credit for the attacks (as was Al Qaeda's own method). The United States was gripped by a perfectly rational fear.

Beginning with that premise and accepting the idea that Al Qaeda had probably not yet secured the weapons but was in the process of doing so, the administration began to focus on this question: If Al Qaeda were to successfully obtain nuclear material or weapons, where would they likely get them? U.S. intelligence, which had already been systematically monitoring the situation through its Counter-Proliferation Office, was now handed a broader task. Given the demonstrated ability of Al Qaeda to operate covertly on a global basis, what were the most likely sources of nuclear weapons?

The fear wasn't idle. There was no question in anyone's mind that Al Qaeda would like to get hold of weapons of mass destruction in general and nuclear weapons in particular. There was no question that Al Qaeda was capable of prodigious feats of covert operations. There was no question that nuclear weapons were potentially accessible and that Al Qaeda would use those weapons if it could. Indeed, in an interview in a Pakistani newspaper in November 2001, bin Laden claimed that he already had nuclear and chemical weapons and would use similar weapons if Washington used them against him. Between the intelligence process and common sense, the feeling of alarm in Washington grew daily. Washington moved into an urgent, preventive mode.

The sense of urgency grew as the battle of Tora Bora ended, because the United States was forced to reevaluate the situation in both Pakistan and Iran. As Tora Bora ended and it became clear that Al Qaeda had not, in fact, been destroyed, an intense nuclear scare was triggered in Washington. Al Qaeda's survival—plus evidence that it was trying to get its hands on nuclear weapons—triggered a statement by Bush in an odd place. Bush visited Poland early in November. In a speech there, he suddenly warned that terrorists "are seeking chemical, biological, and nuclear weapons." The new theme reflected the warnings he was getting from the CIA.

U.S. intelligence began to receive information from western Afghanistan that Al Qaeda members were being permitted into Iran a few days after Tora Bora ended. This surprised Washington tremendously. The administration thought that they had reached an understanding with Teheran. When it became clear that Al Qaeda members were moving into western Iran unhindered, the question in Washington was simple: Had Iran switched sides in the war? Some argued there had been a policy shift, while others contended that it was simply a case of bribed border guards.

If it was simply a matter of border guards and local leaders, that was manageable. But if the government shifted or a major faction was following its own policy, then that was dangerous. What made it particularly dangerous was the CIA's belief that Iran had a serious nuclear development program under way, and no one was quite sure who controlled the program or the site at any given moment. If Al Qaeda was getting into Iran, then either the government or some important faction was aiding them. Given the deep anti-American passion in Iran, Washington suddenly faced the possibility that Al Qaeda might be given nuclear weapons by someone in Iran.

A very similar situation existed in Pakistan. The large majority of Al Qaeda had moved into the tribal areas south of Tora Bora. It was always understood that the Pakistani ISI were close to the Taliban and sympathetic to Al Qaeda. ISI personnel were reported to be in the tribal areas, and instead of capturing and turning over Al Qaeda to the United States they were actually aiding them in moving to safe haven away from the frontier.

At the same time, a major crisis was under way between India and Pakistan. Both countries were nuclear powers. There was serious concern on a number of levels about the degree of control President Musharraf had over Pakistan's nuclear weapons. Security at the weapons sites was in the hands of the ISI. There was some concern that rogue elements could launch missiles at India. There was even more concern that these same elements would provide weapons to Al Qaeda and that Musharraf would have no idea.

The fear of nuclear attack really hit Washington in the last week of October. The CIA had received reports from a Russian source that

Al Qaeda may have obtained a ten-kiloton nuclear device, probably from somewhere in the former Soviet Union, and planned to detonate it in New York. George Tenet immediately arranged to brief the President in the White House. The report was sketchy, with holes and contradictions. But as the movie goes, it was the sum of all the President's fears. Even so, it would have been ignored, except that, at almost the same time, the CIA received intelligence from another source—code-named Dragonfire, according to some reports—also saying that Al Qaeda had a nuclear device.

Neither source, by itself, would have been taken that seriously. However, when two sources, completely unconnected to each other, suddenly come at you with similar stories, you have to stop and listen. Given the heightened sensitivity of the CIA to all such sources, it was not actually that extraordinary that the two reports would come in at the same time. And the level of specificity was not sufficient in the two stories to make them identical. Tenet briefed the President without expecting major consequences.

Analysts at the CIA could take all this from a calm distance, but the President felt he couldn't. If the story was true, he was about to lose New York. More important, no one could assure him that the world's nukes were nailed down. If he wasn't going to lose New York now, in this incident, he had a good chance of losing cities down the road. Bush overrode his staff at the end of October and ordered the nuclear threat to be treated as taking precedence to all other threats.

This was a break point in the war. Until that point, the primary focus was Al Qaeda personnel. As of November 2001, that was no longer the top priority. It now took a close but clear second to the need to stop any nuclear threats against the United States. Stopping another September 11 was important, but it was utterly imperative to prevent a nuclear 9/11. The President was reacting viscerally to limited intelligence. Essentially, the nuclear threat was simply speculation. But in any rational threat analysis, the reliability of intelligence has to be measured against the consequences in case it proves to be true. From that briefing onward, the entire strategy of the war was changed. The obsession with WMD and nuclear weapons became an obsession that defined the war permanently. The change was first felt in U.S. relations with Pakistan in the wake of Tora Bora.

The United States was deeply worried about the members of the ISI, many of whom continued to admire and obey former Director General Hameed Gul, who had led the ISI during the late 1980s when it collaborated with the CIA in Afghanistan. Gul was and remained an Islamist who had close political ties with Islamist parties in Pakistan. Gul was a frequent visitor to Afghanistan and had been on a two-week visit there just before September 11. As the crisis began boiling up in early December, Gul gave an interview in a Pakistani newspaper and said that, "No one can tell us how to run our nuclear facilities and nuclear programs. This is being done in the interest of Pakistan, not the United States. The Taliban will always remain in Afghanistan, and Pakistan will always support them."

CIA Director George Tenet went to Islamabad in early December to confront Musharraf with allegations that Pakistani nuclear scientists, working with and through Gul, had been collaborating with Al Qaeda. He gave Musharraf a list of scientists that the CIA wanted questioned in connection with technology transfers to the Taliban, including several close to Gul. Gul denied these allegations. Tenet demanded that Musharraf get control of the ISI and of his nuclear weapons. Two of the scientists were out of the country at the time, visiting in Myanmar, a country as inaccessible to the United States as any. Tenet demanded that they return.

Musharraf had actually shifted Pakistan's nuclear weapons and materials to six new locations in mid-October, soon after the U.S. air attacks on Afghanistan began. He argued that by doing this he had secured them sufficiently so that the United States need have no concern. He also let it be known that if the U.S. pushed him too hard and he had to give too much too fast, his government could be overthrown, leaving the United States in a much worse situation than it was already in. He pleaded for room to maneuver.

The problem was that additional intelligence was accumulating.

The ISI told the U.S. that it certainly had not collaborated with Al Qaeda in any way, but that they had picked up information that Al Qaeda had already gotten hold of two suitcase nuclear devices through contacts in unspecified former Soviet republics in Central Asia. The ISI gave specifics. It provided the serial numbers of the weapons and the date of manufacture—October 1988. Now another specific nuclear threat was materializing, this time with the ISI driving it.

A suitcase bomb is assumed to yield a ten-kiloton explosion. If you bear in mind that the Hiroshima bomb was thirteen kilotons, it gives you a sense of the devastation it could yield in an urban area. Suitcase denotes size of the device, not its power. A reasonable estimate of a ten-kiloton bomb going off in Midtown Manhattan would be about a half million dead and a trillion dollars' worth of damage. Yet a suitcase bomb is only about 24 × 16 × 8 inches, weighing less than 30 pounds.

If the ISI was right, the United States didn't have an ISI problem: It had an immediate threat on its hands. Suitcase bombs could easily be brought into the United States by numerous routes. If they were already in the hands of Al Qaeda, the situation was indeed desperate, and leaning on the Pakistanis would achieve nothing. In fact, the best chance the U.S. had was to rely on the ISI, which obviously already had operatives on top of it.

The problem was that it was all too neat. The serial numbers did not check out with the Russians—but the Russians had to admit that their record keeping, which had always been poor, was now abominable. The Russians had indeed manufactured such weapons in 1988. But the coincidence of ISI just happening to discover the plot was all too much—particularly when they could not explain coherently why, having gotten close enough to the devices to get the serial numbers, they hadn't seized or destroyed them. The story seemed perfectly aligned to create an ideal political outcome for the ISI. Moreover, the uncertainty as to where the weapons had been obtained seemed an invitation to the U.S. to surge into countries it was counting on for help in the war in Afghanistan. On the other hand, given the zero-risk premises of the Defense Department, how could the United States ignore the report?

This was the intensifying nightmare situation the United States faced as the fighting at Tora Bora ended. The world, rather than becoming clearer, had become enormously murkier. At the same time, the risks were rising astronomically. The United States had no reason whatsoever to believe that a nuclear strike would not take place at any minute in any city in the United States. It could not stop it, it could not predict it, and it could not control it. As New Year's approached, the government was operating in full emergency mode, with all backup sites—from Site R in Pennsylvania to command centers to the west of Washington—fully manned at all times. The administration was in agony.

A number of advanced radiation detectors were deployed around Washington and New York, designed to sense if a vehicle contained a nuclear device. The dilemma was this: Even if the device hadn't been properly shielded by attackers and had been detected, then what was to be done? If the vehicle was intercepted, the attacker could detonate at will. An explosion in Falls Church, Virginia, or in Fort Lee, New Jersey, would be devastating enough. Simply detecting the device didn't show anyone how to prevent detonation from happening.

By mid-December 2001, the United States was being driven by a phantom that it could neither see nor ignore. The possibility that nuclear weapons were already in the United States meant that the people sitting in a meeting in the White House could well be dead at any moment. But there was nothing to be done if that was the case. Unless the FBI got very lucky—and luck did not seem to run with the FBI very much—the chances of finding a nuclear device in the United States were slim. No one wanted to create a useless panic, but no one wanted to go down in history as covering up a nuclear threat, however vague that threat might be. Therefore, the White House issued vague warnings that expressed real fears—but not the intensity of the feeling.

On December 20, Bush held a press conference marking the hundredth day since September 11. He opened with:

Today I'm announcing two more strikes against the financing of terror. We know that Al Qaeda would like to obtain nuclear, chemical, and biological weapons, and we know that oftentimes they do not act alone. Al Qaeda has international supporters, and some of those supporters hide themselves in the disguise of charity. Last year a former official of the Pakistani atomic energy commission set up an organization known as the UTN. UTN claims to serve the hungry and needy of Afghanistan, but it was the UTN that provided information about nuclear weapons to Al Qaeda.

The President went directly after Gul and the nuclear physicists allied with him. Bush made it clear that Al Qaeda posed a nuclear threat and made it appear that effective steps were being taken. The facts were out and prominently displayed, regardless of accuracy and without any real conveyance of the seriousness being given to the situation.

Bush left for Camp David on December 20 and then flew to his ranch, where he would stay until January 6, 2002. While he was out of Washington, the crisis between India and Pakistan raged. Once again, Musharraf was squeezed on all sides and had only one way to turn—to the United States. The Americans told him that they could call off the Indians, but only if he arrested those responsible for the attack on the Indian parliament—as well as other supporters of Al Qaeda. In other words, the United States gave him a choice: break with the ISI's Islamist faction by going after individuals under their protection, or face the very real possibility of nuclear war with India.

This was a line that, once crossed, would be very hard to retreat from. That was precisely what all factions inside the Bush administration wanted to happen. They wanted Musharraf to cross that line, because once across, he would become permanently dependent on the United States. Musharraf crossed the line and started arresting people. For the next few months, the U.S. would use India against Pakistan, and Pakistan would use arrests—and releases—to control the United States. But the key principle was in place: Musharraf was aligned with the United States. He was relying on the Americans to keep the Indians at bay. And the Americans were relying on Musharraf to keep his nuclear weapons under tight control.

There was an intense debate in Washington. Inside the Pentagon, Paul Wolfowitz and the Department of Defense argued that neither the government nor the factions in either country could be relied on to protect their nuclear capabilities. Wolfowitz's view was that the danger of imminent transfer of weapons to Al Qaeda made some sort of action imperative.

The State Department took a somewhat different approach. In their view, neither Iran's Khatami nor Pakistan's Musharraf was interested in transferring nuclear technology to Al Qaeda. They did not deny that there were powerful elements in both countries that might be inclined to do so. But their argument was that if both Pakistan and Iran were simultaneously treated as totally unreliable, the United States would be in an untenable position. They said that the only reasonable path was to strengthen the hand of the Iranian and Pakistani governments and help them keep and increase their control over their nuclear facilities.

This was the first time that the two major factions—Defense and State—had clashed on a policy issue (it would not be the last). In this first disagreement, we can see the basic outlines of a struggle that would continue throughout the war, dividing Rumsfeld from Powell. The view of the Defense Department was that the events of September 11 had created an absolute state of emergency. The United States had to assume the worst case—in this situation, that Al Qaeda was acquiring nuclear weapons. The acquisition of these weapons was absolutely intolerable to the United States, as it would result in a cataclysm. Therefore, any compromise that accepted a degree of risk was unacceptable. The only acceptable solution was one in which the United States could take full control of the situation—and that required a military response.

The State Department did not challenge the absolute character of the threat but focused instead on the limits of American power. From the State Department's point of view, regardless of the extent of the threat, the response had to fit resources. The United States did not have the ability to simultaneously impose solutions on both Iran and Pakistan, even if it was advisable.

The Defense Department countered that this lack of clarity was the heart of the issue. In an unclear situation, it is necessary to assume the worst when dealing with weapons of mass destruction. Therefore, the use of indirect means in a murky situation posed unacceptable risks. The argument about lack of resources, Defense said, failed to take into account the lessons of Afghanistan and Kosovo, which is that major force is no longer necessary to achieve striking outcomes. State, run by General Powell—a former Army general who did not necessarily agree that either Kosovo or Afghanistan had been stunning successes—did not yield ground.

As the New Year approached, the situation in Pakistan became particularly worrisome, because that nation had the most mature nuclear program in the Islamic world and because the intense crises with India and along its Afghan border appeared to be profoundly destabilizing the country. Documents that had been obtained during a raid on Mullah Omar's compound in Kandahar were now being carefully analyzed. Strong evidence was emerging about close links, and some hints of nuclear collaboration, between Al Qaeda and the ISI. In December, Bush made a speech at the Citadel that laid out the new policy: "The authors of mass murder must be defeated and never allowed to gain or use the weapons of mass destruction." Urgency was turning into policy.

The Pakistani situation was by no means under control after the war in Afghanistan, and certainly the broader threat was still as real as ever. When Bush returned to Washington on January 6, there had been no nuclear detonation, but tension remained sky-high. A strategy had to be developed, something that would deal with both dimensions of the problem: Al Qaeda itself and the danger that nuclear weapons would get loose and be used by them.

The Axis of Evil

Everyone knew that the 2002 State of the Union Address was going to be one of the most important in history. It had been only about four months since the attacks of September 11. The Afghan war had been fought and, as far as the media was concerned, won. However, the State of the Union was being written in a condition of increasing anxiety. Between the intelligence-review process, the failure at Tora Bora, the uncertain situation in Pakistan, and the seeming reversal of Iran's position, things were not going very well.

The basic problems were twofold. Before Tora Bora, the United States had some idea of the location of senior Al Qaeda commanders, even if the organization as a whole was opaque. After Tora Bora, the level of specific tactical knowledge on Al Qaeda had actually declined. The U.S. knew little more about the broader organization and had lost Osama bin Laden and the senior commanders.

Second, what intelligence was gathered seemed to indicate that Al Qaeda had or was trying to get WMD in general and nuclear weapons specifically. That intelligence coincided with indications that there were nuclear weapons available for purchase. When the U.S. looked at the entire landscape, it suddenly seemed as if the world was oozing nukes. That might not have been true, but the mind-set in U.S. intelligence was focused on worst-case scenarios, and from that point of view, there was an immediate and real threat of nuclear disaster to the United States. Moreover, what intelligence the United States had from countries in the region, like Pakistan and Iran, was unsettling.

The State of the Union was being prepared under extraordinary pressure. The country was mistakenly celebrating Tora Bora as a U.S. victory, payback for 9/11, expecting bin Laden to be dead or captured any day. The reality was that Tora Bora was a failure and the Afghan operation was, at best, a partial success. The fear of follow-on attacks by Al Qaeda—particularly of nuclear attacks or attacks with dirty bombs—hung heavy. The speech was being written under the specter of nuclear attack.

At the same time that the speech was being written, a strategy was being forged. Part of it was the Bush Doctrine, enunciated immediately after September 11, and turned into the foundation of everything that the administration was doing. The Bush Doctrine focused on the reality that Al Qaeda was neither a nation nor a state, but a global, conspiratorial movement that could be found in many countries. The doctrine simply asserted that the United States would attack Al Qaeda wherever it existed. It would, ideally, do so with the full and active cooperation of the state in which Al Qaeda was operating. If the state was incapable of cooperating for any reason, the United States would attack anyway. If the government was hostile, prevented the attack, or was actively protecting and abetting Al Qaeda, the United States would attack that state along with Al Qaeda.

The fear of nuclear weapons created a parallel and more secret doctrine. The United States could not tolerate the existence of nuclear weapons or facilities that were not under the verifiable control of a government in which the United States had confidence. The possibility that nuclear weapons would be transferred to Al Qaeda was an absolutely intolerable risk to the United States, next to which all other considerations were inconsequential.

The United States therefore viewed every store of nuclear weapons or facilities in one of three ways. First, the nuclear facilities, such as Britain's or Japan's, were under the tight control of a competent and responsible government. The risk of transfer of weapons was negligible. Second, the nuclear facilities were under the control of a government whose ability to control them was uncertain, even if its intention to control them was clear. Pakistan and the Central Asian republics that had once been part of the Soviet Union fell into this class. Finally, there was the class of states who might be inclined to deliberately transfer nuclear weapons or material to Al Qaeda either for ideological or financial reasons. There were three of these on the administration's list in January 2002: Iraq, Iran, and North Korea.

This was the origin of the famous Axis of Evil. It is hard to imagine three more different regimes. Iraq and Iran were mortal enemies of each other. Iraq was a secular, socialist, militarist state, while Iran was religious, mercantilist, and democratic in its own way. North Korea was a Stalinist regime. According to the CIA, all three countries had some sort of nuclear weapons development program. Each country was capable, for ideological, political, or financial reasons, of selling these weapons to Al Qaeda. The U.S. had some indication—not necessarily strong—that there had been some contacts concerning the transfer of technology. Therefore, the three countries were of enormous concern to the United States and were, until they demonstrated otherwise, enemies.

Searching for a Night of the Long Knives

As this nuclear obsession gripped the administration, a series of war games took place within and among the various agencies responsible for protecting the United States from nuclear attack. The government had hurriedly begun taking whatever steps it could to provide some measure of defense. It had deployed sensors, designed to detect nuclear weapons, along key highways, ports, border crossings—and sensitive foreign locations. Called gamma ray detectors and neutron flux detectors, they were orders of magnitude more sensitive than traditional Geiger counters.

The government had also created teams of scientists and technicians, called nuclear emergency search teams (NEST), whose job it would be to deactivate a nuclear device once it was located. Since the people controlling the device would probably resist, the United States took elements of Delta Force and other classified teams and put them on standby, ready to head for the location of a device, take out the owners, take control of the nuke, and protect the NEST units as they deactivated the bombs. When properly configured, these bombs can be detonated in seconds or minutes—or have timers set for auto-detonation.

By November 2001, the pieces were in place—proving that government can act quickly when faced by nuclear catastrophe. A war game was held, involving cabinet-level officials, to play out various potential scenarios for blocking a nuclear attack. All the scenarios resulted in disaster. The problem was simple: The United States is a big country, and there just weren't enough sensors in the universe to cover all possible locations. More important, if a truck carrying a nuclear device was detected heading for Washington or New York, calling in Delta Force and executing an assault would not only take an hour or two—plenty of time for the truck to reach its destination—but the assault itself might cause Al Qaeda to detonate the bomb. Unless the U.S. got very lucky, there was no defense possible.

The only solution was offense, consisting of two integrated parts. The first was a global assault on Al Qaeda. The second was a simultaneously global attack on all nuclear facilities that the United States regarded as either unintentionally unsecure or intentionally hostile. What emerged in American thinking in January, following Tora Bora and the nuclear scares, was a strategy for a global covert and overt assault, taking out all of Al Qaeda and all dangerous nuclear facilities in one fell swoop. One way to look at this was as a global Night of the Long Knives—a short, intense period in which U.S. power would attack and destroy its enemies.

The essential part of the plan was simultaneity. The attacks had to occur wherever Al Qaeda was—and wherever unsecured nuclear facilities were located—across the world. Al Qaeda had the ability to rapidly redeploy assets, and any piecemeal attack would serve to alert Al Qaeda that elements of its organization had been detected. This could result in its speeding up the acquisition of weapons or in using weapons already obtained, under the principle of use it or lose it.

There would be three steps in any successful U.S. operation:

1. Deploying U.S. overt and covert forces to strategic areas around the world, so that they could rapidly stage attacks on potential targets.
2. Identifying nuclear facilities, applying political pressure to solve the problem, and, when that failed, devising suitable military solutions.
3. Mapping out by U.S. intelligence an extremely detailed picture of Al Qaeda deployments around the world—and particularly in the United States—in order to attack them.

The United States was particularly concerned that the governments of the three countries mentioned in the "Axis of Evil" speech might engage in a deliberate transfer of nuclear weapons. They were the wild cards. There were two more that could be added to the list, Libya and Syria, although their capabilities appeared to be more uncertain and their relations with the United States were less volatile at the time. Lastly, there was always a degree of uncertainty concerning the republics of the former Soviet Union and Pakistan.

The Russian problem was different. The Soviet Union had a vast nuclear arsenal and development capability. When the Soviet Union collapsed, countries that had been part of the Soviet Union now had their own arsenal, and the Soviet nuclear accounting system collapsed as well. It was simply unclear whether nukes were missing, and if they were, what their condition was. The Soviet arsenal was a threat because it was dispersed among primarily Islamic-populated states that were not functioning, and because no one was keeping track of the weapons.

There was some evidence that Soviet-era nuclear material was in play—aside from the usually unreliable sources. For example, in November 1995, a bomb was found in Moscow's Izmailvo Park, apparently left by Chechens. It was not a nuclear weapon, but it was a dirty bomb, consisting of radioactive cesium 137 wrapped around a powerful dynamite core. It didn't go off, but if it had, it would have contaminated the neighborhood. That proved that the Chechens at least had access to radioactive material and understood how to use it. In 1998, someone robbed a storage facility in Chelyabinsk in Russia, getting enough material to build a nuclear device.

The United States wanted one of two things from every nuclear state in the world: verifiable evidence that existing stockpiles of nuclear weapons and radioactive materials had been secured, or, failing that proof, a specific plan for dealing with the problem. Each of these was an enormous problem in its own right.

Some countries, like Iraq and Iran, simply denied that they had nuclear facilities. They were unprepared to give guarantees because they said none was necessary. Other countries were prepared to give formal or informal guarantees, but it was simply unclear if they were prepared to honor them. Others were prepared to give genuine guarantees but couldn't enforce them. The risk was intolerable, and the solution was completely uncertain.

The United States prepared to deploy teams into the region whose job it was to help local forces secure nuclear facilities or, failing that, take control of those facilities themselves and, if needed, destroy them. By the time George W. Bush made his "Axis of Evil" State of the Union speech, the United States had made a strategic decision: It was going to do everything necessary to ensure that no nuclear weapon would fall into the hands of Al Qaeda. If that meant destroying nuclear facilities in other countries, the United States was prepared to do that.

At this point the administration made public what they had already decided in private. In an extreme case, the United States was prepared to make a preemptive nuclear strike on an unsecured nuclear facility if that was the only way to destroy it and if it was determined that the site represented a threat to the U.S. In other words, the U.S. response to an unlimited crisis was an unlimited threat.

Most countries of concern to the United States granted access to U.S. agents and troops to search for and secure nuclear facilities. Some did not, and the United States began to think of ways to destroy facilities in these countries—Iraq, Iran, Libya, and, above all, Pakistan. Pakistan was the key, because it had the closest connections to Al Qaeda and the least cooperative intelligence service, in spite of the apparent cooperation of Pakistan's President Musharraf. The United States didn't really think that the Iranians would provide Al Qaeda with nuclear weapons. The Iranians were too cautious, and their own program was too undeveloped. The Iraqis were a greater threat, but they seemed not to have extensive contact with Al Qaeda. The North Koreans were much too concerned with regime survival to risk it—and they were being watched too carefully. Pakistan was seen, of all these countries, as the most unstable, most pro–Al Qaeda, with the greatest threat of nuclear proliferation, making it the biggest problem. It was not the only one, just the most immediate.

The United States had undergone a Nuclear Posture Review in the Defense Department prior to September 11. The issue of that review had been the traditional one—the nuclear balance with Russia or, more precisely, its irrelevance. After September 11, the review took on a new dimension. The United States needed Russian cooperation, and the review shifted from its original intention—forcing Russian reductions in nuclear weapons—to a new issue—using the review process to entice Putin into greater cooperation with the United States.

As the nuclear fear intensified during December and January, and as the new policies on all nuclear facilities (not only Russian) came to the fore, a new issue was thrown to the group undertaking the review. Assume that there is an uncontrolled and uncontrollable nuclear facility in the world and neither conventional air strikes nor special operations are likely to remove the site: What nuclear options are available, as a last resort? The planning group was the logical place to bring the issue, but the answer was actually predetermined by the way the problem was posed.

The nuclear review concluded that, in the absence of any other solution, nuclear weapons could be used to destroy unsecured nuclear storage sites. That conclusion was obvious, but it had technical and political implications. The United States really didn't have nuclear weapons suitable for the surgical destruction of a nuclear site. This was not a humanitarian concern. It reflected the fact that most nuclear weapons development and storage sites are extremely robust—they were built to contain explosions and therefore are likely to resist them. A surface burst against an underground bunker, even a larger weapon, simply might not take it out.

The United States had conventional bombs that actually burrowed dozens of feet underground before exploding. Even without burrowing, it was clear that a new generation of precision-guided, small-yield nuclear weapons was necessary to fully implement the doctrine. Of course, there was no time to build such weapons in the current crisis.

In Washington a crisis will oftentimes kick off a weapons program that will take so long to complete that it will have no impact on the crisis. That is what happened in the Nuclear Posture Review. The United States would be using weapons from the current arsenal, but it was decided that a new round of development would take place.

The administration didn't want to make any of this public, since they knew that the entire doctrine would not only cause controversy but generate panic. The administration was acutely aware of the fact that the public could not be protected from any weapons already in Al Qaeda's hands. It also knew that there was little to be gained by explaining the Nuclear Posture Review and the plans that had emerged from it—it would reveal only that the administration had long-range plans for dealing with the problem but no short-term defensive solution.

In December 2001, when all of this was coming to a head, the administration was not afraid that the new doctrine would be seen as too aggressive. Rather, they were afraid that it would be perceived as insufficiently aggressive. As the story unfolded, this was an important inflection point that affected planning for Iraq. The administration's perception, when the President spoke at the Citadel and when Donald Rumsfeld started talking about releasing the review late in December, was that the public response would be one of fear because the plan left the country tremendously vulnerable.

The administration had a foreign problem as well. The purpose of this new doctrine was not to trigger the use of nuclear weapons but to warn countries like Pakistan and Iran that, in extremis, the United States was prepared to do so. These countries had to be made aware of the reality of the new American doctrine without being made to appear to their own publics that they were submitting to U.S. nuclear blackmail. Also, the Russians, who had once been the center of U.S. nuclear thinking, had to be reassured that the U.S. did not intend to target or coerce them. The U.S. had to ask them to work with the United States while convincing other countries in the former Soviet Union—including countries the Russians effectively dominated—that they had better cooperate.

From a military standpoint, the doctrinal shift was simple save for the lack of an appropriate weapon. From the public point of view, it was a nightmare—not because Bush was afraid that his opponents would object to nuclear coercion, but because the mood of the country was frightened and ugly. Bush did not want to intensify these feelings.

The review was complete by mid-December, and the doctrine was effectively in place. Rumsfeld promised that the report would be released on December 27. No one outside the core group of under-secretaries that really ran the government was aware of what was in it. Then Rumsfeld announced that he had misspoken and that it was a classified document that was going to be released to Congress, and that a declassified version would be released shortly.

The declassified version, released on January 10, contained no mention of the new first-use doctrine. What it did contain was a curious passage, a request for increased spending in preparation for "future underground nuclear bomb tests," if needed. A few careful readers spotted that wording and wondered what it was about. Presidential Press Secretary Ari Fleischer answered this question by saying that the request was made "to make sure the stockpile, particularly as it is reduced, is reliable and safe." Not at all untrue, but not at all accurate. It was not until February 18 that the Nuclear Weapons Council, made up of officials from the Defense and Energy Departments, began studying the development of a nuclear-tipped, earth-penetrating weapon that could destroy hardened underground targets.

The decision to develop a new generation of nuclear weapons was not a significant issue. It was going to be a three-year study that affected nothing. The critical issue was that the U.S. was telling Pakistan and other countries as early as December 2001 that it would not tolerate the existence of any facility that was not under clear control. In late December, when it appeared that India might launch a nuclear strike at Pakistan, Pakistan was facing a nuclear threat from two directions.

When U.S. officials went to mediate the crisis, it was also to deliver this message to Musharraf: Unless U.S. observers, to put it politely, were given access to Pakistani facilities in order to guarantee that nuclear materials were not being taken out by nuclear scientists and technicians close to the ISI, the U.S. would have to take steps to destroy those facilities, steps that would, if no other way was available, include nuclear strikes. But the U.S. did not want to deal with the Pakistan issue in isolation. It had much more ambitious plans.

In the midst of the nuclear crisis with India, the United States created another nuclear crisis for Pakistan. Unless they were able to place observers on Pakistani nuclear sites, which meant taking over those sites, the United States would not only remove any restraints that India felt but would also feel free to strike if necessary. Pakistan faced a nuclear nightmare from a completely unexpected source. The United States wanted control of Pakistan's nuclear capability, and it wasn't bluffing. It wanted that control quickly.

The United States was prepared to do this secretly. It did not want to take down President Musharraf, but it was looking for more than a symbolic gesture. The U.S. wanted sufficient force on the ground to control access to Pakistan's nuclear facilities and explicitly wanted the ISI and their pet scientists kept out. Musharraf assured the U.S. that ISI's control would be limited and that key scientists would be removed. He swore that Gul and his allies would be frozen out. The U.S. had no trust in Musharraf's promises and wouldn't bend. Musharraf was facing catastrophe.

It has never been clear if Musharraf buckled, if the U.S. simply presented him with a fait accompli, or if Musharraf secretly agreed but wanted it to appear that he had been forced. However, at a point in March, U.S. forces (not in uniform and drawn primarily from former SOCOM troops transferred to CIA and units from SAD), along with scientists from NEST, deployed simultaneously to all of Pakistan's nuclear reactors. They rushed to take inventory of what was there and examine records of what ought to be there. The records were scarce. No conclusion could be drawn, but the technology found indicated that Pakistan was certainly in no condition to deliver a small nuclear device to Al Qaeda, given U.S. monitoring of their facilities.

Also found were advanced Chinese plans for other devices that had not yet been built but which would have made Pakistan much more dangerous by increasing the reliability and sophistication of its weapons.

The United States had secured Pakistan's nuclear facilities, although it was only nominally observing them. Musharraf worked with the United States to keep this secret. The ISI, of course, knew what had happened, but this was not the time or place to challenge the Americans. Musharraf was conducting careful purges in the ISI— nothing definitive, but the handwriting was on the wall. The ISI contented itself with playing a waiting game. It was all very quiet among the main players.

Taking out the nukes was important. Taking out Al Qaeda was more important in the long run. While Al Qaeda was running loose, anything was possible. The Pakistani nukes were safe for the moment, but no one knew what Al Qaeda already had in its hands. Al Qaeda was operating in three theaters: the United States, where it had carried out its recent strikes; in Europe, where it organized its operations and frequently recruited members; and finally, in and near the Islamic world, where it organized itself and prepared to take advantage of collapsing governments.

There were three tasks in order for the U.S. to achieve the destruction of Al Qaeda: develop intelligence on where Al Qaeda operatives were, put a force in place to exploit this information, and assign a coordination point for the execution of this strategy—some agency had to run the war.

The last point was the major problem. Running the war in the United States, in Europe, and in the Islamic world was wildly different, and the tasks, by law and diplomatic necessity, belonged to different agencies. The internal defense of the United States against covert threat belongs to the FBI, Coast Guard, local and state police, and so on. By law, the military has no role or rights within the United States, and neither does the CIA. Homeland Security was created by the President to coordinate the fight in the United States, but it was led by an ex-governor, Tom Ridge, who lacked any of the necessary skills and was generally ignored anyway.

In any allied country, the United States was bound by bilateral intelligence-sharing agreements. These agreements were fairly strict in limiting active CIA operations on their soil, and required collaboration with host-country intelligence and internal security forces. This did not mean that there were no CIA covert operations in these countries, unknown to the host government. It did mean that the CIA was not supposed to carry out major assaults or executions in those countries, and that the host countries certainly didn't expect to see U.S. Special Operations teams kicking in doors in places like Paris and Rome. The CIA, therefore, was as involved with joint committee work as covert operations.

Finally, in the Islamic world, the CIA was in many cases subordinate to Central Command—or at least had to compete with Central Command. Given the war in Afghanistan, operations still under way in Iraq, and the basing of U.S. forces in many countries in the Islamic world, the Defense Department held sway. As in the United States proper, there were internal tensions, not only within the Defense Department but also between Defense and other agencies.

The idea of a Night of the Long Knives, in which a sudden, stunning blow was dealt to Al Qaeda and all nuclear threats were eliminated, required the equivalent of a commander in chief: world, as opposed to the regional, commanders in chief. Donald Rumsfeld wanted to control CINCWorld. It was not simply because he was power-hungry or as Secretary of Defense had an institutional imperative for the role. Rumsfeld understood the strategy that was being laid out. It was originating in large part in the Defense Department and it was the only strategy that held any hope for a rapid reduction of the threat to the United States—a threat that appeared to be enormous.

From Rumsfeld's point of view, the threat to the United States had to preempt all other considerations. It was a state of emergency, and considerations like posse comitatus had to be put aside. Without a single coordinated strategy that could control the situation everywhere, the goal of the operation could not be met. It was understood that there were bureaucratic issues in the United States, diplomatic issues in Europe, and tensions between SOCOM and CIA in the Islamic world.

The tasking of available forces all ran through different channels. The United States had, by March, deployed forces in a large number of strategic countries designed to increase its global reach. For example, two U.S. aircraft landed at an airport in Georgia on February 21, 2002, carrying counterterrorism troops. In January 2002, about 600 troops deployed in the Philippines to conduct operations against abu Sayef troops, a movement linked to Al Qaeda. This was years after the Philippines had expelled U.S. forces. By early April, the number of troops had expanded to over 1,000, and the U.S. was building a naval facility on the tiny island of Basilan. U.S. forces were all over Central Asia.

By April 1, 2002, the United States had forces dispersed throughout the Islamic world—both troops and aircraft—that could strike at any point where intelligence indicated an opportunity. The U.S. could reach out and touch anyone it wanted.

Beyond Long Knives

Through April and May, U.S. forces stood by, waiting for the command that never came. The U.S. was never even close to the point where it had a clear picture of where Al Qaeda was in any one theater, let alone in all theaters. By May, it had become apparent that the plan was not going to be implemented. Even worse, it became clear that real opportunities were being missed because of the obsession with a sudden strike rather than a war of attrition.

There was never a point at which the concept was abandoned. Troops were positioned, intelligence was searching, and the U.S. had set up Joint Terrorism Task Forces. The United States was ready. But the concept was inherently flawed. Al Qaeda was not going to allow the United States to gain that sort of clarity on a regional, let alone global, level. It went against the very organizing principle of the group.

Moreover, the United States's fear of loose nuclear weapons had subsided. There was no reason for Al Qaeda, if it had obtained nuclear weapons, not to use them as quickly as possible, because the threat of discovery by the U.S. outweighed the benefit of waiting for an optimal moment. If the reports of October–December 2001 were true, then at least one American city should have been destroyed already. The United States had taken control of all critical nuclear sites. There was no plan for a single dazzling strike to take out Al Qaeda, only a long war of attrition—a war that the United States was not likely to win.

After the exhilaration of the early phases of Afghanistan, the adrenaline generated by nuclear fears, and the anticipation of a knockout blow to Al Qaeda, the realization in May 2002 was that there would be no climactic end to the war. This was not just a disappointment—it also struck at the fundamental U.S. warfighting doctrine. This was the search for the center of gravity, the one point that, if struck properly, would take down the entire system. Al Qaeda had deliberately been created not to provide that point. But it was in the U.S.'s nature to seek it.

The U.S. war effort by May 2002 was fragmenting into a police investigation in the United States, a diplomatic tangle in Europe, and a stalemate in the Islamic countries. The Islamic world still believed that the United States was inherently weak and unwilling to fight. As the U.S. stood back and looked at the picture before it, it became clear that the high point of the counteroffensive had been reached and all that was left was to plink away at an elusive enemy. Al Qaeda had survived the first attack and, in truth, was relatively unscathed. The U.S. still didn't know if there were Al Qaeda forces in the U.S. It knew that there were many cells in Europe—many that it couldn't touch because it had no real proof, and the Europeans were not going to permit a repeat of the Israeli–Palestinian war in Europe.

The United States needed an elegant solution to the problem. For that, it had to have an elegant definition of the problem. The definition it now found was Al Qaeda financing, and the trail led back to Saudi Arabia. In May 2002, the United States redefined the Al Qaeda problem. It was now seen as the Saudi Arabian problem—and the key to Saudi Arabia, it was determined, ran through Iraq.

CHAPTER 11

Searching for a Strategy: Saudi Arabia, Iran, and Iraq

THE UNITED STATES was not going to defeat Al Qaeda militant by militant, capillary by capillary. As the U.S. wove its way from Tora Bora to the Pakistan crisis, it became clear that hunting down Al Qaeda wherever it might be found made for rousing rhetoric but did not make for an operational plan. The United States realized it could defeat Al Qaeda only by taking out its bases of support—its financial, logistical, and personnel systems. That meant that the U.S. had to hit the arteries—and had to deal with Saudi Arabia.

Al Qaeda was, in fundamental ways, a Saudi phenomenon. Its leaders and members were Saudi, its ideology was Wahabi, and its financing drew on Saudi citizens. Al Qaeda was created out of Saudi foreign policy. The problem was that Al Qaeda—or at least Al Qaeda's social and intellectual foundations—were so deeply embedded in Saudi life that it was impossible to cut off support for Al Qaeda without ripping the Kingdom apart. Certainly, Al Qaeda was opposed to the policies of the Saudi Royal Family, and vice versa. Nevertheless, the financial sinews of Al Qaeda flowed from numerous supporters in the Kingdom, and the Saudi government was loath to trigger the consequences of restraining these supporters.

The Saudis simply did not want to participate in the American war to any extent that would have made a difference. This startled the United States, which believed it had saved the Saudis during Desert

Storm. It was the culmination of a policy that had been evolving for a decade. The United States needed a way to pressure the Saudis into doing what the Americans needed—even though it was not in the Saudi interest. The United States pressed, and the Saudis deflected.

The Saudi Dilemma

The central dilemma the U.S. now faced was how to get the Saudis into the war. The problem was that the Saudis did not think the United States was going to win this war. They understood the region and their own country far better than the Americans, and the United States did not terrify the Saudis nearly as much as Al Qaeda did. The Saudis had heard U.S. rhetoric in the past and were not impressed. Somehow the U.S. had to demonstrate just how serious and frightening it could be, and then be in a position to put massive military and political pressure on the Saudis.

This was the origin of the U.S. decision to invade Iraq. There were other strands, such as fear of weapons of mass destruction, concern that Al Qaeda was collaborating with the Iraqis, and a genuine feeling that Saddam Hussein was a monster. But to understand the American decision to invade Iraq, it is essential to understand the American concern, and even obsession, with the course Saudi Arabia was taking amid growing evidence that the Saudis were financing Al Qaeda.

There were deep springs of sympathy for Al Qaeda among Saudis. The government's decision to permit U.S. troops to use Saudi soil to retake Kuwait had created tremendous tension within the Kingdom. The Americans viewed themselves as disinterested liberators. Many Saudis viewed the Americans as foreign, Christian occupiers defiling the land and intervening to save the widely despised Kuwaiti ruling family.

The House of Saud was not a secure entity. It had been in deep competition for dominance over the holy places with the Hashemites, with whom the British had been aligned during World War I. After the war, the British switched loyalty to the Saudis, moving the Hashemi

Bedouin out of the Saudi peninsula to what is now Jordan and Iraq. The Saudis created a complex system of governance through a series of alliances based on intermarriage and distributed oil wealth that created a coalition of tribes, clans, and families undergirding the House of Saud.

That coalition was the foundation of Saudi power, but it also dramatically limited Saudi room for maneuver. Arabian tribes were deeply steeped in a conservative and restrictive reading of Islamic law. The rural tribes of the Arabian Peninsula were the bedrocks of this religious conservatism that was coupled with xenophobia. The Saudis' wealth came from selling their oil around the world, but their cosmopolitan economics constantly collided with the religious sectarianism of the tribal leadership that formed the political foundation of their regime. The Saudi government had always had a difficult time balancing these competing realities.

Following the fall of the Soviet Union and Desert Storm, a suppressed strand of anti-Americanism reasserted itself. More specifically, it wasn't an anti-American sentiment as much as it was an anti-Christian one—couched in general hostility to the non-Islamic world. The United States was not viewed as a secular state that was neutral on religion. Rather, the U.S. was viewed as simply the latest of a long line of Christian Crusader powers that had made war on Islam. Islamic religious sentiment held that resistance to Christian encroachment was a moral obligation.

This was not the official view of the government or the dominant sentiment within the Royal Family. Quite the contrary, both of these groups felt themselves threatened by this sentiment, since it also targeted them as being intimately involved with foreigners. In its most extreme form, this view held that the Saudi leadership was hypocritical, claiming to be Islamic but actually collaborating with Christians. The Saudi government would have liked to see the conservatives disappear. However, the political tradition of Saudi Arabia involved accommodation rather than confrontation. The Royal Family had prospered by accommodating, rather than resisting, the very different views, interests, and passions that comprised the Saudi political system.

In the 1970s, the Saudis had helped create the mujahideen movement for the Americans to help oppose the Soviets. In the 1980s, they had fueled it with recruits and money. These recruits were fighting not for the United States but for their own religious principles. Having energized this movement, the Saudis did not know how to shut it down. Nor, in the final analysis, did they want to. The political costs would have been tremendous.

The key figure in all of this was a Saudi prince, Turki al Faisal, who became head of Saudi intelligence in 1976. A son of the late King Faisal and the brother of the Saudi foreign minister, Turki al Faisal had guided Saudi intelligence for a quarter century. He was responsible for overseeing Saudi Arabia's role in recruiting and supporting the mujahideen in Afghanistan and, later, for trying to manage the situation in both Pakistan and Afghanistan. He had long been considered a friend of the United States, having been educated there, and having had close relationships with key American figures, including George Bush the elder and Bill Clinton. He was regarded as a key collaborator and friend of the CIA.

It would not be accurate to say that Turki al Faisal lost control of the weapon he had created. It was not his idea to create it (it was Jimmy Carter's), and the weapon was never truly under anyone's control. After Desert Storm the movement intensified and, lacking other pressing enemies, focused itself on the Americans—and in particular on the United States's presence in Saudi Arabia. The critical point came in June 1996, when Khobar Towers, housing U.S. Air Force personnel, was blown up, killing nineteen Americans.

The United States expected to have the full cooperation of Saudi intelligence and the government in the wake of the Khobar bombing. It sent FBI agents to Saudi Arabia to participate in the investigation, expecting to have direct access to anyone being questioned and to all physical evidence. To the surprise of the Americans, the Saudis denied American personnel access to the investigation, and in fact seemed reluctant to press forward with the issue. Turki al Faisal was put on the spot. He was caught between his American friends and the Royal Family.

Khobar Towers was one of the first major actions of the movement that would solidify into Al Qaeda. It was a movement that had a great many supporters in the Saudi Kingdom. The same people who contributed money to support Wahabi schools in Afghanistan and Pakistan had donated money to Al Qaeda. This was not government money, but it was money that came from important sectors of Saudi society. The political cost of cracking down on these people would be substantial. The public perception of all of this was that Turki al Faisal wanted to rein in the Islamist radicals, but that others, particularly Interior Minister Naif, who had his finger on the pulse of Saudi society, would not permit him.

At Khobar Towers the underlying tension between the United States and Saudi Arabia first came to light. It was subtle. The government was not anti-American by any means, and it did not want to see the Islamist movement drive the United States out. At the same time, there was a deep fear that trying to suppress that movement would result in an explosion, since the Islamist view of the world was deeply embedded in Saudi society.

The United States looked to Turki al Faisal as the expert on Al Qaeda, and as Al Qaeda intensified its operations, at Khobar Towers and beyond, the U.S. felt that he had failed to share intelligence he must have had. Turki al Faisal explained that the United States was overestimating his knowledge. Having been put into motion, Al Qaeda had become impenetrable—it had created a system for vetting members so that it was impossible to slip anyone inside.

Two weeks before September 11, Turki al Faisal suddenly and unexpectedly formally resigned as head of Saudi intelligence. There was never a clear explanation as to why he left his post, nor was there any explanation of why it happened just before September 11, or even an indication that the events were linked. Nevertheless, after September 11, U.S. intelligence tried desperately to piece together what had happened. The Saudi connection was clear, but Saudi intelligence could not respond. Turki al Faisal's replacement, Nawaf bin Abdul-Aziz, was not an intelligence professional, and Saudi intelligence was obviously in turmoil. U.S. intelligence wondered if the entire point of removing Turki al Faisal was to disrupt intelligence cooperation with the United States, especially since he and Saudi intelligence were the U.S.'s primary window into Al Qaeda. Conspiracy theories flourished, but the fact was that Saudi Arabia was, to a great extent, opaque to U.S. intelligence. Without a guide like Turki al Faisal, no one really knew what was going on.

Saudi money became even more important as the failure of plans to engage Al Qaeda became obvious. New recruits and money were flowing into Al Qaeda's coffers, and the source of that money was in Saudi Arabia. From the beginning of the war, U.S. intelligence had targeted Al Qaeda's financial flows for interdiction, under the reasonable theory that cutting off the money would destroy Al Qaeda. The U.S. started by trying to track Al Qaeda money spent in the United States. The process of money flows was bewildering. Every convenience store with a Western Union money-transfer center could be used for this purpose.

Laws could be passed to interdict the flow of money, but Al Qaeda was extremely sophisticated. They transferred relatively small amounts of money through fairly primitive systems, and there was no way to cut off the money completely at the destination point, the United States. The money had to be cut off at the source. The primary source was Saudi Arabia, and the U.S. was not receiving meaningful cooperation.

In January 2002, while the United States was focusing its attention on dealing with both the nuclear crisis and the assault on Al Qaeda, the Saudi government quietly informed the United States that it would like U.S. forces to be removed from its land. The Saudis had allowed their facilities to be used during the Afghan war, but the United States was now mobilizing for a much broader series of operations in the Islamic world and Saudi Arabia did not want to be drawn into this process. It had financial problems at home because of low oil prices, tensions within the Royal Family, and tensions with the clergy. The American presence had lost its attractiveness. By March, the United States had reluctantly complied and was moving equipment from Saudi Arabia to Qatar. The split between the United States and Saudi Arabia that had begun slowly following Khobar Towers had now become a reality.

The problem the United States had was that it could not let the rift end there. Saudi Arabia was still the key to the American war on Al Qaeda, and the U.S. could not win that war without the Saudis. Furthermore, the Saudi Peninsula itself contained many Al Qaeda personnel. The Empty Quarter along the Yemeni border was active with Al Qaeda training camps and other operations. U.S. troops were moved into all of the countries surrounding Saudi Arabia—Yemen, Oman, Qatar, Bahrain, Kuwait. All of these countries feared Saudi power, and their rulers feared Saudi fundamentalism as well. The more the Saudis retreated inward, the more the United States was drawn, and eagerly entered, these other countries. During the spring of 2002, Yemen in particular became a battleground between U.S. Special Forces and Al Qaeda operatives—with the action on occasion spilling across the border into Saudi Arabia itself.

It was not exactly a war between the U.S. and Saudi Arabia. It was far more complex than that. The Saudis were trying their best to avoid a confrontation with anyone—Al Qaeda or the United States. Al Qaeda was happy to accommodate the Saudis—it simply wanted Saudi money and Saudi soil for base camps. It did not want a confrontation with the Saudi government. The U.S. did not want a confrontation with the Saudi government either, but did want to get to Al Qaeda. It was a case in which intentions simply didn't matter very much. The net result was that Saudi Arabia and the United States were on a collision course.

As the U.S. began to get control over the Pakistan situation (at least to the extent of having Musharraf accede to U.S. demands over arresting terrorists and giving the United States access to Pakistani nuclear facilities), the focus of the United States turned overwhelmingly to the Saudis.

By February 2002, even as the United States focused on the global assault on Al Qaeda, extreme frustration with Saudi Arabia grew.

The Saudis felt this process intensely. Prince Bandar, the longtime Saudi ambassador to the United States, was reporting back to Riyadh of the changing mood in the administration. The Saudis publicly blamed the tension on what they called "neoconservatives," when what they meant were Jewish policy intellectuals in the administration, led by Paul Wolfowitz, the Deputy Secretary of Defense who was the chief architect of the U.S. war. The Saudis were telling anyone who would listen that the neocons were poisoning U.S.–Saudi relations.

The administration was controlled not by the neocons but by people who had a history of close ties with the Saudis. Dick Cheney, for example, had worked extensively and harmoniously with the Saudis while he was Secretary of Defense during Desert Storm, as well as during his stint as the head of Halliburton. Colin Powell had also been close to the Saudis. George W. Bush himself had become close to a number of important Saudis while working in the oil business. The Saudis tried to present the problem as something generated by the neocons, but the truth is that it was the straight conservatives—who had been friends with the Saudis—who had the problem.

In the few months since September 11, U.S. intelligence had developed a substantial amount of information revealing that Saudi citizens and many significant figures in the Saudi establishment had, with the knowledge of Saudi intelligence, provided financial support to Al Qaeda and related groups. Some may have thought they were simply engaged in charitable work, while others may have known the real purpose of the donations—but Saudi intelligence knew the truth of the matter and did nothing. Moreover, senior government officials had to know as well.

It was this intelligence that drove men like Bush, Cheney, and Powell, who under other circumstances would be accused of being in the Saudis' hip pocket, to turn on the Saudis and demand a fundamental shift in their policy. The Saudis did not reject the demand but rather deflected it. It was this deflection that most concerned the administration. It was clear that the Saudis weren't planning to solve the problem—or, more precisely, couldn't solve the problem.

One example of this inability occurred in February 2002. An Intifada had been raging in Israel. It had begun in the fall of 2000, following the collapse of the Clinton administration's peace initiative at Camp David. The Intifada predated 9/11 and was only tangentially related to it. Al Qaeda had certainly made an issue of the Palestinians, but not all that much more than it had made an issue of Kashmir or even Chechnya. Al Qaeda took a traditional view that each generation had to protect all the lands that had converted to Islam, and the loss of Israel was as significant—and no more—than the loss of other lands.

Historically, the Saudis had not been all that concerned about Israel or the Palestinians. They had provided only token forces in previous wars and had actively opposed the Palestinian radicals who dominated the movement prior to the rise of Hamas. For the Saudis, Israel had never been a central concern—until February 2002, when they suddenly discovered that they would not be able to collaborate with the United States on Al Qaeda until after a peace settlement was reached in Israel. The Saudis had discovered that the Palestinian issue could actually be useful to them.

The United States wanted Saudi assistance on Al Qaeda. The Saudis were under tremendous pressure internally from their own conservatives. If the Saudis simply helped the United States, they would be wide open to charges of collaboration. If, on the other hand, the Saudis extracted, from the United States, an agreement to impose a reasonable peace on the Israeli–Palestinian conflict, they could persuasively argue that the quid pro quo of Al Qaeda for Palestine was worth it. They therefore asked the United States to do something about Israel immediately.

This appeared to be a plausible position. Many commentators, particularly in Europe, echoed the Saudi line, arguing that the real reason Al Qaeda was powerful in the Islamic world was the manifest injustices being perpetrated against the Islamic world, with the case of

Israel under Ariel Sharon being the greatest example. The Saudis argued, and were supported by many, that it was impossible to ask the Saudi regime to crack down on Islamic fundamentalists while the Israelis were brutalizing the Palestinians. Also, it was impossible for the Arab world to turn on Iraq, for example, while the U.S. refused to support sanctions against Israel.

Beneath the surface of this extremely plausible argument was another reality. The Saudis knew that the kind of proposals they were floating were not only unacceptable to Israel, but would be rejected by the Palestinians as well. The Saudis were proposing acceptance of the partition of Palestine into two states—with Israel having far more land than the UN had allocated them in 1948. The Palestinians had rejected that plan in 1948 and had reaffirmed that rejection in 1967, when the Khartoum summit asserted the famous "three no's" in the wake of the 1967 Israeli victory: "No recognition of Israel. No negotiation with Israel. No peace with Israel."

The Saudis knew that Europeans and Americans sympathetic to the Palestinians believed that this position was simply rhetorical and political and not a core Palestinian value. The Saudis knew better. They could read the Palestinian press in Arabic and knew that the plan they were thinking about was going to be rejected, in various ways, by everyone involved. The idea of a Palestinian settlement prior to cooperation with Al Qaeda essentially meant that there would never be cooperation on Al Qaeda, since there would never be a Palestinian settlement. However, it would divert attention from the Al Qaeda issue and toward the Israeli–Palestinian conflict, buying the Saudis some breathing space. Thus, the Saudis suddenly started generating peace proposals—the broader, more breathtaking, and less practical, the better.

The U.S. administration understood the Saudi strategy. They knew that the Saudis had far greater concerns than the Israelis, and that the argument was a plausible explanation for why the Saudis would not be able to comply with American wishes. It was designed to put the burden of any breach with the Kingdom on the United States. The administration, however, was having none of it. The pressure stayed on. The Saudi hope—that the administration could be deflected from its course—was failing.

The Saudis urgently needed to find room to maneuver without appearing to be uncooperative. They started a major public relations push designed to lock in the administration. In February 2002, Crown Prince Abdullah kicked off the campaign. First, Abdullah made a speech that hinted that Saudi Arabia was prepared not only to establish diplomatic relations with Israel, but also to proceed to full normalization, if the Israelis were prepared to withdraw from the occupied territories. At first, no one noticed the speech. Then, as it began to get public attention, Bush telephoned Abdullah to tell him that he welcomed the proposal and that he was sending a senior U.S. delegation to Riyadh to discuss it. Bush knew that he couldn't appear to be too negative, particularly because it would give the Europeans an excuse to back off potential U.S. demands.

The delegation would include Assistant Secretary of State William J. Burns, who headed Near Eastern affairs, and George Tenet, the head of the CIA. Tenet was the last man Abdullah wanted to see in Riyadh. Under the Clinton administration, Tenet had been given the task of monitoring Israeli and Palestinian compliance with U.S. peace proposals and processes. He was the U.S. specialist in the nuts and bolts of the peace process. However, by sending Tenet to Riyadh, the administration put the Saudis in the one position they didn't want to be: having to explain themselves to someone who knew what he was talking about.

Protocol required that Tenet meet with his Saudi counterpart, the head of Saudi intelligence. Tenet was going to sit down in a room with Turki al Faisal's successor and ask for information and explanations. Evasion would be difficult if not impossible, especially if the Saudis wanted to avoid a break with the United States. The administration was playing the Saudi game. They were publicly focusing on the Israeli–Palestinian problem, but their not very well-hidden agenda would be the focus of the meeting.

Abdullah decided to flank Bush by playing an even bigger card: Tom Friedman, columnist for the *New York Times*, influential, knowledgeable about the Middle East, Jewish—and eager to play a hand in revolutionizing Arab–Israeli relations. Abdullah invited Friedman to dinner and floated an idea to him—total recognition of Israel and normalization of Arab-Israeli relations in exchange for Israeli withdrawal from the occupied territories. Simple, persuasive—and impossible. Friedman bit hard, writing a column about it on February 17. Suddenly, everyone was talking about the revolutionary Saudi proposal—a total end to the Israeli–Palestinian conflict. Very few asked the question why the Saudis were suddenly floating the idea in February 2002 rather than any other time in the past.

The *New York Times* celebrated the proposal, and serious thinkers around the world took it seriously. The administration was furious with the Saudis—the Saudis had consulted nobody about the idea, which meant that this radical proposal didn't even have the backing of Abdullah's own government. In addition, Abdullah hadn't even talked to other Arab states, let alone to the Palestinians. His recommendation failed to address critical questions, from the status of the Temple Mount to the future of Palestinian exiles. The Saudis had not done their diplomatic homework, nor had they really done more than pose a sentiment. But they had tried to place the United States on the defensive.

The Saudis, as usual, had nothing at risk and were not in a position to bring those who were at risk—like Hamas and Syria—to the table. Moreover, the proposal was couched in such a way that the Saudis themselves were not going to back it until there was a consensus, and the administration knew the Saudis were not going to build one.

Rather than deflecting the administration, the Saudi peace proposal intensified Washington's deepening suspicions about the Saudis. Not only were the Saudis still a problem regarding Al Qaeda, but they were not willing to do anything about it—and in addition, they were trying to maneuver Washington into deeper problems than it already had. This was the main goal of the Saudis' Israeli–Palestinian initiative. The administration began to raise, in earnest, the question of whether the

U.S.-Saudi relationship had any future. That posed a second, more serious question: If the Saudis were no longer to be thought of as allies, and the Saudis were at the center of the Al Qaeda problem, then what should the United States do about Saudi Arabia?

The Iraqi Lever

One of the reasons for Saudi disregard of the United States was a conviction, shared with much of the Islamic world, that the United States was a military weakling. For Americans, it is difficult to imagine such a perception—especially since Saudi Arabia had witnessed the power unleashed in Desert Storm. But Desert Storm was the perfect example. Having taken months to assemble a force to fight Saddam, the United States executed a campaign whose primary purpose appeared to have been the avoidance of casualties. More to the point, rather than continue the war to defeat Saddam Hussein completely, the U.S. ended the Gulf War prematurely.

This was simply one of many American military failures brought on by fear of casualties. Included in the list were:

- The blunder at Desert One in 1980.
- Reagan's decision to withdraw troops from Beirut after the bombing of the embassy.
- The withdrawal of U.S. troops from Somalia after a handful of casualties.
- A decade of ineffective air action against Iraq.
- Extremely weak military responses to the bombing of the embassies in Africa and the USS *Cole* attack.
- The Afghan war, which was regarded by Americans as a success but was seen by most of the Islamic world as simply another half-hearted, incomplete mission.

The Islamic world did not take the United States seriously as a military power—and the Saudis were no exception.

The United States needed a military victory of substantial proportions. This was not driven by bloodlust or some cowboy mentality. It was a matter of credibility, an integral part of the political reality in the region. Being perceived as weak, the United States was not feared nearly as much as Al Qaeda, which was seen as small but deadly, and likely to prevail over the United States in the long run. The United States had no hope of defeating Al Qaeda unless it could shift this perspective. It needed to win a war.

It also needed to be in a position to influence events in the region militarily. The United States had a series of bases on the Arabian Peninsula. Each of these bases was under the political control of the host government, including U.S. bases and facilities in Saudi Arabia. The host countries could decide whether the United States would be permitted to use those bases for conflicts on a case-by-case basis. The United States was severely constrained in its exploitation of these facilities by the interests of the various states.

Moreover, the basing system did not provide solutions throughout the region. From western Afghanistan to the Mediterranean, the United States had allies and air and naval bases. It even had some ground troops in Kuwait. But it did not have the ability to stage larger-scale, multibrigade, or divisional attacks. That meant that countries like Syria and Iran—and, for that matter, Saudi Arabia—did not perceive the United States as a significant threat. Therefore, the Saudis did not see the need to adjust their policy on Al Qaeda to the extent the United States wanted.

The U.S. began to see the war on Al Qaeda as a long-term war. As the tremendous terror of weapons of mass destruction subsided to an ongoing gnawing fear, and as the realization grew that the global defeat of Al Qaeda was not going to be possible, the issue turned to a longer-term strategy. This new focus would not so much solve the Al Qaeda problem as create a process that would undermine the operational foundations of Al Qaeda by forcing nations in the region to redefine their behavior.

From a purely military point of view, Iraq is the single most strategic country in the Middle East. It borders on six other countries: Kuwait, Saudi Arabia, Jordan, Syria, Turkey, and Iran. In other words, from Iraq—and with its forces in Afghanistan—the United States could influence events in countries that ranged from the Himalayas to the Mediterranean and from the Black Sea and the Caucasus to the Red and Arabian Seas. Like its predecessor Mesopotamia, Iraq is the pivot of the Middle East.

An American occupation of Iraq would create an untenable situation for Saudi Arabia. The United States would have Saudi Arabia literally surrounded by not only air and naval forces, but by ground forces as well. The thought of an American occupation of Iraq had never been seriously considered by the Saudis. The assumption was that the Americans would not carry out such a maneuver except under extreme provocation, and then only with Saudi cooperation. The assumption was that the United States would not be able to execute an invasion without the use of Saudi territory and facilities. From the Saudi point of view, the Iraqis had not provoked the United States sufficiently, and since Saudi Arabia would not participate in such an attack, the Saudis did not see this as a serious option.

The Saudis simply misread the emerging American strategy. They did not understand that the Americans regarded the Saudis as a strategic problem that had to be solved. The Saudis never believed the U.S. would rupture their relationship, and they failed to see that, in spite of repeated signals from the United States, Saudi behavior since September 11 had already done just that. The Americans were looking at a potential Iraq campaign not in terms of preserving their relationship with the Saudis, but in terms of redefining it.

Given Saudi resistance to the United States, the obvious, straightforward path would have been an invasion of Saudi Arabia. The problem with the obvious path was simple. Apart from military problems inherent in invading the larger country, the United States did not want to displace the House of Saud. It wanted to change the Saudi government's behavior. An invasion that would have deposed the Saudi government and Royal Family would not have reduced support for Al Qaeda flowing out of the Kingdom. It would have unleashed it. The United States needed the Saudis to use its power to suppress Al Qaeda. Destroying that power would have achieved nothing. Quite apart from the danger of disrupting oil supplies—which was important but not central—the United States had to follow an indirect path, using Iraq as a platform from which to coerce Saudi Arabia.

From the American point of view, the occupation of Iraq would give the United States two critical levers over the Saudis. The first, and most important, was the very real presence of several U.S. divisions along the Saudi Arabian border with Iraq. The Saudis were used to hostile divisions along that border, but they also were used to American power protecting them from those forces if necessary. The idea that American forces would constitute the threat from Iraq was outside any security paradigm the Saudis had ever considered.

The second lever was oil, although not the way in which many critics of the war talked about it. The United States had never had an interest in directly controlling Persian Gulf oil. As long as the oil continued to flow at market prices and the supply was not interrupted, the U.S. understood that the cost of military action would dwarf any potential savings in the price of oil.

Moreover, in the generation that had passed since 1973, the economics of global oil had shifted dramatically. First, supply and demand were not only in balance, but no small group of nations controlled a disproportionate share of that oil. Second, these countries had gone from being economically robust to extremely weak. As oil prices dropped, they found it more and more difficult to service the massive international debts they had undertaken to buy social peace and attempt economic diversification. Saudi Arabia, in particular, was in no condition to impose an oil embargo. It needed the income at least as much as the global economy needed oil.

The U.S. had no interest in seizing Saudi oil fields—the Saudis were financial hostages already. In fact, Saudi Arabia had such a weak economic hand that the United States looked at Iraqi oil as a potential lever against Saudi Arabia. Iraq had enormous reserves, and while its infrastructure was decayed, bringing some Iraqi oil on line quickly was possible. Bringing enormous amounts of Iraqi oil on line after a year or so was entirely within the realm of possibility as well.

Saudi Arabia desperately needed to keep the price of oil above $20 a barrel, and preferably at or above $25. That was a fundamental national interest. It was also critical to the Saudis that Iraqi oil be kept off the market—and the sanctions on Iraq achieved that. The prospect of Iraqi oil moving freely onto the market unnerved the Saudis, to say the least. The prospect of its surging onto the market—guarded by U.S. troops, managed by U.S. companies, and sold in quantities not seen for well over a decade—posed a terrific economic threat.

A U.S. occupation of Iraq would, in theory, influence other countries as well. Iran, in particular, was of strategic importance. It could affect events in Afghanistan and was also believed to be providing sanctuary to at least some members of Al Qaeda. Iran had three strategic interests. It had an interest in the destruction of the Iraqi government and armed forces. It also had an interest in eliminating the American presence in the region. Finally, it had a historic conflict with Sunni Islam, and particularly with Sunni Wahabi power in the Arabian Peninsula.

The Iranian foreign-policy interests were inherently contradictory. Iran had gotten the worst of it in the war with Iraq. It could not bring about Iraq's destruction without the United States. It certainly didn't want to see a powerful United States in the region, but it also didn't want to see the Saudis outmaneuver the Americans and therefore become even more powerful in the Islamic world. Finally, the Iranians were willing to go after Al Qaeda, but only if they felt the United States was committed to the game. They simply weren't certain.

Iranian intelligence had been organizing the Iraqi Shiites—who dominated Iraq south of Baghdad and constituted the majority of Iraqis—since the failure of an American-inspired uprising in 1991. In fact, the United States was unaware of the extent to which the Iraq Shiites had been systematically organized by Iran—from the leadership who had been given sanctuary in Iran, to the local level in the villages of the Tigris and Euphrates Rivers. The Iranians knew that in the event of the fall of Saddam, they would be in a position to fill the power vacuum—and that the Americans would need the Shiites if the U.S. was to achieve its goals.

The Iranians had a fundamental national-security interest in the destruction of Iraqi power. The Americans would leave eventually, so Iran was willing to signal the Americans that an invasion of Iraq would not at all displease them, and that in return for the destruction of the Mujahideen e-Khalq—an anti-Iranian paramilitary force funded by the Iraqis—they would collaborate with the United States against Al Qaeda.

Iran wanted the United States to invade Iraq. It did everything to induce the United States to do so. Its strategy was to provide the United States with intelligence that would persuade the United States that invasion was both practical and necessary. There were many intelligence channels operating between Teheran and the United States, but the single most important was Ahmad Chalabi, the Defense Department's candidate for President of Iraq. Chalabi, a Shiite who traveled extensively to Iran before the war, was the head of the Iraqi National Council, which provided key intelligence to the United States on Iraq, including on WMD. But what it did not provide the U.S. was most important: intelligence on Iranian operations in Iraq or on Iraqi preparations for a guerrilla war. Chalabi made it look easy. That's what the Iranians wanted.

The primary vector for Chalabi's information was not the CIA, but OSP under Abe Shulsky. OSP could not have missed Chalabi's Iranian ties, nor could they have believed the positive intelligence he was giving them. But OSP and Shulsky were playing a deeper game. These were old Cold Warriors. For them, the key to the collapse of the Soviet Union was the American alliance with China. Splitting the enemy was the way to go, and the fault line in the Islamic world was the Sunni-Shiite split. The United States, from their point of view, was not playing the fool by accommodating Iran's wishes on Iraq. Apart from all of its other virtues, they felt that the invasion would create a confluence of interests between the U.S. and Iran, which would have enormously more value in the long run than any problems posed by the Iraqi invasion. From the standpoint of OSP—and therefore of Wolfowitz and Rumsfeld—Chalabi's intelligence or lack of it was immaterial. The key was alignment with Iran as another lever against Saudi Arabia. And there were more immediate effects as well.

Getting access to Iranian intelligence on Al Qaeda was essential to the United States. The Iranians had a library on them. The Iranians were cagey in sharing intelligence, but not unwilling. Motivating the Iranians to cooperate was the key. Invading Iraq and supporting the Shiites would give the Iranians what they wanted. In the long run, this would cause other major problems for the United States. In the short run, the reasoning went, there was Al Qaeda. Moreover, anything that would help guarantee that Iranian nuclear technology did not get into the hands of Al Qaeda was worth the effort. This wasn't friendship; it was mutual interest.

Finally, there was Syria. Syria had always fished in the muddied waters of Palestinian politics. Like Iraq, Syria was ruled by a Baathist government, but one that was an enemy of Iraq. Syria's Assads and Iraq's Husseins had had a blood feud going back a generation. Syria's primary interest was in Lebanon, which had historically been part of Syria and which had been effectively absorbed into Syria by Hafez al Assad during the brutal Lebanese civil wars. Above all, the Syrians wanted to retain their sphere of influence in Lebanon.

To do that, however, Syria would inevitably be drawn into the complex factionalism of Lebanon, which included groups with a history of terrorist actions. Syria's position in Lebanon was complex. It should be remembered that Syria intervened in Lebanon on behalf of Christian factions with whom the Assads had been doing business for years—and against Yassir Arafat and his Fatah faction, which was powerful to the south of Beirut. The point is that any simple explanation of Syria's motives is bound to be wrong. They have played a deep and complex game.

They have also played a dangerous game, from the American point of view. The Assads are part of a small Muslim sect called

Alawites. Historically, many Alawites survived, as did others in the Levant, by buying, selling, and smuggling. From drug deals in the Bekaa Valley to the leisure industry on the Beirut coast, Alawites were involved in anything where money could be made. Ideologically, they opposed Israel and supported Hezbollah—a Shiite group aligned with Iran. Practically, Syrian and Israeli businessmen could meet in Nicosia, Cyprus, and do business. Money talked, ideology walked.

The problem was that Al Qaeda had money. Bashar Assad, the son of Hafez who had died a few years before, had nothing in common with Osama bin Laden. Assad had been an ophthalmologist living in Paris before he was brought back by his father to succeed him. He was secular to the bone. He—and especially the men around him— were businessmen. The CIA had information about Al Qaeda personnel not only passing through Syria but also using it for operational planning and, possibly, training.

The Syrians were not supporters of Al Qaeda or the United States. They rather liked the battle raging between the two. It not only served as a good source of revenue from Al Qaeda, but as far as the Syrians read the situation, the American need for allies in the Muslim world would cause them to keep Israel on a short leash. While the United States was fighting Al Qaeda and the Israelis were tied down in their internal Intifada, Syria was free to consolidate its position in Lebanon and make a nice piece of change on the side. Besides, the Syrians, having provided forces to Desert Storm, were simply not impressed by American will and capabilities. Syria was a perfect example of the problem the United States had to solve.

If the United States were to occupy Iraq, Syria would face enemies on all sides—the Israelis to the southwest, the Turks to the north, and the Americans to the east. They would be completely isolated and threatened by powers that could individually crush them. By occupying Iraq, the United States would be in a position to influence and coerce Syria as well.

The U.S. had been thinking about Iraq for over a decade. The Iraq question had dominated the first Bush administration as well as the

Clinton administration. It had been one of the first issues reviewed by the second Bush administration as well. Ever since 1991, the United States had maintained a constantly updated contingency plan for invading and occupying Iraq. But it had always been looked at as a stand-alone operation. In other words, U.S. Iraq planning had always taken place in a context in which Iraq was to be dealt with by itself.

Ever since Desert Storm, when the U.S. declined to wheel north toward Baghdad, the U.S. had always reached the same conclusion— Iraq was not only not worth the price, but toppling Saddam would harm U.S. interests. The issue wasn't Saddam. He was known to be a homicidal maniac. The problem was that the foundation of U.S. strategy in the Persian Gulf had always been maintaining the balance of power between Iraq and Iran, in order to protect the security of the Arabian Peninsula. The U.S. knew that if either country had the upper hand in the region—as Iraq did in 1990—it would try to seize part or all of Arabia. That meant that the United States would have to inject massive force in order to deter invasion. It was far more efficient for the United States to maintain a balance of power between the two countries. Therefore, the United States always declined to act on plans for toppling Saddam.

By the spring of 2002, U.S. strategy had changed in several ways. First, the paramount consideration was Al Qaeda. Second, the Saudis were no longer seen as an American client state that required protection but as an enabler of Al Qaeda requiring coercion. Third, Iran was seen as a potential ally against Al Qaeda. Thus, what had been previously undesirable was now emerging as a very logical step.

Strategic Decisions

By February 2002, there were elements in the Bush administration who were arguing for an invasion of Iraq. Some had wanted to invade as early as October 2001, in a knee-jerk reaction to September 11, but they were overruled. By late winter 2002, this hard-core group was being joined by a broader coalition, including Vice President Dick

Cheney. They made the following case: First, war would demonstrate American will and resolve. Second, war would get rid of Iraqi weapons of mass destruction. Third, it would eliminate the opportunity for Al Qaeda to collaborate with Saddam. Fourth, the destruction of Saddam would be good simply because he was unspeakably evil and deserved to be deposed. Finally, the occupation of Iraq would give the United States military leverage throughout the region.

However, there were several major problems with invading. First, apart from the administration's occasional public assertions, there was no obvious connection between the occupation of Iraq and the destruction of Al Qaeda. Iraq still appeared to be a complete, stand-alone operation, without any effect on the broader war. Second, the United States was still in the middle of diplomacy with Saudi Arabia in the hopes of persuading it to cooperate. Third, the possibility of a global strike on Al Qaeda and WMD had not yet evaporated, and the Iraq operation had to be considered within that context. Finally, the United States did not have forces in place to invade and occupy Iraq. The case for invasion was far from won.

One approach was put forth by the Air Force, Special Operations Command, and Defense Department civilians, who argued that what happened in Afghanistan could be repeated in Iraq. This fit into the general feeling that heavy forces were obsolete, that the Iraqis were not serious enemies, and that there was no need to slow down the timeline in order to build up forces.

Their argument was this: The Northern Alliance did not defeat the Taliban. Rather, the Taliban was defeated by airpower, which broke their morale and caused them to flee. The Northern Alliance was able to move into the vacuum. Had they not been an experienced fighting force, but an unarmed group of peasants, Special Forces could still have guided them in taking the abandoned and undefended cities of northern Afghanistan. It wasn't the Northern Alliance that made the difference. It was the ability of airpower to crush resistance.

Iraq presented Special Forces with the same opportunity that Afghanistan did. The Kurds in the north had been armed and trained by U.S. Special Forces for a decade. In the south, there was a massive Shiite population who had also worked with U.S. Special Forces in the past. If airpower could shatter Iraqi conventional force, these two ethnic groups could move into the vacuum. In fact, the argument went, an attack on Iraq would actually be easier than an attack on Afghanistan because Iraq was more developed and was, therefore, more vulnerable to air attack.

Opposition to this plan came from the Army and the State Department—not incidentally, run by a former Army four-star general, Colin Powell. The Army always had a jaundiced view of the claims made for airpower, and nothing that happened in Afghanistan persuaded them otherwise. It argued that Afghanistan was a typical Air Force/USSO-COM operation. All the easy parts were done, the hard parts were unfinished, and after all the declarations of victory, the Army was left holding the bag without a clear mission or enough troops.

Powell basically said that if Afghanistan was the model, the United States really couldn't afford another victory like that. General Eric Shinseki, the Chief of Staff of the Army, also argued that whatever happened in Kosovo wasn't the Air Force's doing. The battle-damage estimates made by the Air Force during the war were completely overstated. The level of destruction was much less and not nearly enough to explain the Yugoslav capitulation.

The Army faction contended that an invasion of Iraq in 2002 would require a multidivisional force similar to the one fielded in 1990. Iraq would have to be invaded by a force large enough not only to engage and destroy the Iraqi Army but also to occupy, pacify, and govern the country. From the Army's point of view, the other faction was interested only in the first, easy part of the war, and would leave the tough part to the Army.

This military debate took place in something of a vacuum. No final decision had been made to invade Iraq, even though everything was moving in that direction. There was a consensus that at some point Iraq would have to be dealt with, but the argument that it should be dealt with immediately had certainly not been agreed upon. Indeed, the decision to go to war in Iraq started to emerge only as the impossibility of the piecemeal destruction of Al Qaeda became apparent.

This was not a sudden realization, but rather, one that developed in the course of the late winter and spring of 2002. There were two sides to this. First, the sense of desperation over WMD started to decline, if not really dissipate. The Pakistani nukes were under control. The Russians were improving their accounting of their weapons. The Iranians were signaling that they were certainly not prepared to take any steps to transfer weapons to Al Qaeda. The nightmarish fears of the previous fall and early winter had given way to a sense that things were, at least temporarily, under control. Certainly, fear of preemptive nuclear strikes had dissipated.

On the other side of the ledger, the lessons of Tora Bora and the problems of other such operations like Operation Anaconda drove home the lesson that finding and killing the senior cells of Al Qaeda was not going to be easy. Moreover, the United States was not having extraordinary success in mapping out the global network of Al Qaeda, either. To be sure, they were capturing and killing some leaders, and some individuals were falling into their hands, but the war against Al Qaeda was turning into a game of bluff and counterbluff.

The United States was constantly confused by Al Qaeda. The problem was not only Al Qaeda's stealth, but that Al Qaeda was adept at playing head games with U.S. intelligence. They would deliberately plant intelligence on the Americans, sometimes via a Web site, sometimes through tales told by captured Al Qaeda personnel who appear to have been armed with myths and fables to tell if they were captured. The Americans could be driven crazy by a Middle Eastern–looking man and a video camera taking pictures of the Golden Gate Bridge, especially when an Islamic Web site also gave a hint that a bridge would be taken down. Between Al Qaeda's opacity and their ability to jerk U.S. intelligence's chain, the U.S. was being systematically exhausted and desensitized by a constant stream of intelligence that could neither be ignored nor fully analyzed.

On the American side, secret arrests of potential Al Qaeda members were driving Al Qaeda up a wall. The United States had very little information as to who was or wasn't a member of Al Qaeda. By arresting people almost at random, they were certain to be arresting some Al Qaeda. The FBI and CIA might not know they were holding an Al Qaeda member, but Al Qaeda would. Al Qaeda would never be sure what the U.S. did or didn't know about their arrestees. They would also never be certain what the arrestee would divulge under torture—which Al Qaeda had to assume would be administered. Therefore, the FBI was constantly arresting people that were Al Qaeda without knowing it and Al Qaeda was constantly adjusting its organization to cope with what might be a serious breach in security.

This was happening on a global scale, and each side was keeping the other completely off balance. Al Qaeda was having serious difficulties launching new operations, less because of Afghanistan than because of the unpredictable behavior of the FBI and CIA. On the other hand, the United States was flying blind while trying to convince Al Qaeda that it had 20/20 vision. In fact, by the spring of 2002, more than six months after September 11, the United States really didn't have much more of a sense of the extent, location, capabilities, and intentions of Al Qaeda than it did on September 10.

By April 2002, a debate was raging inside the administration as to what to do next. It was a debate suffused by a feeling of helplessness. Afghanistan had been a limited success at best; the covert war was a stalemate. There was a deep crisis within the administration on subsequent actions, and it was in a context in which the administration could not know, but had to assume, that Al Qaeda would strike again.

Something else had been noticed in the administration. There had been a great deal of talk about the "Arab Street" and the idea that it was about to rise up in support of Al Qaeda. The fact was that at least in this sense, Al Qaeda had failed miserably—there was no rising in the Arab Street. No Islamic governments had fallen, though most had not thrown themselves wholeheartedly into the American coalition, either. Most Islamic governments were firmly on the fence, responding to pressure where they felt it, moving carefully back and forth, but except for those firmly in the American camp—such as the sheikh-doms on the edge of the Arabian Peninsula—none of them had moved decisively either way. It was as if the Islamic world were waiting for one side or the other to take control.

There had been a great deal of discussion that decisive action by the United States would increase anti-American sentiment and support for Al Qaeda. A different argument was made inside the administration, coming from Paul Wolfowitz and his staff but resonating strongly in the White House. This argument said that anti-Americanism in the Islamic world was rampant and embedded. Its origins were in historical animosity to Christianity, to the behavior of European colonialists, and to the occupation of Islamic lands by Israel and India. Even if Israel as a whole was destroyed and Kashmir ceded to Pakistan and Chechnya given independence, the animosity toward the United States would remain. The idea that it could be reduced by passivity failed to account for the origins of the sentiment.

There was one variable that could shift: the level of activism. A Muslim could hate the United States, but whether he joined Al Qaeda as a result didn't depend on his level of hatred, but rather on whether he perceived Al Qaeda as being able to defeat the United States. Islamic anger at Christianity, Hinduism, and Judaism were powerful and permanent, but they turned into political and military action only when weakness was perceived. Following this reasoning, the way to prevent increased active support for Al Qaeda was to create a sense of overwhelming power.

The decision to invade Iraq was partly driven by the historic weakness of prior U.S. military encounters in the region. At least in the minds of the administration, the inability to engage Al Qaeda effectively left no alternative but to invade Iraq.

It was also essential, from the standpoint of the Defense Department, that apart from being perceived as militarily capable and willing to endure hardship, the United States must not be perceived as being constrained by alliances. The Defense Department did not object to coalition building. It did object to coalition building that reshaped the battle in order to minimize its ferocity. From the point of view of the Office of Secretary of Defense, it was the ferocity of the battle plan that was of the essence.

President Bush clearly stated that the U.S. was prepared to go to war in Iraq with or without coalition partners. In particular, OSD argued that the U.S. did not need the support of Saudi Arabia. Feeling American pressure, the Saudis had asked the United States in January to withdraw their troops from Saudi soil, and the U.S. quietly complied. The Saudis had not expected an American withdrawal; they thought, rather, that the U.S. would change its invasion plans. The Saudis assumed that the U.S. would never jeopardize its military relationship with Saudi Arabia. This was the Saudis' trump card, and when used, they were certain that Washington would back off.

The Saudis had developed a very refined method of managing Washington: They stayed away from the Israel question, except in a very formal, perfunctory way; they cultivated key decision-makers in Washington and created webs of financial relationships with a range of people outside the government. Finally, and most important, they allowed the United States to use Saudi territory for military operations. They assumed that if they signaled a military breach, the United States would find a basis of accommodation with the Saudis and cancel plans for an invasion of Iraq. To the Saudis' shock, the U.S. went ahead not only with withdrawing but with plans for invasion. This is where the light assault strategy became important. It didn't need the Saudis' participation. Practical or not, it introduced the idea that war didn't depend on agreement from the Saudis.

By March 2002, the U.S. was starting to move its equipment in Saudi Arabia to Qatar. The U.S. had, as early as February, hired contractors to start moving equipment out of Prince Sultan Air Base, a major U.S. facility in Saudi Arabia. Both sides tried to keep it quiet. There was a game of chicken taking place. The Saudis had completely miscalculated the mood in Washington, having assumed that anti-

Saudi feeling had been confined to the Defense Department. They had not grasped the extent to which Dick Cheney—a close friend of the Saudis—had changed his view on them.

Washington was hoping that Riyadh would realize the situation was getting out of hand and call a halt to it. Washington was more aware of the situation in Riyadh than the Saudis were of the situation in Washington. The Americans knew that the Saudi government was under terrific pressure from militant Islamists to get the Americans out of the Kingdom. Nevertheless, Washington hoped that the Saudis could manage their internal situation. The Saudis couldn't. They had hoped that the U.S. would capitulate on key demands, allowing the Saudi government to claim victory inside the Kingdom and the American security blanket to remain.

As the withdrawal was taking place, there were calls for an immediate invasion of Iraq. At this point, Colin Powell intervened. The press was filled with stories of how Powell opposed the invasion and was clashing with Donald Rumsfeld. The truth was more complex. Powell did not inherently oppose the invasion. He had little confidence in the CIA's ability to deal with Al Qaeda, and he did not reject the notion that the United States had to demonstrate its military capability. However, he did not think that Afghanistan had been a great success, and he clearly did not condone the risk-taking that was inherent in the OSD/USAF/USSOCOM plan.

From his point of view, the invasion of Iraq was fundamentally different from the invasion of Afghanistan. In Afghanistan, the occupation of the country was not an issue. No one expected to be able to occupy it. The goal in Iraq, however, was occupation. Moreover, Powell had always been concerned with the potential strength of at least some of the units of the Iraqi Army. He had worried about them in 1991, and he continued to worry about them in 2003.

Powell's thinking was that of an Army officer trained in armor and in heavy, combined arms operations. In sheer numbers, the Iraqis had a substantial armored force. They were defending on interior lines with collapsing lines of supply as they withdrew. The U.S. was faced with a swamp in the south, the Euphrates River line to cross, as well as substantial urbanization south of Baghdad. Then there was Baghdad, a city of five million that could be defended by an even mildly motivated force.

Powell had no doubt that the U.S. could defeat the Iraqi Army. But he thought that the light plan was based on two assumptions that could not be verified until the battle was joined. First, it assumed that the Shiites and Kurds would go on the offensive under U.S. direction. Second, it assumed that airpower alone could shatter Iraqi armor formations and infantry defending the towns and Baghdad. Powell was trained to plan for the worst, and he argued that planning for the worst in this case would require a much more substantial force. In addition, the occupation and pacification of the country would require additional force. Powell conceded that the Iraqi Army had deteriorated substantially since 1991, when over 500,000 coalition troops were needed to take Kuwait alone. However, he still believed that as many as 300,000 troops would be needed to take Iraq now.

A diplomatic imperative therefore grew out of Powell's military analysis. If 300,000 troops would be needed, then the United States had to build a coalition. Three hundred thousand troops would strain U.S. manpower availability and perhaps push it beyond its limit. Therefore, some troops would have to be supplied by allies other than Britain. If Powell's analysis was correct, then the U.S. did not have enough combat force to take Iraq, hold Afghanistan, and maintain a sufficient reserve for action anywhere else. The United States would need allies. The British could be counted upon, but even they wouldn't bring enough force. The U.S. would need additional force from Europe.

This is exactly what Rumsfeld and the DoD didn't want. First, if Powell's plan was to be implemented, the U.S. would have to build up its forces in Kuwait and Turkey in a process that would take at least four months. That meant no invasion would be possible until the fall at the earliest, and that was assuming the deployment would be more rapid than any before. Second, in Rumsfeld's and the DoD's opinion, building a coalition would undermine the core psychological effect they thought was necessary—showing that the United States could be effective without the help of others.

Rather than rushing into war, as was claimed later, George W. Bush actually dithered while the press misunderstood the issue. There was no debate over whether or not to go to war. That had been decided months before. There was, however, a debate over what strategy to use. The more the administration examined events in Afghanistan, the less confident it was of the model. As the temperatures would rise in Iraq in May, the viability of the light option would decline. Donald Rumsfeld's view was increasingly seen as too risky. The uncertainties of the Shiites and of Iraqi resistance were seen as excessively dangerous. In a very quiet but effective way, Powell was winning the argument.

One of the key figures in the debate had been General Wayne Downing, who had been head of SOCOM and had been brought out of retirement after September 11 as Deputy National Security Advisor. Downing had been a strong advocate of the light attack plan, arguing that a fast attack was essential and that the Afghan model would work in Iraq as well. Downing's argument, shared with other key advocates, was that the logic behind an invasion of Iraq also called for a quick invasion. The alternative plan could not be mounted for several months, during which time the entire momentum of the American war effort would appear to be bogged down.

On June 27, 2002, Downing suddenly resigned. His resignation was important—not because he was the most important advocate of the plan, but because his resignation signaled that at least one decision had finally been made. The OSD/USAF/SOCOM group had been defeated by the Army/State Department coalition. The administration had decided that an Afghanistan-style invasion of Iraq was too risky, and that if an invasion was to take place, it would follow the Desert Storm model. More precisely, a compromise was worked out. The invasion would be heavier than Rumsfeld wanted but not as heavy as Powell thought was necessary.

Apart from risk, the decision was influenced by a serious logistical problem that had emerged, one that would have undermined any quick strike. It concerned precision-guided munitions, the backbone of U.S. airpower strategy. One of the most important types of PGM were the Joint Direct Attack Munitions, or JDAMs. A JDAM is really nothing more than a Global Positioning System and a tail-fin guidance system attached to an ordinary iron bomb. More than 25 percent of the 17,000 pieces of ordinance dropped in Afghanistan were JDAMs. The roughly 5,000 dropped in Afghanistan in April 2002 represented nearly half the available stock. Estimates made during the summer of 2002 assumed that somewhere between 10,000 and 15,000 JDAMs would be needed in Iraq. The standard production rate was less than 1,000 JDAM kits a month. That meant that it would not be until early 2003 that a sufficient reserve was available to launch the war. Production was pushed to about 1,500 a month in May and continued to expand, meaning that sufficient stocks would be available by November. It also meant that there could be no war in the spring of 2002.

The logistical question was everything. JDAMs were a critical item, but the U.S. military was short of a host of other systems. The drawdown that had occurred during the 1990s left the United States military on a short leash. The Afghanistan War, launched as quickly as it had, had burned through matériel rapidly, particularly requirements for the Air Force and naval aviation. The carriers were a huge problem as well. In July, three of the twelve U.S. aircraft carriers were at sea, three were in training cycles, and the rest were undergoing repairs in port. Training and repairs for several more carriers were scheduled for completion by late autumn. That would give the Pentagon the minimum five carriers considered necessary for an attack.

The United States was simply not ready for a lightning attack, no matter how badly it was needed. And given the inclination to go with a heavier force, time was needed to get the force into position. The earliest a light war could be launched was November. And when the entire range of logistical issues was considered, January–February was the most realistic period for an attack.

By midsummer 2002, the pattern of reserve mobilizations, deployments of troops to Europe, carrier maintenance, and procurement schedules made it quite clear that the United States was on its way to war. The Defense Department was partly moving in anticipation of a decision, but the debate over the next step was reaching its inevitable conclusion by August. The United States was going to invade Iraq with a multidivisional force that would be based primarily in Kuwait, with a secondary thrust coming out of Turkey. It was not quite Desert Storm—it was more like Desert Storm Lite—but it was certainly not a replay of the Afghan strategy.

By the end of the summer, the decision to invade Iraq had been finalized. Powell's vision for war strategy had prevailed. His war strategy also opened the door for his diplomatic strategy. There was a paradox built into his position. Powell the General wanted to repeat Desert Storm. He felt that it was the safest and surest path to the occupation of Iraq. Desert Storm had used Saudi ports and bases for the attack. Ideally, the next invasion would do the same, but Saudi Arabia was unwilling to host these troops. The rationale for the invasion of Iraq was to bring the Saudis into the U.S. anti–Al Qaeda coalition. If Powell could get the Saudis to collaborate in the war, they would also collaborate against Al Qaeda—and that would make the invasion of Iraq unnecessary. In other words, Powell was saying that Saudi cooperation was necessary for an invasion in Iraq. One of the goals of such an invasion would be to force Saudi Arabia to cooperate with the U.S. If it cooperated, the U.S. wouldn't have to invade Iraq. Powell was setting up a situation in which the invasion of Iraq would become unnecessary.

The chosen military strategy gave Powell at least four but no more than six months to resolve the paradox—to get the Saudis to collaborate and avoid invasion. In order to do this, Powell and the United States had to undertake a massive chess-like strategy to convince the Saudis that there would be an invasion. (The Saudis were convinced the U.S. would not go to war if most of the European nations were opposed.) Here was the paradox: In order for there not to be a war, the Saudis would have to believe that it was inevitable and change their behavior. In order for the Saudis to believe in the inevitability of war—and thereby avoid war—the Europeans had to support the U.S. war plans. This was the incredibly complex challenge that faced the administration in September 2002.

The decision to invade Iraq was not a good one and very few in the administration thought it was. It was simply the best decision available given the limited menu. It was the best of a bad lot. Taking out Al Qaeda through covert operations was not a practical option. Getting Saudi Arabia to incur the political wrath of its radical elements by cutting off financial support was also not going to happen unless the United States forced them to do so. The United States faced the option of hoping for the best or making the best of a mediocre strategy. In a sense, Iraq reminds us of Guadalcanal. No one wanted to be there and no one really cared about it. It was, under the circumstances, the best available option. Now, wars must not be presented that way to the public and allies. So the administration had to become wildly enthusiastic about the idea.

The European Game

The reason for the war was complex and difficult to explain. The process of public explanation undermined the war's utility. If the President was to say that the reason for invading Iraq was to prove that the United States was really much tougher than people thought, and that the occupation of Iraq was intended to intimidate neighboring countries, it would undermine the United States's ability to attain either goal. During World War II, for example, the core American strategy was to allow the Soviets to bleed the Germans dry so that the United States could then land in France and defeat a weakened Germany. It was certainly true, but it was not something that could be said publicly. Roosevelt preferred to speak in terms of the Four Freedoms and the United Nations rather than publicly embrace the actual strategy. Indeed, his strategy and his ideals were not incompatible. Nevertheless, explaining his strategy was not something to be done in polite company.

All nations, especially democratic ones, are torn between the realities of foreign policy and the need to mobilize public opinion around ideals. This is made even more complex when it is simultaneously necessary to build a coalition of foreign nations while attempting to influence the behavior of enemies. It is frequently impossible to publicly reveal the strategic purpose for taking action, and necessary to invoke powerful symbols to justify them. In the best circumstances, the realities of strategy and the symbols invoked are not incompatible.

This was a crossroads for the administration—perhaps one of the most important of the war. The decision to invade Iraq had been made, but now the case had to be made for its necessity. It was difficult to express the real, complex reasoning, and making it public would detract from the strategy's effectiveness. However, as difficult as it was, the truth had the advantage of being the truth. There were other, easier explanations possible that were not altogether false (in the sense that the administration thought them important reasons by themselves), but they weren't the driving reasons. The administration had to decide whether to go public with their actual reasoning or to go with a simpler, more easily expressed view.

The administration had two explanations it could give that would ideally be both true and persuasive without revealing the real reason. One explanation was that Saddam Hussein had collaborated with Al Qaeda. The other was that Iraq had weapons of mass destruction and had to be disarmed. Both would have been good reasons for invading, but neither was exactly the truth.

During August and September, senior members of the administration tried out both justifications for the war. The Al Qaeda argument was, of course, enormously powerful. September 11 had occurred less than a year before. If it could be shown persuasively that Saddam Hussein was in some way complicit in that attack, there would be very few in the United States who would oppose the war, and among foreign nations, few who could justify resisting the attack. The problem was that there was not only little evidence of any collaboration, but good reason to believe there hadn't been very much, if any. The best evidence for collaboration was the claim made by Czech intelligence that a member of Al Qaeda had met with representatives of Iraqi intelligence in Prague and that they might have discussed September 11. That was a very thin strand on which to hang the invasion. It could not be verified; nor was it proof of conspiracy.

Moreover, Al Qaeda had absolutely no use for Saddam Hussein. Hussein was seen as the antithesis of an Islamic ruler—secular, corrupt, and untrustworthy. As we have seen, Al Qaeda's strategy was to avoid becoming dependent on any national intelligence service while making use of what assistance was available. Al Qaeda might have purchased services from Iraqi intelligence—the Iraqis were available for the right price—but it is impossible to believe that bin Laden and his lieutenants, as obsessed with security as they were, would entrust Iraq with any real information about what they were planning to do.

This was a point made forcefully to the United States by European intelligence services. One of the goals of U.S. public diplomacy was to bring the Europeans into the coalition; any argument that the European intelligence services would reject out of hand was, by definition, a nonstarter. The claim of collaboration between Iraq and Al Qaeda was neither true nor persuasive. An argument could have been made that future collaboration was possible, and that an invasion was necessary to prevent that, but the question would be raised: Why single out Iraq?

By early September, this justification had begun to disappear in the administration's public utterances. It was replaced by the claim that the invasion was necessary because Iraq had weapons of mass destruction. These weapons, the argument went, were dangerous in and of themselves, and even more dangerous should they be transferred to Al Qaeda at some future date. The only certain way to prevent this was invasion, since the air attacks carried out by the Clinton administration in December 1998 had not eliminated them.

This appeared to be a more persuasive argument than the Al Qaeda one. First, it was well known that Iraq had used chemical weapons—considered a weapon of mass destruction—during the Iran-Iraq war.

Therefore, there was no question that Iraq had these weapons and no reason to believe that they had destroyed them. Second, Iraq had an ambitious program to build a nuclear weapon, using a French nuclear reactor. The Israelis had destroyed that reactor in 1981, but there was substantial intelligence that Saddam remained interested in securing nuclear technology. Finally, there was some evidence of Iraqi research into biological weapons. The names of the scientists working on biological projects in Iraq were well known to U.S. intelligence.

The general consensus that Saddam had weapons of mass destruction was reinforced by his systematic resistance to United Nations inspections through the years. In 1998, he had expelled UN inspectors and refused to allow any further inspections, an act that resulted in the Desert Fox air campaign launched by Bill Clinton in December 1998. Saddam's behavior was incomprehensible unless he had weapons of mass destruction to hide. It was the universal consensus of the international intelligence community. At the very least, it suggested that he had chemical weapons and was trying to obtain other, more lethal weapons.

The administration believed that this represented an airtight and persuasive justification for an invasion. Saddam was known to be a brutal tyrant, and there was nothing about him that could appeal to even the most virulently anti-American European. Also, weapons of mass destruction would represent a threat to the entire region, including Saudi Arabia, who ought not object to their eradication. Finally, there were UN resolutions barring Iraq from having these weapons, and Saddam was not complying with the inspection regime required under these resolutions. This gave the U.S.—or so the administration was prepared to claim—UN sanction to deal with the problem.

The United States was not planning to invade Iraq because of WMD. That much ought to have been apparent to the most casual observer. If one country is afraid that another country has WMD and might use them, you don't start threatening them with war months before you are ready and wage a very public countdown to a proposed attack date. If you really believe a country has WMD, you say nothing and make no threats until you are ready to strike, and then you strike without warning. U.S. behavior was incompatible with U.S. claims. Just as significant, Israeli behavior didn't make sense if Saddam really was developing nuclear weapons. Israel had destroyed the Iraqi reactor in 1981. Its policy had never changed. If Iraq had ever been close to having deliverable WMD, Israel would have attacked.

The United States believed that Iraq had chemical weapons and that these could potentially be mounted on Scud missiles. The U.S. did not believe that Saddam had nuclear weapons, although it believed he had a nuclear program of sorts. The United States thought Saddam might have some biological weapons—in other words, the U.S. did not think there was an imminent threat from Iraqi WMD, nor did the Israelis.

The U.S. was certain of one thing: No one wanted Saddam Hussein to have any weapons of mass destruction, and no one really wanted Saddam to remain in power. Therefore, although invoking WMD did not assure the United States of broad support, it at least removed the possibility of broad resistance. The beauty of the WMD argument is that while it was a cover, it was also a self-sustaining justification. Unlike the Al Qaeda justification, the United States believed that the WMD explanation was both true and ultimately irresistible. The U.S. could build a coalition around it.

The United States miscalculated, in large part because it failed to understand the geopolitical consequences to others of an Iraqi invasion. The great powers (major regional powers without the ability to influence events globally) understood that the United States had to wage its war on Al Qaeda. They were prepared to cooperate fully in a war designed to track down Al Qaeda around the world. However, an invasion of Iraq would shift the global balance of power so dramatically that these great powers could not tolerate it. In other words, the great powers opposed the invasion for the same reason that the United States wanted it.

An invasion of Iraq would make the U.S. the preeminent power in the Middle East. The United States would have Saudi Arabia surrounded. Iran would be surrounded. U.S. forces would be present—and effectively occupying—most of the smaller sheikhdoms of the Persian Gulf. The U.S. would dominate the area between the Mediterranean and the Hindu Kush; it would control the pivot of Eurasia. This, along with absolute control of the seas, would give the United States a global empire that was unprecedented in history. It is important to understand that this was exactly the American strategy, except for the fact that the United States was focused on defeating Al Qaeda and didn't regard its presence in the Middle East as an end, but merely as a means to an end. It didn't want an empire. The great powers were prepared to concede that this was the current American intention, but they also understood that even with the defeat of Al Qaeda, the U.S. would still control the region and would be unlikely to relinquish that power. American intentions were not the issue. The reality of what would be created as an unintended consequence was the problem.

Different nations had different concerns. For Russia, the critical issue was oil. Russia had become one of the world's largest exporters of energy, and it badly needed the price of oil to remain high. Keeping Iraqi oil off the market in amounts large enough to maintain global energy prices was of a vital national interest to the Russians, in spite of some development projects they had in Iraq. The Russians worried that the U.S.–Saudi conflict would result in the U.S. trying to crush the Saudis by pouring Iraqi oil on the world markets.

The Russians knew that surging Iraqi oil production was easier said than done, but they had also learned never to underestimate American technical prowess. If the U.S. did surge Iraqi production, Saudi Arabia would not be the only victim. If oil prices tanked, Russia's economy tanked with them. Therefore, Russia had no interest in seeing the United States occupy Iraq and every interest in keeping them out of there. The Russians were already coping with Americans all over Central Asia. They did not need them in control of the Middle East as well.

China was much less concerned with the specifics of American domination of the Middle East than they were with the general imbalance of power. The United States and China had had a terrific face-off before September 11, when the Chinese forced an American aircraft to land on Hainan Island. Donald Rumsfeld had said, just before September 11, that the United States was going to reorient its entire defense policy to focus on Asia—which meant to counter the growth of Chinese power. This was the last thing China needed.

In that sense, September 11 was a welcome relief for China, since it diverted American attention and relieved pressure on China. At the same time, China had a serious Islamist problem of its own. Xinjiang province was predominantly Muslim, and a significant rebellion was under way there, which included bombings around China. China wanted to weaken the Islamists but didn't want to see Americans dominating its western frontiers or increasing its power dramatically. As much as it welcomed the relief following September 11, it understood that U.S. victory in the war on Al Qaeda would leave China extremely vulnerable to U.S. power.

The French position was the most interesting. Ever since Charles de Gaulle, France had been deeply concerned about its declining position in the world. France saw the rise of American power, particularly after the end of the Cold War, as a threat to its national interest—in particular, to its critical economic and strategic interests in the Middle East. France had absolutely no desire to see an increase in American power. It had a national strategy of blocking the rise of American power in any way possible.

France also understood that it was in no position to resist that increase in power. The only realistic possibility for resisting and shaping it was to create a coalition that shared French interests. De Gaulle had always been cautious about a united Europe, fearing that it would submerge France in a multilingual, multicultural empire. The problem that de Gaulle had was that France alone could not solve the problem. Following de Gaulle, France became committed to a united Europe as a means of achieving its goal. French strategy was twofold: Europe would counterbalance the United States. And France, in collaboration with a psychologically subordinate Germany, would control Europe.

France saw the U.S. intention to invade Iraq as both a threat and a golden opportunity. The threat was that France would be further marginalized in the region and become even less significant globally. The opportunity was that the threat would allow France to galvanize Europe into changing from an economic unit into a more unified political unit with a foreign policy defined by France. French president Jacques Chirac understood that there was deep, incipient anti-American feeling in Europe. The United States was a powerful, ascendant, self-confident nation. Europe was neither a nation nor self-confident. There was tension on every level. France viewed the proposed invasion of Iraq as an opportunity to pursue its own agenda of building Europe into a force equal to the United States.

The U.S. expected France to play its traditional game with American military adventures, which was to balk and criticize, and then ultimately go along. The entire point of the WMD rationale was to put France in a position where it could not reasonably object to the undertaking. The CIA routinely shared intelligence with French intelligence, and they knew that the French evaluation of Iraqi capabilities were the same as the American. The United States expected the French to agree to the American plan or have to explain to the United States (and the world) why France regarded Iraqi WMD as tolerable.

This was the point where things began to go awry for the Bush administration. The United States miscalculated two things. First, it miscalculated the extent to which France feared the rise of American power, and the extent to which it feared that the American response to September 11 was already threatening French and European interests. Second, the United States did not see that the French regarded the American action as the perfect opportunity to galvanize Europe. Instead, the U.S. thought the French were up to their old games. The administration did not recognize that France was playing a new game.

It was because the United States failed to understand French plans that it committed a critical error. The Bush administration did not simply link its invasion to the proven existence of Iraqi WMD. They linked it to United Nations resolutions requiring Iraq to permit inspections to prove that there were no WMD. In other words, the U.S. was not demanding action because Iraq had WMD. Rather, it was demanding action because the Iraqis weren't cooperating with inspections. This created a huge hole in American diplomacy. The French did not have to assert that Iraq had no WMD. They knew they couldn't do that. France had merely to assert that until inspections were thoroughly carried out, the United States had no basis for invading Iraq.

The French knew perfectly well that the United States was going to invade. French intelligence in Washington was accurately reporting the mood of the administration, while French military intelligence could clearly see the beginnings of the military buildup that would lead to the invasion. They knew a decision had been made and that the invasion would take place regardless of UN mandate. Finally, they knew that the Americans believed that they would get UN approval. The Americans believed they could make deals with Russia and China involving other issues of greater interest to them. The French also knew that the Americans mistakenly believed that the French would ultimately agree, or at worst abstain. This allowed the French to lay a trap for the Americans—although they ultimately trapped themselves as well.

The U.S. intended to invade Iraq no earlier than January 2003, and most probably in February. The war could not begin earlier for logistical reasons. The United States could claim, with some justification, that there were sufficient prior resolutions to enable the United States to invade Iraq without new UN Security Council resolutions. It would have caused an uproar, but it did not invite total, public repudiation. The United States looked at the position taken by France— and shared less vigorously by Russia and China—and saw no reason not to accept a new UN resolution that demanded that the Iraqis agree to a new round of inspections or face war.

From the American point of view, one of two things would happen. In the most-likely scenario, the Iraqis would block inspections or delay them so flagrantly that their violation would be self-evident and war would ensue. In a less-likely scenario, the inspections would be permitted to proceed unimpeded, in which case the Iraqi WMD would be discovered and war would be justified. The United States saw agreeing to a new UN resolution as a no-brainer, and believed that it would defuse criticisms of the U.S. and serve as the foundation of a strong coalition.

On November 8, after weeks of maneuvering, the United Nations Security Council passed a unanimous resolution calling on Iraq to permit resumption of weapons inspections. The resolution called for the inspectors to report back to the Security Council in sixty days on Iraqi compliance with the resolution. At that point a second resolution would be required to permit an invasion, but the United States felt comfortable that it had reached a suitable understanding with the other members to move forward. Sixty days from November 8 was January 6, 2003, the earliest date on which an invasion was possible anyway. From the American point of view, diplomacy and war plans were perfectly synched.

The key here is that the U.S. thought it had made a deal with France. It would give France the November 8 resolution, accepting that the issue was inspections. In return, France would, if Iraq resisted the inspection process, side with the United States in a second resolution. The U.S. thought it had the guaranteed support of France. The French, however, were quietly sandbagging the Americans. Though they hadn't told the U.S., the French intended to declare the inspection protocol a success regardless of what was happening.

Between November 8 and January 6, the French worked to create an antiwar coalition in Europe. They had an ally in Germany, which for reasons of internal politics as well as a shared interest in a greater Europe was opposed to an American war in Iraq. The United Kingdom, of course, was allied with the United States. British reasoning on the war was complex, but it ultimately boiled down to this: Historically, Britain tried to maintain a balance of power. The stronger the pull of Europe, the more the British sought the American counterweight. The British wanted to manage their relations with both sides in such a way that they could avoid being overwhelmed by either. Working with the United States on security matters while cooperating with Europe on most economic matters was a rational policy. As a result, a struggle was under way for the soul of Europe, with the UK on one side, but less than aggressive in making the case to Europe, and France and Germany on the other, with Russia, generally aligned with France and Germany.

Iraq played its role precisely as the Americans expected. Saddam read the international situation as in his favor. He knew the French well, particularly Jacques Chirac, through prior dealings. The Iraqis understood from the French and Russians, through a variety of channels, that they would not relent in their opposition to the war. They also heard from the Saudis that they were opposed to war. The Iraqis' intelligence from Turkey also told them that Turkish participation was uncertain. From the Iraqi point of view, with the European continent firmly opposed, the Saudis opposed, and Turkey up in the air, the likelihood of an American attack strictly from Kuwait was limited. Iraq thought the Americans were boxed in.

The Iraqis did not fully cooperate with the inspectors, nor did they refuse to cooperate. It was in their interest to buy as much time as possible. They also understood that the French and Russians—permanent members of the Security Council—would help them buy time. Their method was simple. The November 8 resolution had demanded that Iraq submit to inspection. The precise definition of what constituted compliance was, obviously, subjective. As long as some progress was being made, the French would argue that no proof of weapons had yet been found, the inspection regime was the best path to resolving the crisis, and anything was better than war.

The longer the Iraqis played the game of minimal credible compliance, the more time the Iraqis thought the French and Russians could buy them. When the inspectors' reports were filed on January 6, everyone understood exactly what would happen. The Americans would claim the Iraqis had not complied with inspections and that there was evidence of WMD. The French would insist there had been compliance but no evidence of WMD as yet—although there might be at a later date, at which time the question could be reconsidered. Thus, when January came, the Americans predictably wanted a resolution that would authorize war; the French, Germans, and Russians rejected it, saying the inspection process was working and should be allowed to continue.

The crisis did not come to a head in early January. The United States was not ready for war. To the fury of Donald Rumsfeld, who had been critical of the plan from the beginning, U.S. ground forces were not yet in place for the attack and would not be until late February, in Kuwait, and possibly later in Turkey, depending on the Turkish mood. There was no way to move and therefore no way to abort the debate.

For France, January was a moment of opportunity. The United States had made it clear to everyone that it was going to invade Iraq regardless of the view of the United Nations or its NATO allies. European public opinion polls were overwhelmingly opposed to the war. The French government felt that this was the perfect moment to try to create a unified European foreign policy—under French guidance, to be sure—that would evolve from a unified stand on Iraq into a unified European position on the United States and its role in the world. The Iraq crisis was going to be the nucleus out of which a unified European foreign policy would emerge.

In tandem with the Germans, France turned up the pressure to create a European consensus. With the two major powers united, and public opinion aggressively antiwar, the French plan seemed irresistible. Pressure built toward a unified statement throughout January 2003, as the American buildup surged and the sense of impending war intensified. Oil prices had risen dramatically, and economists were claiming that the war would result in economic calamity.

The United States appeared to have played directly into the hands of the French on January 22, when Donald Rumsfeld made a speech in which he referred to France and Germany as "the Old Europe."

What he appeared to be saying was that France and Germany represented moral decay and weakness. It was, in particular, a dig at the French, reminding them of their failure in World War II and before.

Rumsfeld's speech appeared to be a massive blunder, typical of Rumsfeld, in which his intemperate comments would simply further enrage European politicians and public opinion. In fact, it was carefully considered and intended to take advantage of a process that U.S. diplomats and intelligence had been noting carefully, but had been overlooked by the media: the growing concern in Europe about a Franco-German axis, allied with Russia, dominating European foreign policy.

What Chirac and German Chancellor Schroeder had failed to realize was that their vision of a Europe united under the guidance of Berlin and Paris, with the collaboration of Moscow, was the worst conceivable outcome for many European countries, particularly in Eastern Europe. Memories of German and Soviet occupation in these regions were still fresh, and France was not remembered particularly fondly either. Between 1938 and 1989, Eastern Europe was dominated by Berlin and Moscow, while Paris had failed to live up to its commitments. In January 2003, most of Eastern Europe favored economic relations with Europe but also desired security arrangements with the United States. The French plan, therefore, was not only unattractive, it was a repulsive historical nightmare. This was the key point the French and Germans had missed in their planning.

Rumsfeld and the administration realized that the French and Germans were actually isolated. The "Old Europe" speech was intended to drive a public wedge into European unity. To the extent that any speech could succeed, it did. Several other major countries in Europe who had dealt with France and Germany on economic matters were not eager to expand relations into other areas.

On January 30, 2003, an extraordinary editorial appeared in *The Wall Street Journal*. In it, eight European countries publicly broke with the Franco-German bloc and endorsed the American position on Iraq. They were: Spain, Portugal, Italy, the United Kingdom, Denmark, Hungary, Poland, and the Czech Republic. This was a huge chunk of Europe, and soon after, almost all of Eastern Europe had turned against the French. In the end, the only countries siding with France, Germany, and Russia were Belgium, Sweden, Greece, and Belarus. This was not an insignificant bloc—France, Germany, and Russia were a large chunk of Europe—but it was a group of leaders without followers. American diplomacy and geopolitical reality had effectively split the European bloc down the middle.

On February 17, Chirac, realizing that his strategy had collapsed, exploded at a press conference at a European Union meeting. He assailed the Eastern Europeans, saying they had "missed a good opportunity to keep quiet" and failed to demonstrate "well-brought-up behavior." He concluded by saying, "If they wanted to diminish their chances of joining Europe, they could not have found a better way." Chirac had done exactly what the U.S. had wanted—he had solidified opposition to France in Europe and driven home to the Saudis that the war could not be stopped. The paradox of all of this was that the French regarded Bush as an uncontrolled cowboy, while Bush read Chirac as an impetuous bumbler and was counting on him to overreact. It was Chirac who couldn't control his public behavior. The administration had been hoping for one of Chirac's patented performances, and Chirac gave it to them.

France, in no uncertain terms, was a godsend to George W. Bush in the United States. The White House benefited from—and encouraged—anti-French feeling in the U.S., and more than any other European country, France was disliked in the U.S. Partly this had to do with perceived cultural arrogance by the French, but the deeper root was the sense that Americans had died to rescue the French from their own incompetence and corruption in the two world wars, only to be rewarded by French ingratitude afterward. France's opposition to the Iraq war solidified prowar sentiment in the United States like nothing else could. As in Europe, the idea that being antiwar meant being pro-French was a genuine political force.

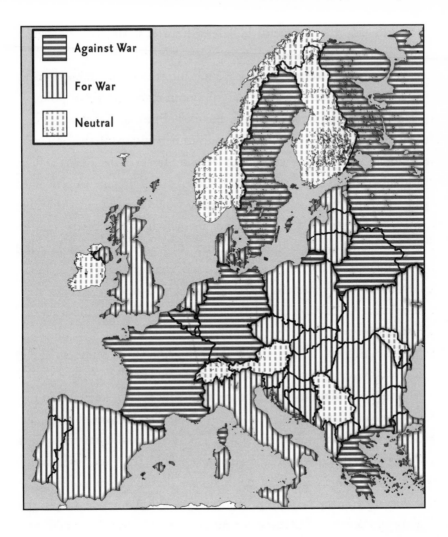

Two interesting notions took hold that Bush could not shake. The first was the idea of unilateralism—that Bush was acting without international support. The second was the idea that he was rushing into the war. Neither idea could be supported empirically. The United States had substantial international support, although not with two of its traditional allies—France and Germany. Moreover, far from rushing into war, Bush waited nearly a year from the time the idea was first seriously considered—to the dismay of some of his advisors.

Nevertheless, the notion of unilateralism and haste took hold and would not let go.

There was a strange weakness built into the Bush administration at exactly the place where it was supposed to be strongest: political management and image making. Bush's political advisors were congenitally incapable of managing public perception of the administration's foreign policies in the United States or in Europe. The administration simply seemed bewildered when it came to articulating what the reality of the U.S. position was. Given the fact that the war's justification (WMD) was not in fact the fundamental reason behind the war, the administration urgently needed clever public relations management. Their inability to overcome the obvious fallacies—such as unilateralism and haste—would not serve them well should they ever have to overcome the real duplicity in the war—its justification.

All of this was in the future. February 17, in effect, represented the end of diplomatic efforts to get UN approval. The UN Security Council resolution that the United States wanted would be vetoed (but the UN Security Council had not approved the Kosovo war either). The Iraqis would continue to maneuver. The French and Germans would hold their positions, and the Russians would try some last-minute strategy. But this was a war that had been decided upon months ago. It was now in the final preparation stage. The Army was still straggling into position, but there was nothing at this point that could stop the war.

Countdown to War

The U.S. was now focused on analyzing Iraq's military strategy. On paper, the Iraqis should have been able to put up a spirited defense. They had a substantial military force, including armor. They had a river line for defense, heavy urbanization south of Baghdad, and best of all, they had Baghdad itself—a major, world-class city with a population in excess of five million and a crowded suburb. The United

States Army had not taken a world-class, multimillion-resident city against vigorous, multidivisional resistance in its history. Casualties in such an environment would be extreme. The value of airpower against defenders fighting house to house would be minimal. It would be the toughest sort of fighting imaginable.

The Iraqi read on the United States was the same as that in the rest of the Islamic world: The U.S. could not withstand casualties. It followed from this that the ideal Iraqi strategy would inflict the maximum number of casualties. That meant that the Iraqis should slow and disorganize the American advance along the Euphrates and create the main line of defense near and in Baghdad. The goal would be to force the United States to make a choice between massive casualties and a negotiated settlement.

From the beginning, there was something odd in the Iraqi deployment. There was not enough force around Baghdad. The Republican Guard Divisions were scattered and the rest of the army concentrated to the northeast of Baghdad. There was a defense of sorts in place, but it was not optimized for conventional war. This was particularly strange since Iraq had extensive experience with U.S. airpower and knew it would have great difficulty maneuvering large forces once the war began. U.S. airpower would destroy any moving target—the bigger, the better.

There was also one factor that nobody, probably not even the Iraqis, could anticipate: how well the army would fight. Nothing is less predictable than morale. In 1967, the Egyptians were utterly routed by the Israelis, almost without resisting. Six years later, in 1973, the Egyptians conducted a brilliant and complex crossing of the Suez Canal that stunned the Israelis. Armies can change their quality rather suddenly, and nothing is more changeable than morale—the willingness to stand and fight. The debate in the U.S. military and intelligence communities focused on morale. It was understood that if the Iraqis chose to fight, they could make it a tough battle. What nobody knew was whether they would. Predictions ranged from complete and immediate capitulation to a repeat of Stalingrad.

Nor did anyone know whether Turkey would allow the U.S. to use its territory to attack Iraq. This was not as crucial as it seemed. Almost all of the Turkish-Iraqi border was mountainous, making it virtually impossible to accommodate large military formations. The only area where a buildup could have taken place was at the point where Iraq, Turkey, and Syria meet, around the Turkish town of Slipji. The road between Slipji and the Turkish ports, if it could be called that, runs along the Turkish-Syrian border—and at some points it is the border. That means supplies would be passing within inches of Syrian territory. The idea of launching a major armored offensive into Iraq from Turkey was far-fetched. No one thought that Turkey could actually be a major front. Even so, the Turkish decision not to participate was a political problem. The Turks had two interests in the war: the Mosul oil fields and preventing Kurdish independence. The U.S. wasn't guaranteeing them anything, so the Turks opted out.

On February 25, General Tommy Franks arrived at Camp As Saliyah in Qatar—the headquarters of U.S. Central Command in the region. Franks's arrival indicated that war, while not imminent, was coming close. On the same day, the United States began air strikes on Iraqi rocket launchers in the critical Basra area as well as on a range of other targets. Things were clearly heating up.

The major explosion, however, was to take place in Washington. Army Chief of Staff General Eric Shinseki, while testifying before Congress, said that the United States would have to keep hundreds of thousands of troops in Iraq after the war, saying that it was a "significant piece of real estate" torn by ethnic tensions. Obviously, the United States was intending to permanently base a large force in Iraq. That was the entire unspoken point of the invasion. However, Shinseki was saying much more. First, he was saying that the occupation of Iraq would not be easy. Second, he was saying that there was not enough force in-theater to fight the war.

This exploded into a public argument between Donald Rumsfeld and the Army. Rumsfeld felt that there were already too many ground troops in the region. He still didn't like Desert Storm Lite. The Army, on the other hand, still felt there wasn't enough force in the region. They didn't like the number of forces allocated to the battle plan, and they didn't believe the CIA's estimates of resistance after the war. It was not that they had different or better intelligence, it was just that the Army and CIA looked at the world very differently. If things fell apart, it was the Army who would be left holding the bag. Rumsfeld, predictably, exploded at Shinseki's testimony, and Shinseki backed off publicly. However, as the run-up to the war began, an argument loomed that would become very significant after the war started to rage—not a question of how difficult it would be to defeat the Iraqi Army, but how difficult it would be to pacify Iraq.

On February 27, two days later, the Iraqi Army began what appeared to be a series of strange maneuvers. Two important Iraqi divisions, the Baghdad and the Adnan, were based north of Mosul, facing the Turks. As it became more apparent that the Turks would not be part of the war, the Adnan started to move southward. But it did not move to the south of Baghdad or into Baghdad itself. Instead, it stopped at Tikrit, Saddam's hometown. It was increasingly obvious that in spite of the absence of a Turkish threat, a major Iraqi force was being kept north of Baghdad. It appeared as if the Iraqis were expecting to lose Baghdad but were planning to keep fighting after its loss.

This was accompanied by a strange announcement from Baghdad: Saddam Hussein was leaving the defense of Baghdad in the hands of his sons, while he himself went to another location to oversee the war as a whole. The command facilities of Iraq were in and around Baghdad. Saddam did not like to announce his movements, let alone the devolution of command to his sons. But in the course of the next few days, it became clear that Saddam was not only transferring command to his sons but giving his regional commanders—some reshuffled to new assignments—control over their troops. It was not clear where Saddam was going and not at all clear what he was doing.

There was a fixed notion within the U.S. military and intelligence community: The destruction of the Iraqi Army south of Baghdad and the occupation of the city would mean the capitulation of Iraq. There would be unrest and violence but no organized resistance—no national redoubt in the north and no guerrilla war. However, the Iraqi deployment and movement of troops seemed to indicate that Saddam was thinking about continuing the war somehow after the fall of Baghdad. He was preparing not for a last-ditch battle in Baghdad, but for something else. What that would be was unclear. In fact, the U.S. basically dismissed the idea that he had any plan. Some analysts went so far as to say that he had no plans for resistance at all, but that did not explain the shuffling of his forces.

As March began, there was mounting pressure on the United States to begin the war. It came from two directions. One was the weather. Summer in Iraq starts early and gets hot. U.S. troops would be fighting in suits designed to protect them against the chemical weapons that Iraq was assumed to have. With the soldier wearing the suit in MOP-4 continuities, fully buttoned up, the temperature inside the suit could be 20 to 40 degrees Fahrenheit hotter than outside. When the air temperature went to 90 degrees, the suits were unbearable. That temperature could come as early as late April, which meant the war had to be over before then if possible. The most optimistic estimates forecast a war of 30 to 60 days, which still meant getting the war under way as quickly as possible to beat the heat.

On the political front, the pressure was building as well. There was not going to be any UN resolution. That was clear by the first week of March. U.S. troops were not going into Turkey. The constant criticism by France and Germany was having some effect. The appearance, if not the reality, of isolation was beginning to get to the American public. Bush's ratings were not hemorrhaging, but they were leaking. It was time to move. But the fact was that there were still major logistical problems. The Army simply didn't have everything in place yet. Tension between Rumsfeld and the Army was coming to a boil. But by March 10, U.S. forces in Kuwait had moved out of their base camps and begun forward-deploying along the Kuwait-Iraq border. Rumors swirled of Russian diplomatic initiatives and Saddam Hussein's possible exile.

These rumors did not please the United States. It must be clearly understood that the United States did not want Saddam to go voluntarily into exile, leaving behind a Baathist government. It did not even want Saddam to leave and allow the Americans to move in peacefully. The idea of a sudden capitulation was a nightmare to the United States. It was not that the Bush administration was bloodthirsty. Far from it; they were terrified of both American and Iraqi civilian casualties. But, paradoxically, Bush's prime goal was to win a war and win it big. The strategic goal was always supplemented by the psychological goal: shock and awe. This, in turn, struggled against the public relations goal: minimize casualties but stun the Islamic world with your force. The very complexity of the mission was its greatest weakness.

On March 16, the United States and its coalition partners delivered an ultimatum. If a diplomatic solution was not reached by Monday, March 17, the United States would feel free to commence hostilities at a time and place of its choosing. In effect, Bush was giving the French one last chance to reverse their position and endorse the war, even sending a token force. Inside the administration, there was a belief that at the last moment, when they saw they could no longer stop the war, the French would cave and join the United States. Chirac refused to give.

U.S. vice president Dick Cheney gave the American verdict on the French maneuvers, further driving the contentious wedge: "It is difficult to take the French seriously and believe this is anything other than just further delaying tactics." When the deadline for the French passed, the United States issued another deadline: March 19, at 8:15 P.M. EST, just before dawn in Baghdad on March 20. If Saddam Hussein and his sons had not left Iraq by that time, the U.S. would launch a war. To Washington's relief, Iraq immediately rejected the demand.

Diplomacy was over. The war was about to begin.

CHAPTER 12

The Iraq Campaign

THE IRAQ CAMPAIGN BEGAN in a way different from all other recent U.S. wars. There was no extended air campaign against Iraqi facilities and forces. The U.S. had relatively few allies. In fact, the alliance was more reminiscent of World War II than of Desert Storm—the Brits and the Aussies were there with the Americans. Some Poles and Czechs showed up along with the Hungarians, and, of course, the Spaniards and Portuguese were there as well. But it was very much, in Churchill's words, a war of the English-speaking world.

In fact, the war's beginning was not only different—it was strange, and it began with a deception. There was an important reason for that. The CIA's read of the situation in Iraq was that it was a highly centralized, personalized regime. If you cut off the head, the body would collapse. While Saddam was alive, it had become clear, his generals and civilian subordinates would not deal with the United States. They feared Saddam's security service a lot more than they respected the CIA's ability to keep a secret. However, if Saddam was dead—or if they thought he was dead—they might be more inclined to deal.

No one was quite certain where Saddam was. Weeks before the war began, Saddam started relocating on an unpredictable basis, flooding the system with personal doubles, faked radio signals, bogus cell phone calls, and so on. Saddam knew that he would be the target of an American attack, and he also knew—or rather, believed, since his paranoia had become his main analytic tool—that his own subordinates would be his biggest threat in a war. He was not certain who would betray him, but he believed that someone would. Therefore, Saddam disappeared.

Even his most senior commanders weren't sure where he had gone. This gave rise to some interesting thoughts at Central Command and in Washington. It was not necessary that Saddam actually be dead to trigger negotiations or chaos. It would be sufficient if senior Iraqi military commanders believed he was dead or had severe doubts about his status. And since no one was quite sure where he was, because no one had seen him in quite a while, it was possible to stage a military action that might be sufficiently convincing that people would assume he was dead. For example, if a building believed to house Saddam was blown up, with attendant silence from Saddam for a couple of days, the Iraqi commanders might believe he was dead. And if they thought he was dead, it was believed, they might make a deal with the United States—which would make the U.S. invasion of Iraq a lot less dangerous.

From the beginning, the United States built "information operations" into its war plans. Run out of an entity known as Joint Information Operations Center (JIOC) in San Antonio, information operations was an amalgam of computer hackers and psychological warfare specialists. Unlike traditional psychological warfare, information operations was designed to use all means to destabilize the enemy at a strategic level. This ranged from manipulating internal e-mail messaging, to creating and disseminating massive disinformation campaigns, to turning off the enemy's Web sites and substituting their own.

At the outset, Donald Rumsfeld committed himself to disinformation campaigns. His view was that Al Qaeda was engaged in psychological warfare and that the only counter to that was more-sophisticated psychological warfare. There are many tools in the psy-war toolkit, and lying is always one of them. The JIOC was tasked with the role of the dissemination of truth—and lies—in such a way as to undermine the ability of the enemy to wage war at the strategic level. Therefore, the lies had to be very convincing. As was said about Allied invasion plans at Normandy, the invasion force had to be surrounded by a "bodyguard of lies." There is no other way to wage war.

There were a number of places where the U.S. believed Saddam might be hiding, one being a compound to the south of Baghdad. There were many other possible places, but for this plan to work, specificity was essential. It had to appear that the Americans actually knew where he was. A volley of attacks randomly distributed would tell Iraqi generals that the Americans were hunting. A carefully aimed attack on a target that could contain Saddam, plus on a few other command-and-control structures and air defenses, would make it appear that the Americans knew what they were doing. The key was that it had to appear as if the location of Saddam was known.

The war began just before dawn, Baghdad time, on March 20, 2003. About forty Tomahawk cruise missiles were fired at targets west of Baghdad—and at a building south of Baghdad. It was about 10 P.M. EST when the missiles started to impact. Bush made a short speech at about 10:15. Shortly thereafter, White House advisors started to brief the press on what had really taken place.

According to the White House, an intelligence agent (at various times reported to be Iraqi or British SAS) who was watching a house known to have been used by Saddam Hussein saw Saddam enter the house. He reported in, and the report was immediately routed to Langley. CIA Director George Tenet rushed to the White House in midafternoon, and there ensued a four-hour meeting during which the CIA urged the President to launch a strike before the "target of opportunity" was lost. For some unexplained reason, the President hesitated to strike and then finally gave the go-ahead at about 8 P.M. The missiles were launched along with two F-117 stealth fighters. White House officials, speaking on background, said they obviously didn't know whether Saddam was dead but they certainly hoped so. As Washington went to bed and Baghdad woke up, both knew that the war had begun. But the remainder of the war turned on a single question: Was Saddam Hussein alive or dead?

Washington knew it hadn't hit and killed Saddam—not unless by sheer luck Saddam was actually there. At the same time that Tenet was rushing to the White House with the "news" of the "target of opportunity," indicators being collected at Stratfor all pointed to the war beginning that night. At about 3 P.M. EST, when Tenet was supposedly reporting new information to the President, Stratfor had reliable intelligence from multiple sources that confirmed it.

In Washington, the major media missed all this because they were so oriented on senior government officials, who did an excellent job in misleading them. But outside of Washington, where war preparations could not be hidden, where consultations with allies had to take place, where movement of equipment could not be hidden, indications had started to pile up on Tuesday, and by 3 P.M. EST on Wednesday it was unmistakable.

Stratfor was told that the President had reserved airtime for an address on network television for 9 P.M. that night. The only news that was important enough for the President to deliver to the nation at that time would have been the beginning of the war in Iraq. The White House had quietly informed key allies that the war was going to begin hours before we heard it. We knew Israel was beginning preparations against strikes that night, including going to a defense condition for civilians called "silent radio." If there is danger of an attack in Israel, a designated radio station broadcasts only a signal and is otherwise silent. That allows people to sleep through the night, confident that a loud noise—followed by news and instructions—will wake them if necessary. Going to the silent radio condition is far from an ordinary occurrence in Israel. It went to this condition at sundown. The Israelis were concerned that Saddam would respond with Scuds and WMD before the night was over.

The Bush administration was hoping for real movement in Baghdad. Senior officials had boasted before the war that they were in direct contact with Iraqi generals via e-mail and other means, but that was simply information operations—aka lies. It was designed to increase Saddam's paranoia. If the U.S. had actually been in contact with Iraqi generals, it would be the most tightly held secret in the world. The CIA had tremendous problems making contact with Iraqi generals for a simple reason. Saddam Hussein had survived many possible coups by executing anyone he even slightly suspected of being disloyal. The CIA had tried to launch several coups in Iraq and all had failed. A sensible Iraqi general was not going to bet on the CIA over Saddam Hussein.

In addition to not having any real idea where Saddam was, the United States also had no real idea how the Iraqi generals might react. The attack was carefully planned in advance, down to the timing and the post-attack spin. There was no special intelligence indicating that Saddam was in the house where he had reportedly been spotted. Nor, indeed, was there any indication that if Saddam was dead, the generals in Baghdad would capitulate. In fact, it was not even clear that the generals in Baghdad controlled the troops in the field. Saddam had turned over control of those troops to regional commanders.

But it was worth a shot. Since the U.S. didn't know exactly where Saddam was, there was a very remote chance he was in that house. Even if he wasn't there, the attacks on command-and-control facilities in the west of Baghdad (combined with jammed radio frequencies) might isolate him so that people thought he was dead, and that would be almost as good. If the generals, believing Saddam was dead, opened negotiations with the United States for a capitulation, that would be perfect. If Plan A didn't work, Plan B, conventional war, was still there, with nothing lost in the bargain. This was a low-risk, high-payoff plan.

Plan A didn't work. Within a few hours, Saddam was on Iraqi television, addressing the nation, quite alive. The United States then started generating stories that the speech had not actually been given by Saddam Hussein but by a double. There was a great deal of speculation outside Iraq, but inside Iraq the generals knew he was alive. Any plans of capitulating at that point were squashed by Saddam's television address.

Still, there was the hope that the threat of an attack would result in someone in Iraq doing something to make the war easier for the United States. No one was quite clear on what they were hoping for, but anything was possible. On March 20, Donald Rumsfeld announced that the "shock and awe" campaign had been postponed, pending developments in the Iraqi leadership. Instead of a massive air attack, the United States held back, waiting. On the ground, U.S. and British forces began to move toward the north. Elements of the 7th Cavalry engaged some Iraqi tanks. The ground war had begun as planned, but the first major engagements were still a day or two away.

Washington was still hoping that its campaign to destabilize the regime might work. When Rumsfeld announced the suspension of the "shock and awe" campaign, it was not due to any specific intelligence. The reasoning was that if the United States held back, Saddam might believe Iraqi generals were negotiating with the U.S. and start executing them. Or the generals, fearing that Saddam would snap, might decide to kill him. Or they might decide to kill each other. Who knew? The point was that there was no cost in jerking the Iraqis around. The worst outcome would leave the United States in no worse a situation than it had been.

Washington was trying to play with the Iraqis' minds by introducing the very idea of a "shock and awe" campaign. The media loved the concept, which had zero military content but sounded great on the air. The fact was that the United States had many more aircraft in-theater during Desert Storm than it did in 2003, and the Iraqis had already lived through a major American bombing campaign. The munitions used this time would be more accurate, but there would be fewer of them. So "shock and awe" was less a description than a hope. To be more specific, it was designed to scare the daylights out of the Iraqis. It was also more effective as a threat than as a reality—so it was hoped that postponing "shock and awe" officially would have an even more frightening effect.

The use of psychological warfare is essential in war. Its greatest weakness, particularly in democratic societies, is that it is very hard to be discriminating in the message. Lying to the Iraqi government was logical and necessary. Threatening death and destruction is as ancient as war. The problem was that the American media and public could never quite distinguish between the lie and the truth. Thus, for example, reporters kept asking when "shock and awe" would begin, and would look around at air strikes saying that they were neither shocked nor awed.

The central feature of the opening phases of the U.S. effort was information operations. From the beginning of the war, the administration had been absolutely open and honest about the fact that they planned to lie. The problem was that when they did begin to lie in order to confuse the enemy—and potential coalition partners—they could not do so without also lying to the American public. In September 2001, Donald Rumsfeld frankly quoted Churchill during a press conference, saying, "In wartime, truth is so precious that she should always be attended by a bodyguard of lies." The media, whose job it was to sort these things out, never understood that lying in war is an operational necessity. Whenever the media discovered a new lie, they would act as if the government's intention was to deceive—which, of course, it was.

Worst of all, the process of lying to deceive the enemy imperceptibly turned into lying to hide failures and disappointments. Just as in World War II, when censorship was used to protect vital secrets—and embarrassing mistakes—information operations in the hands of the leadership turned from confusing the enemy to shielding the leadership from criticism. What began as a crucial part of warfare turned into the management of public opinion.

Combat

The Allies rewrote the book on warfare during the Iraq war. The air war was confined to the decapitation strike and sporadic attacks on command-and-control facilities, many of which had already been attacked during the previous months under the cover of the no-fly-zone campaign. While the air war was sporadic, the ground war was launched almost at the same time as the decapitation strike. U.S. special operations teams were already spread out in the south, along the path of the forces scheduled to advance. And American special operations teams had already penetrated western Iraq from Jordan, hunting for Scud missiles and watching the Syrians. In fact, western Iraq had already been effectively occupied by coalition special operations teams before the war in the south began.

The attack out of Kuwait was divided into two distinct thrusts. One thrust, primarily by the British, pushed directly to the north toward the port town of Umm Qasr and the major city in the south, Basra. It had to advance through difficult ground, swamps, and numerous river lines in the Delta region. The other advance, primarily American, was the main thrust toward Baghdad. It came out of western Kuwait and drove toward the Euphrates River and An Nasiriyah, then up the south bank of the Euphrates, which was lightly settled.

Allied forces began to move forward at about the same time the first missiles hit—another sign that the attack was coordinated. The troops moved forward carefully. They were not certain about what was in front of them or how intensely they would be resisted. A major question was whether or not the Iraqis were going to use chemical weapons. That uncertainty forced both the U.S. and British troops to remain in chemical defense suits. It also meant that they would probe carefully. While the U.S. and Britain had a fairly good idea of whom they were facing, no one knew exactly what the Iraqi troops were going to do.

For the next three days, the air war seemed strangely quiet. The fact was that the Allied command was waiting. There had been some question in the minds of the Iraqis about whether the U.S. was prepared to go to war in the face of what the Iraqis thought was unremitting global opposition. The United States had gone to war. More important than air strikes (which the Iraqis were used to), it became evident by Friday that a major armored thrust was developing up the Euphrates. As the Third Infantry Division pushed forward, led by cavalry units, they encountered Iraqi resistance. By Saturday, the news that a major American force was moving forward would have reached Baghdad command. The United States knew that this was the last moment for the Iraqis to either capitulate or overthrow Saddam and negotiate. Saturday came and went. There was no political feeler out of Baghdad.

On Sunday, March 23, the war took on a new cast. First, Donald Rumsfeld conceded the obvious, which was that there were no high-level negotiations taking place with anyone in Baghdad. With that announcement, the psychological phase of the war ended and the next, primarily military, phase began. Sunday marked the end of the fencing. The U.S. was now moving toward pure warfighting mode.

It had also become evident that at least some Iraqi forces were going to stand their ground. A U.S. supply column made a wrong turn and was annihilated. That was the first indication that there was someone out there looking for a fight. At the same time, as U.S. armored spearheads passed through Iraqi positions, as doctrine required, troops coming up behind them encountered pockets of resistance. Around the towns of An Nasiriyah, As Samawa, and An Najaf—all along the Euphrates River—U.S. troops found themselves engaged in very real combat.

There had been a great deal of speculation before the war—bravado, really—claiming that the Iraqis would collapse completely and offer no resistance. Therefore, what was surprising was not that the Iraqis fought well but that they fought at all. The expectations had been set so low (not only by the media but at times by the administration itself) that any sort of resistance caught everyone by surprise. Questions started to be raised about whether the plan had failed. By Monday, the media began questioning whether the administration had failed to plan properly, whether there were enough forces on the ground, and whether U.S. troops were properly equipped and trained. A small media frenzy started.

As anyone familiar with warfare knows, the measure of a plan is not whether it is adhered to but whether the war is won. A plan is a document that prepares you for war and can guide you, but it is not a blueprint and must never become one. What was happening on the battlefield was no threat to an American victory over Iraqi conventional forces. Armor is supposed to bypass enemy resistance. Second-echelon troops, typically infantry, come up, engage the isolated pockets, and reduce them. If the plan was to take control of the south bank of the Euphrates River as far north as Karbala, it was on track.

But the plan could not and did not posit what the Iraqis would do. As it was, the Iraqis offered isolated pockets of resistance that were effective for a short period of time but trivial from a strategic point of view. The problem was not what Rumsfeld had said about the war. He was actually quite careful to hold open a range of possibilities. Rather, he projected such an aura of authoritative confidence that the media interpreted it as omniscience and omnipotence. When events showed that he had neither, he was attacked by the media. This hardened Rumsfeld's attitude, and he began to get angry and defensive. Where he had previously been blunt but honest, he shifted slightly toward defensive and exasperated. This process that began during the first week of the Iraq war would have serious consequences when the guerrilla war began—and Rumsfeld's responses would become even sharper and more evasive.

The real issue now was how and when to apply airpower. Rumsfeld had tried to cow the Iraqis by raising the specter of a "shock and awe" air campaign. In fact, the first week of the air war had been fairly light. As U.S. forces moved up the western bank of the Euphrates toward Karbala, the air campaign focused on supporting the advancing troops tactically. The strategic air campaign didn't begin until around a week after the war started, when it became clear that the Iraqis wouldn't collapse. This was the true war—the kind of war the U.S. likes to fight. In the last few days of March, U.S. airpower stepped on the pedal.

By April 1, two thousand sorties a day were being flown against the entire range of targets that one would expect. This was a Desert Storm level for sorties. Meanwhile, the United States was halted south of Karbala, with its Third Infantry Division preparing to cross the river. However, there was resistance around Karbala, and intelligence

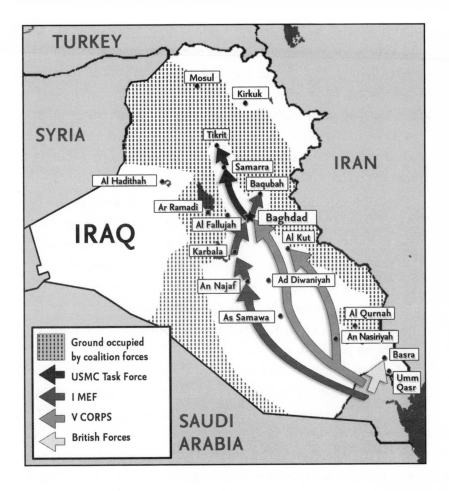

was reporting several Republican Guard divisions on the move south of Baghdad. The United States, probing forward carefully, trying to get the measure of Iraqi resistance, badly wanted to destroy the Republican Guard outside of Baghdad. The overwhelming fear was that the Republican Guards—and the more capable Special Republican Guards—would retreat into Baghdad. That would be the worst case.

On April 1, no one—not at Central Command, not at the CIA, and certainly not at the White House—had any idea about the intentions of the Iraqi forces. Views ranged from a belief that the Iraqis were about to stage a massive counterattack, to the idea that they were digging in for a last-ditch fight south of Baghdad, to the idea that they were waiting in Baghdad, to the idea that they had completely disintegrated. For all of its intelligence capability, the United States did not know what the situation was five to fifty miles ahead of its troops. Speculation began to grow in the media about massive resistance in Baghdad—the worst-case scenario. Rumsfeld attempted to gruffly dismiss these fears. But in fact, it was as unknown as whether the Iraqis would launch chemical weapons.

Something quite strange began happening. Iraqi divisions that had been plotted carefully on maps started to disappear. Iraqi forces that were thought to be there one day simply weren't there the next. As U.S. forces probed carefully toward Baghdad, they found that there was almost nothing in front of them. There was some resistance with a few sporadic and sometimes intense firefights. But the kind of resistance one would have expected from a multidivisional force was nowhere to be found.

By April 5, U.S. forces had crossed the Euphrates and moved to the southern gateway of Baghdad. Again, the Iraqi forces that were thought to be there weren't. This did not relieve Central Command. If the Medina Division, to name one, was not south of Baghdad, then it had to be in Baghdad. Intelligence reports inside Baghdad were confused, as they would be in any city, which is an extremely difficult place from which to extract tactical intelligence. Visibility is good for a block or two but not much farther. One thousand men could be inside a building five blocks away and you'd never know it. Soldiers on the ground in a city the size of Baghdad are blind, and you can't see inside of buildings from the air.

Some reports said there weren't any forces in Baghdad. Others said there were but what forces did exist were moving north out of the city.

It was in this spirit of absolute confusion that the battle for Baghdad began. On Sunday night, April 5, the United States, desperate to know the situation in Baghdad, took a necessary risk. It sent armor from the Third Infantry Division on a reconnaissance in force through western Baghdad. The purpose of the maneuver was simply to draw fire and map out at least some of the Iraqi strongpoints in the city. All of the advanced capabilities of the United States could not know which basements housed teams of infantryman with antitank missiles. Sending part of the Third ID into the city, it was assumed, would reveal something.

The reconnaissance revealed hardly anything. No significant fire was drawn. That might indicate that there was no one in the area they traversed but there were troops elsewhere. Or it might indicate that there were no troops in the city. It could even mean that there were troops throughout the city but that they were highly disciplined and holding their fire. No significant military intelligence was gathered. The concern was heightened by fighting that was still going on around Karbala to the south. An American sergeant was quoted by Reuters as saying, "I don't think they stand a chance, to be honest, because we just have overwhelming firepower. But they've certainly got balls, you have to say that."

The one thing people didn't expect U.S. sergeants to be saying about Iraqi troops more than two weeks into the war was that they had balls. Resistance along the Euphrates River line had been locally intense, and the fighting at Karbala was considerable. The thought was growing that if the Iraqis resisted in Karbala, they may be tough in Baghdad. However, no one could predict what would happen next—and the anxiety soared.

So they kept probing, looking for the forces that prewar intelligence and intelligence during the war told them had to be there, which certainly had not yet been killed or captured. A debate started. From a military point of view, the best solution—certain to work—was to surround the city and starve the enemy out. From a political point of view, this was entirely unacceptable. No one wanted to see starving children on CNN. The other alternative was to attack the city directly, causing massive civilian casualties and probably a lot of U.S. casualties. April 6 and 7 were extremely tense days. No one was certain how the situation would be resolved.

By April 7, the situation had become even stranger. Several other U.S. armored probes had moved into the city from various directions along several axes of attack. None of them were hit by anything more than sporadic gunfire. The Iraqis were either holding their fire or no one was home. But where were they? The discomfort was not simply about not knowing. It was about not understanding.

Before assaulting Baghdad directly, the United States had one more move it could make. It knew that Saddam had not been killed in the opening attack, but it was still hoping to nail him and convince the resistance in Baghdad that he was dead. In the afternoon of April 7, U.S. missiles slammed into a restaurant in the Mansour district of Baghdad, demolishing the building. At first, it seemed to be another accident of war. That night, the United States announced that the attack had taken place because intelligence operatives reported that Saddam Hussein, his two sons, and about thirty other senior government officials were attending a meeting in a restaurant in or near the building.

Why Saddam would choose to meet with his entire government in a restaurant rather than in his numerous, well-fortified bunkers was not clear. However, the destruction of the building was so total that it wouldn't be known for days whether he had been killed or not. Not much would be left of him in any case. This was perfect from the American point of view. The story was out that Saddam might be dead, and there was no way to disprove the story quickly. U.S. troops were surrounding Baghdad. The psychological blow was struck. By then, Iraqi television was intermittent at best, and Saddam could not simply pop up again.

On April 9, U.S. forces began the occupation of Baghdad. There was no resistance in most of the city. To be more precise, U.S. forces didn't go where there might be resistance. There were no Republican Guards or Special Republican Guards. There were no Husseins. There was just a large, crowded city without any organized military force. Baghdad didn't so much resist as buffet American troops with sheer disorderliness when they arrived. Endless rumors swirled that Saddam had made a deal with the Russians for safe conduct to Syria, that he had been killed in the fighting, that he was in Tikrit planning resistance. Facts were hard to come by.

As the statue of Saddam Hussein was toppled, the U.S. was not certain of what had happened. Saddam's whereabouts were unknown, as was his army's. Except for mopping up in the north, the U.S. thought the war was over. But there was still uncertainty, as even U.S. intelligence wasn't sure what had happened. Suddenly, after preparing for one of the biggest battles in decades, it was over before it began. It was strange and everyone knew it. Victory was tempered by unease.

Intelligence Failures

The successful conclusion of the conventional campaign in Iraq did not end the war. Very quickly the United States found itself in a web of unanticipated circumstances that affected its strategic position in the world. The web consisted of three major intelligence failures on the part of the United States, no one of which would have been enough to trap the U.S. even temporarily, but all of which, taken together, trapped the United States during the occupation of Iraq.

The three intelligence failures were:

1. The failure to understand the degree to which the Iraqi Shiite population had been organized and was influenced by Iranian intelligence.
2. The failure to understand the fact that Saddam Hussein, anticipating both war and the collapse of Iraq's conventional forces, had prepared a postwar guerrilla campaign.
3. The failure to find any weapons of mass destruction in Iraq whatsoever.

U.S. intelligence estimates in 2003 were divided into two views. In one view, there would be spontaneous uprisings by the Shiites in Iraq that would aid the campaign. The other view was that the Shiites, cautious and disorganized, would not rise but would accept U.S. and

British help in becoming organized and would fully participate in American plans for a postwar Iraq.

There was no uprising. As the British began to move toward Basra, rather than a Shiite uprising, they found the population carefully staying out of the fight, while dedicated Sunni fighters from the Baath Party's elite troops stood and fought the British to a standstill for days. When the British entered the city after having finally disposed of the Iraqi troops, they discovered that they were neither celebrated as liberators nor needed to organize the city. The city was already organized politically, as was the region, with a Shiite sheikh firmly in charge. The Iranians had done their job well. Knowing that at some point Saddam would either fall or the U.S. would invade, the Iranians had created a situation on the ground that defined political reality.

At this point, a sharp political disagreement occurred between the British and American military. The British commander, relieved to find relative order in Basra in spite of the damage from fighting, turned over control to the local sheikh. The U.S. Department of Defense was furious. It went deeper than the fact that the British had gone against the U.S. strategy of controlling postwar Iraq through the military. It had as much to do with the Defense Department simply not knowing the degree to which the Shiites were organized. In other words, the British never had the option of imposing direct military government on Basra when the city fell; there was already in place a lightly armed—but fully in control—Shiite shadow government, and the U.S. had completely failed to anticipate it.

As the Euphrates cities fell to U.S. control, American commanders started to realize the same thing. Their plans for civil affairs troops to come up and take command of the major Shiite cities of An Nasariyah, Al Najaf, and Karbala were not so much thwarted as irrelevant. These cities, too, had functioning governments, under the control of either local tribal leaders or the Shiite religious hierarchy. A liaison was established, but the idea that the Americans were in charge was simply rejected.

Indeed, as if to drive the point home, major demonstrations started taking place in Shiite cities shortly after the main fighting ended in the north. The point was not to hinder the Americans but to make a critical point: The Americans had defeated the Iraqi army, but they were not in control of the Shiites. All of this began to sink into the Defense Department and CIA. On April 23, the Defense Department announced that Iranian-trained Iraqi Shiites had crossed into southern Iraq and were active in An Najaf, Karbala, and Basra. The report was correct. Iraqi Shiites who had lived in exile in Iran, and had been trained and financed by the Iranians, were indeed pouring into Iraq. What was omitted was that this was not the first wave. Far from it—their predecessors had been in Iraq for years, only the CIA did not realize how many or how effective they were until U.S. troops got there.

The second major intelligence failure involved Saddam's long-range war plan. There was something peculiar in the deployment of Iraqi troops prior to the war—a concentration of forces to the north and northeast of Baghdad, an area where the U.S. was not going to be attacking until after the fall of Baghdad. Also, there was the announcement that Saddam would not be commanding the Iraqi forces himself and that he would be in a special location outside of Baghdad while his sons fought the war. Saddam was no fool. He had fought the Americans before, and he knew that they could be effective. Saddam fully understood that the Americans would beat him, and he neither tried to reach an accommodation nor went into exile. Clearly, he had something on his mind.

Intermittent attacks on U.S. forces never stopped. The attacks continued throughout April, increasing in intensity through May and June and through the summer. Political manifestations of this resistance emerged as early as April 11, just two days after the statue of Saddam Hussein had toppled. A group called the National Front for the Liberation of Iraq sent a statement to several European governments announcing that the NFLI consisted of armed resistance groups scattered around Iraq and Arab volunteers from outside Iraq. Whatever the NFLI was—and many such groups popped up in the next few months—they laid out what was coming. There would be a resistance based on the Baath Party and elements of the Republican Guards and Special Republican Guards, and another resistance built around foreign troops, mostly jihadist.

The fact that communiqués were being issued in Europe only two days after the fall of Baghdad points to an inescapable fact: The resistance had been planned before the war began. Arms caches were created, safe houses were designated. Leaders were designated along with areas of responsibility. Communications protocols were laid down—mostly human rather than electronic, to avoid detection. The plumbing of a guerrilla war was laid down. With the fall of Baghdad, it began to be executed.

The United States had expected ongoing acts of violence. The fact that there were intermittent attacks on U.S. troops throughout April did not, by itself, indicate that a guerrilla war was starting up. Such attacks were the least one would expect after conquering a foreign country. Thus, given the lack of strategic intelligence on the guerrillas, tactical intelligence could point to a guerrilla war or random chaos with equal persuasiveness.

As May dragged into June, and the number of attacks increased rather than declined, it became increasingly difficult to maintain the idea that these were simply the remnants of a defeated army. If that were the case, incidents ought to have been declining. In fact, they were increasing in both frequency and effectiveness, ranging from ambushes to bombs. It was clear that a low-grade guerrilla war was indeed under way.

The Iraqis were running a guerrilla war on a fairly small scale, conducting hit-and-run raids on the U.S. and foreign troops in order to sap their morale and demonstrate the guerrillas' presence and effectiveness to the Iraqi people. It was difficult to imagine a situation in which they would be able to widen the conflict even under the best of circumstances because the terrain was such that larger formations, company- and battalion-size, could be identified and defeated by U.S.

firepower. Iraq didn't have jungles, and conducting large-scale combat in Baghdad was not a real possibility.

Indeed, the war was confined to a relatively small area around Baghdad called the Sunni Triangle. It never spread to the Shiite south, and the Kurds in the north were having nothing to do with it. Less than a third of the country was affected. Twenty attacks a day at most, with only two or three effective, against a force as large as the Americans in the Sunni Triangle were not strategically significant. These attacks were irritants and unfortunate, but they could not force the United States to make strategically significant readjustments—in other words, the U.S. was not going to withdraw.

The main damage was political. One of the reasons the United States had invaded Iraq was to demonstrate the effectiveness and ferocity of the United States military. The inability of the United States to put an end to the guerrilla war began to resonate in Islamic countries, where it appeared that the predictions by Al Qaeda about the ineffectiveness of American forces were being borne out. Moreover, as the American media became more critical of U.S. policy in Iraq, the perception began to spread that the old American disease—abandoning a fight as soon as it got tough—might be coming back.

The last thing the United States needed at this point was an interminable guerrilla war in Iraq, and yet the signs of this were looming. The entire equation was being upset. Syria, for example, had encountered a sudden crisis with the United States in April as U.S. forces tried to seal the Syrian–Iraqi border and firefights broke out between coalition and Syrian troops. The Syrians, seeing the handwriting on the wall, began to tilt toward accommodating the United States, handing over some senior Iraqi leaders who had sought refuge there. As the guerrilla war intensified and the U.S. seemed to be getting bogged down, the Syrians recalculated their position and started to decrease, or even end, cooperation with the United States.

The strangest part was the response from Donald Rumsfeld and the Defense Department. At the beginning of May 2003, Rumsfeld announced that the United States was considering reducing the number of troops in Iraq to 30,000, effectively sending 100,000 troops home. Rumsfeld began talking about a group of fanatics and dead-enders fighting the Americans, denying vigorously the presence of an organized guerrilla resistance. No matter how many attacks there were, or how self-evidently well organized, Rumsfeld insisted that nothing unexpected was going on and that there had been no miscalculation. On June 18, he went so far as to assert that he had always been expecting problems like these.

As late as June 27, when Rumsfeld was asked whether the assailants were guerrillas, he replied, "I don't know that I would use that word." He said thousands of people had been turned out of prison, portraying the attackers as the "dead-ender" remnants of the Baathist regime and criminals. Rumsfeld also said that all major cities had crime, and "you've got to remember that if Washington, D.C., were the size of Baghdad, we would be having something like 215 murders a month."

Rumsfeld's denial was rooted in the strategic purpose of the war. It was also rooted in the failure of intelligence, even at such a late date, to develop a clear strategic or tactical portrait of the guerrillas. However much it may have violated common sense, Rumsfeld's denials cohered with the intelligence he was getting. To be more precise, the original intelligence had not, in late June, been overridden by a new intelligence analysis, because U.S. intelligence continued to lack sources among the guerrillas—just as it had lacked them among the senior Iraqi command. Based on the strategic guidance, it was—by a stretch—possible to believe that there was no guerrilla war. Possible, but not easy.

In fact, everyone knew that something was badly wrong in Iraq. Tommy Franks, who had commanded CENTCOM during Afghanistan as well as the Iraq campaign, was scheduled to be relieved later in the summer. Franks was tired and not responding to events, torn between the denial of reality in Washington and the fact that everything he was doing on the ground seemed to be working against him. Sweeps and searches in suspected villages weren't trapping guerrillas, but they were angering the population. Nothing had prepared Franks for the problem he was facing—not the intelligence guidance he had received before the invasion nor the guidance he had received since then.

The decision was made to relieve Franks early, sending in John Abizaid to replace him. Franks was offered the job of Chief of Staff of the Army to replace Eric Shinseki, who had infuriated Rumsfeld when he said that hundreds of thousands of troops would be needed in Iraq. Franks turned it down—he had had enough. Abizaid, born in Lebanon and an Arabic speaker, was fresh. He was also not about to be sucked down the fantasy hole by the Defense Department. The change of command was announced in late June, with the formal change of command taking place on July 7. However, change was already in the air when Paul Bremer, Administrator for Iraq, publicly asked for an increase in the number of troops in Iraq—going directly against Rumsfeld's claims.

Finally, on July 16, John Abizaid stated the obvious, which was not a trivial matter under the circumstances. He announced that the United States was facing "what I would describe as a classical guer-rilla-type campaign against us. It's a low-intensity conflict in our doc-trinal terms, but it's war however you describe it." He also said, "We're seeing a cellular organization of six to eight people armed with [rocket-propelled grenades], machine guns, et cetera, attacking us at some times and places of their choosing, and other times we attack them at times and places of our choosing." After months of guerrilla warfare, the United States had now finally conceded that there was a guerrilla war under way. It also admitted that there had been a major intelligence failure.

At this point the first two major intelligence failures intersected. First, it is not possible for an outside power to defeat a guerrilla movement on its own. The idea that a twenty-year-old American sol-dier standing at a checkpoint could distinguish between civilians going about their normal business and a guerrilla is absurd. In any successful counterinsurgency, there must be a substantial indigenous force that has an interest in allying itself to the outside power. Absent that, the situation is extremely difficult, even hopeless. In Iraq, that indigenous force was the Shiite community.

A second problem was that the Shiites could, if they so decided, make the U.S. position in Iraq completely untenable. In July, the guerrilla war was confined mainly to the Sunni Triangle. Should the Shiites go into the streets, as they had demonstrated they could and would do on a number of occasions, the strategic basis of the American occupation of Iraq would dissolve. The U.S. might be able to maintain its position in Iraq in the face of a rising limited to the Sunnis. It would be impossible to remain in Iraq, however, if the Shiites turned to an intifada against the Americans.

By failing to understand Saddam Hussein's war plans, as well as the degree to which the Iraqi Shiites had been organized by the Iranians, the United States now found itself in a guerrilla war it could not cope with. As a result, the U.S. had become highly dependent on the plans of the Iraqi Shiites. The Americans needed their help in suppressing the guerrillas, but even before that, they needed the Shiites not to go into the streets and completely collapse the American position. Already in this vulnerable predicament, the Bush administration now faced an even more unsettling prospect—it became extremely dependent on the Iranians.

U.S.–Iranian talks had been under way since the end of the Iraq campaign in a number of venues. Initially, it had been the United States's intention to confront Iran in the same way it had confronted Saudi Arabia and Syria—threaten or imply military action in order to force policy changes toward Al Qaeda and an abandonment by Iran of their nuclear weapons program. By the summer, however, the talks were less about what the United States wanted than what the Iranians wanted. The U.S. was in no position to threaten Iran.

Iran was not opposed to helping out the United States. But its price was high. The Iranians had an interest in a Shiite-dominated Iraq that would be either within the Iranian sphere of influence or at least a neutral buffer. Iran and Iraq were historical enemies, and the opportunity to solve the Iraqi problem transcended all ideological and theological differences. All Iranians, regardless of faction, wanted to see that happen.

The Iranians wanted a U.S. guarantee that the postwar government would reflect the makeup of Iraq. This meant a Shiite-dominated government. The Iranians were prepared to give the U.S. rights to bases in Iraq, limit their own nuclear weapons programs, and turn over any Al Qaeda members they might have been holding in Iran. In return, the Iranians would ensure that the Iraqi Shiites would remain quiet. They would not guarantee Shiite participation in the war against the Sunni guerrillas until after an Iraqi government suitable to them was formed, but they offered intelligence sharing. In the end, the U.S. could hardly turn down the deal. If the U.S. refused and the Shiites rose, the U.S. would be driven out of Iraq and the Shiites would still wind up dominating the country. This was the only path out.

The United States still had primary responsibility for suppressing the Iraqi guerrillas, and the more effectively the United States did this, the greater their negotiating leverage with Iran and Iraq's Shiites. If they could start taking down the guerrillas, the Sunni tribal leaders would reconsider their support for the guerrillas. That would allow the United States to have some bargaining chips to use with the Shiites—however limited they might be.

The guerrilla war continued to intensify through the summer. Abizaid had called a halt to the massive search operations. For most of the summer, the United States appeared to be a deer caught in headlights. However, thinking and planning was going forward at an intense pace. It was quickly recognized that the core problem was the U.S. lack of intelligence, and by the end of the summer two things began to happen. First, the CIA surged agents into Iraq during August and September. The agents came with the same ammunition they had in the early days of Afghanistan—extremely large amounts of money. Second, and just as important, the military was authorized to distribute money as well. Civil affairs personnel, military intelligence, Special Forces—all were given money to distribute. The goal was to buy information.

The strategy was designed to take advantage of the key weakness of the Baath Party and the guerrilla movement: its corruption. Baath ideology had long since degenerated into irrelevance. Iraq had been ruled by a coalition of avarice. From the top down, money and power were intertwined, and money could buy both power and loyalty. In such an organization, money could easily purchase information, and it did.

On October 6, National Security Advisor Condoleezza Rice was appointed to head a new entity called the Iraq Stabilization Group. The ISG was charged with overseeing overall strategy in Iraq. Rumsfeld was furious over the appointment and publicly lashed out. But by this time, the President had lost confidence in Rumsfeld—at least to the extent that he had any confidence in his ability to close down the guerrillas. Rumsfeld's hostility to the U.S.–Iran relationship, coupled with his identification of the failures of the summer, had made it impossible to leave him in charge of Iraq. However, politics militated against dismissing him—he was simply pushed aside. It was public enough for Washington and its allies to notice, yet quiet enough that the general public didn't notice.

By October, the U.S. campaign to use money to drive a wedge between the guerrillas and their Sunni supporters was under way. The U.S. was moving from being almost completely ignorant of the guerrilla operational structure, to developing some real insight as to who they were, where they were operating, and to a lesser extent, what they were planning. This, finally, was information upon which the U.S. could act.

The guerrillas were fully aware of what the Americans were doing—and how well. Although the guerrillas were being portrayed as wildly successful in the Western media, they did not share that view of themselves. The one thing they wanted—a generalized uprising among at least the Sunni population—didn't happen. The attacks during the summer killed some Americans but didn't achieve any of the guerrillas' political goals. Looking at the American counterattack, they understood that over the coming months their position would deteriorate.

The guerrillas were trapped in a number of ways. There were limits on the size of operations they could carry out. If they massed their forces, they would be massacred. They were very worried about a Shiite intervention and were already dealing with hostile Kurdish forces. They were also being squeezed by jihadist foreigners who were formally fighting the same enemy but wanted to supplant the Baathist guerrillas with an Islamic force. The jihadists were less supporters than an alternative group who were quite happy to see the Baathists in deep trouble.

The guerrillas viewed the shifts in CENTCOM command and in Washington control as ominous signs. The money on the street was a sign of how fast the Americans were learning. The guerrillas, knowing that time was no longer on their side, understood that they had to come up with a strategy that would reverse the process. Most important, they needed to do something that would convince their Sunni supporters that taking American money in exchange for intelligence was a ticket to the cemetery.

The guerrillas did not have many effective options. In fact, they had only one—to increase the tempo of operations dramatically, to convince the world that they had the Americans on the run. The goal was to get the Western media to believe that the Americans were losing the war, to get the Sunnis to believe the same thing, and to get the Shiites to buy in as well. The problem was that the guerrillas had limited resources—from weapons to men—that they were using up rapidly. If they were successful, they would have a chance to gain new equipment and recruits. If they failed, they would simply be speeding up the inevitable.

They decided to pull a Tet. The Tet Offensive in Vietnam in 1968 was another Hail Mary, a desperation move designed to generate an uprising among the Vietnamese masses and undermine confidence in the war effort in the United States and around the world. It consisted of scraping together whatever was in the cupboard and throwing it at the Americans in an effort to redefine the war. Militarily, it was a disaster from the North Vietnamese standpoint. Within Vietnam it was a disaster as well. Not only was there no rising, but the pictures of exe-

cuted officials that came out of the city of Hue terrified the population. The only place it was successful was in the United States, where
the uprising was perceived as a sign of American weakness. Tet
brought down Lyndon Johnson and locked in place a negotiation policy that accepted the principle of North Vietnamese military power.

The North Vietnamese were very lucky with the political outcome;
the Iraqi guerrillas weren't. While the North Vietnamese had several
hundred thousand men in the field, the guerrillas in Iraq had fewer
than 5,000 by credible Defense Department estimates. An offensive
would cost them a large number of irreplaceable men. The Iraqi guerrillas knew they were going to slam into a large brick wall, but it was
their hope that the sound they made would convince the world that
the wall was crumbling.

The guerrillas increased their operations dramatically in October,
but their goal was to truly blow out the Americans in November, the
month in which Ramadan occurred in 2003. The constant, intensifying attacks on U.S. troops and targets, combined with the very visible
casualties to Americans, created the sought-after crisis in Washington.
Bush went to Baghdad at Thanksgiving in a show of solidarity with
the troops.

Less visible were the intelligence inroads being made by the Americans. Their program of buying intelligence was working, and the new
rounds of the guerrilla offensive were exposing the guerrillas to
deeper intelligence scrutiny. Their attacks were being analyzed and
prisoners were being questioned. Ironically, just as the situation
looked the bleakest, the United States was actually penetrating the
security shield around the guerrillas. Political perceptions of a failed
policy were actually masking the fact that success was finally within
reach.

The penetration of the Sunni infrastructure took place with
remarkable speed. The conclusion of the Ramadan campaign by an
exhausted Baathist guerrilla force at the end of November signaled
the beginning of the American counteroffensive. It was not an offensive of tanks and planes but a skillful exploitation of the intelligence

gathered over the past sixty days, plus everything that was learned from watching the guerrillas hurl themselves against the brick wall. U.S. forces conducted raid after raid—sometimes Army, sometimes Special Operations, sometimes CIA troops. Guerrilla squads were taken apart; some of the guerrillas were captured or killed. Some lost their sanctuaries, expelled by Sunni sheikhs fearful of being cut out of the postwar world by the Americans, who now seemed likely to win the war.

On December 14, Saddam Hussein was found hiding in a hole because of a series of bribes paid to a number of senior Baathist officials. His sons had been killed months before. Saddam's capture did not harm the guerrillas; rather, it was the harm done to the guerrillas that allowed the United States to capture Saddam. But the capture of Saddam symbolized the decline of the Baathist guerrillas. The Ramadan offensive had failed. The command structure of the Baathist guerrillas had been broken.

CHAPTER 13

The Great Reversal

THE NEW YEAR had been greeted in Washington with a great deal of hope. The world was moving its way. In Iraq, the U.S. penetration of the Baathist guerrilla structure had led to a massive decline of significant guerrilla activity. The foundation of U.S. strategy for the occupation—the alliance with the Shiite community—remained in place. A sense of impending victory was in the air, and discussions were focused on the next and final phase of the war on Al Qaeda: the battle in Pakistan's northwestern territories for the destruction of Al Qaeda's command structure and the capture or death of Osama bin Laden.

During January, February, and March 2004, the Iraq war seemed under control. The Shiites remained aligned with the United States. Sunni leaders were entering into discussions with the United States over their future role. Foreign jihadists, led by Abu Musab al-Zarqawi, remained active, but as painful as their attacks were, nothing they did threatened the occupation. The war was not over, but it was being won.

The strategic situation seemed even more promising. Almost all Islamic governments had, reluctantly or not, lined up with the United States. Even Libya was in the process of shifting its position, clearly seeing the handwriting of U.S. victory on the wall. Al Qaeda was on the defensive, under pressure from the U.S. in Afghanistan and Pakistan and being harried by global intelligence services. It was on the offensive in Saudi Arabia, where it was at war with the Saudi regime, which had switched its position because of the U.S. invasion of Iraq. There was a sense that the U.S. had turned the corner on the war that had begun on September 11, 2001.

The sense of victory, however, sometimes makes the victor careless. It took the United States a while to come to the conclusion that it was in a guerrilla war. Starting in the summer of 2003 and culminating in the Ramadan offensive of October and November 2003, the United States had become increasingly dependent on the Iraqi Shiites. Had the Shiites risen in the fall of 2003, the U.S. would have found itself in an untenable position: It could not manage simultaneously Sunni and Shiite uprisings. It therefore negotiated a deal with the Shiites in Iraq and Iran. It was never a public deal (much of it consisted of winks and nods), but it was a very real deal nonetheless.

The heart of the deal was the principle that the government of Iraq would be dominated by the Shiites. This was a tremendous offering to the Shiites and their Iranian allies. In November 2003, however, the United States thought this was a very inexpensive price to pay for stability in Iraq and help against the Sunnis. It was the core of all U.S. planning, encouraged by Ahmed Chalabi, who had been the United States's—or at least the Pentagon's—candidate to lead Iraq. Chalabi was himself a Shiite, and was very close to the Shiite leadership in Iraq and Iran.

By December 2003, the U.S. was feeling buyer's remorse. The apparent collapse of the Sunni insurgency was causing a reevaluation of their position among the Sunni leaders—the tribal elders and political leadership. The Sunnis understood the relationship between the U.S. and the Shiites and were starting to believe that the guerrillas who had their origins in Saddam's elite forces were not going to be successful, and that the Sunnis were going to be completely locked out of the administration of Iraq. Having oppressed the Shiites for a generation, the Sunni leaders were terrified of payback.

A broad section of the Sunni leadership, some bribed, some on their own, started serious conversations with the American command in Baghdad. By the New Year, the United States had begun to believe that an entirely new reality was emerging and that the deal with the Shiites was neither necessary nor wise. Certainly, if the Sunnis were in general rebellion, then the deal was necessary. However, if a substantial portion of the Sunnis were prepared to collaborate with the Americans, then it was a bad deal. The U.S. could craft a broader coalition and it would not have to make the kind of strategic concessions to Iran that would follow from a Shiite-dominated government.

Therefore, the United States began to tinker with the deal. The core issue was the makeup of the Iraqi government that would take over on June 30, 2004, and that would oversee the creation of the Iraqi constitution. The United States had a great deal of influence as to who would be in that government and how it would be run. That, in turn, would determine how elections were organized and largely decide who would win those elections.

The Shiites thought they had a deal with the United States about the June 30 government—they would dominate, just as they had been permitted to dominate the Iraqi Governing Council that the U.S. had installed after the invasion. The United States started tinkering with the formula, devising a system in which a proposal by the government could be vetoed by two or three provincial governors. That meant the Shiites would be permitted to govern Iraq but Sunnis and Kurds, each of which controlled several provinces, would be able to block them. The Shiites would not only be blocked on their immediate governance, but would be severely limited in writing the constitution.

In other words, the United States was reneging on the original deal. Now that the Sunnis had collapsed, the United States didn't need the Shiites or Iranians. The U.S. was not precisely violating the terms of the agreements—at least if one looked at it closely—but was certainly violating the essential deal.

The Americans made some basic assumptions. First, they assumed that the Sunni guerrillas were finished. Second, they assumed that the Shiites, having seen what happened to the Sunnis, would have to swallow and live with the double cross. Third, they assumed that Zar-qawi, linked to Al Qaeda and furious with what he saw as the Shiite betrayal, would hammer at the Shiites with suicide bombings—as in fact happened—and that this would increase the Shiites' dependency on the United States. To put it simply, the Bush administration was feeling good in January 2004 and was getting very confident in its dealings with the Shiites.

Grand Ayatollah Ali al-Sistani understood the American game completely—as did the Iranians. He did not want a confrontation with the Americans, but he also knew that if the game played out the way it was going, he was leading the Shiites into a trap. He had to do something. The Iranians also had to act, as their strategic plans were about to blow up in their faces.

On the morning of December 26, 2003, a tremendous earthquake devastated the city of Bam in Iran. United States relief assistance was promptly accepted by Iran: a change in behavior on both sides. From the American point of view, this was a tremendous opportunity to improve the U.S. relationship with Iran. The United States suggested that Elizabeth Dole and another unnamed but very major U.S. digni-tary—rumored but never confirmed to be George Bush Sr.—visit Iran as a symbol of American concern. The U.S. expected the Iranians to welcome the visit—in fact, in rapid backchannel communications the OK had been given. Publicly, however, the Iranians rejected the visit, leaving the United States embarrassed and confused.

By late December, the Iranians were smelling a rat. Their intelli-gence organization was outstanding in Iraq, and they knew that the U.S. was talking closely with Sunni leaders. Through Ahmed Chalabi and other Shiites on the IGC, the Iranians knew that the U.S. was tweaking the plans for the June 30 government. The U.S. genuinely didn't think what was being discussed ought to affect U.S.–Iranian relations—these were thought of simply as technical adjustments—but the Iranians saw their hope for a Shiite state in Iraq (the only thing they truly cared about) in jeopardy. They slammed the brakes on U.S.–Iranian relations so hard that Washington spent days trying to figure out what was going on. The U.S. was even more startled when, two months before scheduled elections in Iran, the Guardianship Council of Iran—a clerical group that oversaw Iranian politics— disqualified almost all reformist candidates from running in the election. The people the U.S. thought were its friends were now suddenly out of power.

As early as mid-December 2003, as the Sunni offensive was collapsing in Iraq, Ayatollah Sistani demanded that instead of an interim government being created by the Americans on June 30, Iraq move directly to elections. These calls were intensified at the same time that the Iranians began to reposition themselves. Sistani knew the Shiites would win any general election—both by demographics and because the Sunni region was so chaotic that most wouldn't vote. Sistani was no democrat. He really wasn't interested in the election. What he was saying to Washington was simple: Stick with your original deal or there will be trouble. Washington argued that there wasn't enough time, sidestepping Sistani's real point.

From the middle of January 2004 onward, demonstrations in the Shiite areas intensified. Sistani called for an end to them on January 23 and got it. He was trying to show the Americans that he had complete control over the Iraqi Shiites—he could create demonstrations; he could stop them. He was trying as hard as he could to get the attention of the Americans, and get them to understand that if they abandoned their agreement with him, they would have far greater problems with the Shiites than they ever had with the Sunnis. The American mood was summed up by Maj. Gen. Raymond Odierno, commander of the 4th Infantry Division, when he said, "The former regime elements we've been combating have been brought to their knees." From the perspective of Washington and the U.S. military on the ground, the U.S. was in control in Iraq and could dictate to Sistani.

On February 12, a delegation from the United Nations arrived in Iraq to review the election demand. They concluded, reasonably, that an election by June 30 was not feasible. Several days later, on February 18, Paul Bremer boldly announced that the U.S. would block attempts to make Sharia (Islamic law) a guiding principle in the new constitution. Abdel Mahdi al-Karballai, a representative of Sistani, responded by saying, "Islam is the source of law, and so it should be in a Muslim majority country." Al-Karballai warned that only Iraqis had the right to veto any legislation and that no one else had the right to interfere in the Iraqi constitution. Bremer responded by saying that Washington was not challenging Islamic principles as one of the sources of legislation for Iraq's new governmental system. Bremer was trying to straddle the positions, hoping not to face the core issue: Shiite religious rule.

The fact was that the U.S. was right back where it was immediately after the war: It felt it had the situation in hand. It was reopening any commitments it had made and it was reexamining its options. It was in charge and knew it. The problem was that the U.S. was reading the situation incorrectly. It was in much better shape than it had been in November, but its position was still vulnerable and weak. Worse, it was making enemies it didn't need and alienating friends it might need. There was a kind of manic depression to the administration's approach, a vacillation from desperation to hubris. It was now in a moment of hubris.

The Global Counteroffensive

At the beginning of March 2004, the situation for the jihadist movement was looking grim both in Iraq and around the world. Apart from some fairly ineffective attacks in the Islamic world, Al Qaeda itself had not been heard from for quite a while, and there was a growing sense, both within U.S. intelligence and in the Islamic world, that its back had been broken. The Sunni guerrillas were seen as crushed; the Shiites were viewed as backed into a corner. Al Qaeda in Iraq was focused on the Shiites. The diplomatic tendency also seemed in favor of the U.S. As combat in Iraq declined, most non-Islamic states seemed content to move on to other issues. The U.S. seemed on the verge of a global victory and was focusing on the last act, in Pakistan.

This fact was not lost on either Al Qaeda or any of the Iraqi factions. They knew they were in trouble, that they were either going to act soon to reestablish their credibility or they would be finished. Money would dry up along with recruits. Al Qaeda, in particular, was operating in a world where it had not only failed to topple a single regime but was being hunted by the intelligence services of those regimes. The entire movement had to try to redefine the game.

The redefinition began on March 11, 2004, when a series of explosions tore apart a Madrid train station. A complex operation involving a multinational team and a coordinated plan of attacks, it was clearly the work of Al Qaeda, and there were 1,700 casualties. It was highly effective using limited resources and minimal creativity. It also was a sudden, unexpected body blow to the U.S. political position.

Al Qaeda struck Madrid just before its scheduled March 14 elections. Spain's government had been a mainstay of the American warfighting coalition in Iraq, and while it had sent relatively few troops, its presence was significant both militarily and politically. The Spanish elections proceeded on schedule. The government of Prime Minister Jose Maria Aznar lost and a socialist government—committed to withdrawing Spanish troops and support from Iraq—replaced it.

Part of the reason for the defeat is that Aznar insisted that the attack had been perpetuated by a Basque separatist group known as ETA, which had never carried out an attack like this. Aznar's insistence that it was ETA was interpreted not only as dishonesty but also as an attempt to divert Spanish attention from the fact that Al Qaeda had struck Spain in retribution for its support for the United States in Iraq. Since the majority of Spaniards opposed the invasion of Iraq, the devastation in Madrid was seen as Spain paying a price for American folly. The government fell, a new government was created, and it ordered the withdrawal of Spanish troops from Iraq.

Al Qaeda had gotten precisely what it had hoped for. Obviously, its operatives knew that they were attacking three days before an election. They knew that Spain was a main ally of the United States and that the Spanish public opposed the war. They were clearly hoping to topple the government, and they did. Their broader ambition, however, was to split the U.S. off from its allies.

As we have seen, regardless of Franco-German opposition to the war, the U.S. had fairly widespread political support in Europe. At the same time, this support was inherently unstable: The European public was not happy with it. As long as they did not have to pay much of a price, and particularly while the U.S. was improving its position in Iraq, the underlying opposition was quiet. But if the price was going to soar, so would opposition—and the position of European governments would change. Al Qaeda's attack on Spain threatened that dynamic, and even triggered serious discussion in countries like Poland as to whether a presence in Iraq was sensible.

The entire atmosphere in which the U.S. had been operating was changed. From speculation that Al Qaeda had been destroyed, the discussion moved to where Al Qaeda would strike next. From discussion that France and Germany had made a mistake in opposing the war, the debate was shifting to whether other European countries had made a mistake in supporting it. Al Qaeda, sensitive to European sensibilities (it tapped into huge Islamic communities throughout Europe), issued a communiqué in which it offered to suspend attacks on European countries if they agreed to withdraw from Iraq. Al Qaeda was trying to pry the United States away from its "coalition of the willing."

Al Qaeda also intensified its operations inside Saudi Arabia. The Saudis had shifted their position toward the United States in February 2003 once it became clear that the war would take place. They had begun to use their intelligence and security services to do what the United States wanted—disrupt Al Qaeda support operations inside Saudi Arabia. Al Qaeda and its supporters struck back, increasing the tempo of their attacks, one result of which was the Madrid attack. U.S. intelligence also detected plans and movements of Al Qaeda personnel globally, issuing constant, increasingly frequent alerts. By April, it was clear that the Bush administration's hopes of Al Qaeda's demise were extremely premature.

The United States discovered in April that the Sunni guerrilla movement had not been crushed either. The U.S. had known that the jihadist movement under Zarqawi was fully operational, but it had been under the impression that the Sunni guerrillas who had traced their lineage back to Saddam's intelligence forces and the Baath Party had been shattered, if not fully destroyed. On March 31, 2004, this was proven to be false as well.

Fallujah, west of Baghdad, had always been a hotbed of Sunni guerrilla activity. On March 31, four U.S. civilian contractors traveling in Fallujah were ambushed and killed. Unlike in other attacks, their bodies were mutilated and displayed. It appeared as if the insurgents were actually trying to draw American attention to the city. On April 6, U.S. forces accepted the challenge and closed in on Fallujah in Operation Vigilant Resolve. Simultaneously, other Sunni insurgents launched attacks around the Sunni Triangle, some operating in formations as large as a hundred fighters. As the U.S. Marines moved toward Fallujah, a major Sunni offensive began to unfold.

At the same time, in an unprecedented move, an uprising began in Shiite territory. Just prior to the start of the Fallujah rising, Paul Bremer had shut down a newspaper operated by Muqtadr al-Sadr, the leader of a Shiite group called the Mahdi Army. Al-Sadr was viewed by senior Shiite leaders as an upstart who was alleged to have incited the murder of another Shiite cleric. On April 5, under pressure from the Shiites to do something about al-Sadr, Bremer issued an arrest warrant—one day before the assault on Fallujah was to begin. Bremer did not understand what was about to happen. In fact, he had bee led into a trap by Ali al-Sistani, who had bided his time since being rebuffed on the election issue.

Al-Sadr responded to the newspaper closing with demonstrations, and to the arrest warrant with a general uprising far more powerful and widespread than had been anticipated. More significant, he issued a statement on April 7 saying that his cause and the cause of the Sunnis was one. The one thing the U.S. didn't want seemed to be happening: A joint Shiite–Sunni uprising appeared to be taking place.

It was so effective that at a certain point in April the road between Baghdad and Kuwait was cut, causing no strategic damage to the U.S. but creating a sense of panic in Washington. U.S. intelligence had not anticipated what was unfolding and no one was prepared for it—yet another in a long line of intelligence failures.

The trap was laid by al-Sistani, who with other leading Shiites hated and feared al-Sadr and pressured Bremer to take steps against him. They also knew from al-Sadr's personality and through their intelligence (particularly through Iranians who had worked closely with al-Sadr) that he would fight rather than surrender. It is not clear whether Sistani knew the Sunnis were planning a rising in advance, although we suspect strongly that he did. It is also possible that he did not know but reacted speedily when the revolt started in late March, after the 82nd Airborne handed over control of Fallujah to the U.S. Marines. In any event, by pressuring Bremer to act, Sistani triggered exactly what he wanted—a Shiite rising that was not his responsibility, to all outward appearances.

With so much perilously at stake in the Sunni Triangle and throughout Shiite Iraq, and with the U.S. position in danger of collapse in the face of the broad, explosive uprising, the Americans had no choice but to reach out to their erstwhile ally, Ali al-Sistani. The U.S. sent emissaries, including Ahmed Chalabi, to talk to Sistani. For precious days, Sistani did nothing. He wanted to extract the maximum price for his services, and he wanted the Americans to feel the pain.

Sistani hated al-Sadr and wanted him and his army destroyed—by the Americans. Although he privately encouraged the Americans to do so, it was clear that once the fighting was done, Sistani would turn around and condemn the U.S. for its actions. He was prepared to act quietly in concert with the Americans, even use his forces to control al-Sadr in places. But he was setting up the U.S. to both do the bulk of the work and take the blame for it, while Sistani picked up the support that al-Sadr had by savaging the United States.

With hostages being taken and executed, and chaos reigning throughout the country, Sistani assumed that the United States had no choice. Even if it understood what was in store for it—which it certainly did—it was going to have to act the role that Sistani had designed for it, or see Iraq go up in flames. Sistani did nothing for three critical days, to maximize the effect of the situation. Then on April 9, Sistani made an important, if nondecisive, gesture. Elements of al-Sadr's Mahdi Army clashed with the Badr Brigade loyal to Ayatollah Ali al-Sistani south of Baghdad. Sistani was finally intervening, paving the way for the full-bore American assault and everything that would follow from it.

This was the point where the Americans strayed from the script. The main figure urging the Americans to follow Sistani's suggestion was, of course, Ahmed Chalabi. Stratfor revealed in February 2004 that Chalabi was actually an Iranian agent working closely with Iran's Shiites. By April, this was generally accepted in the Bush administration and by the U.S. administrators in Iraq. The fact that it was Chalabi carrying the message caused the U.S. decision-makers to recoil: They smelled the trap and knew that they needed to make a different move.

In a stunning move, on April 11 the United States announced a cease-fire—not with Sadr's group, but with the guerrillas inside of Fallujah. For the first time in the Iraq campaign, the U.S. had entered into negotiations with the Sunni guerrillas, who had been treated with contempt only shortly before. There was a military reason for this: The guerrillas were well dug in in Fallujah and the Marines did not relish the prospect of digging them out. But there was a political reason as well: It was a clear message to Ali al-Sistani that he had overplayed his hand, and a message to Ahmed Chalabi that his skillful manipulation of American policy in favor of the Shiites was at an end.

The negotiations in Fallujah were a turning point in the war. Irreconcilable enemies found that it was possible to negotiate with each other, and that it was possible to reach an agreement—shaky at first, but becoming increasingly solid. When the United States started negotiating, it went all out: It not only recognized the de facto reality that the guerrillas controlled Fallujah, but it created a structure for giving them effective control over the city. It went so far as to bring in a former Baathist general to oversee the peace—and take command of the guerrillas, with quiet American blessing.

Sistani assumed the United States didn't understand that he had more to fear from Sadr than did the Americans. It turned out that the Americans did understand. From Sistani's point of view, he was trapped in the worst of all worlds. First, he was dealing with Sadr, and the Americans were not taking care of the problem. Second, the Americans were demonstrating unprecedented flexibility. Instead of ramming their heads into the wall over and over again, they were engaged in a much more sophisticated process than had ever before been seen. Instead of Sistani holding the balance of power between Americans and Sunnis, the Americans controlled the balance of power.

The Sunni offensive had been much smaller than that in November. By early May 2004, it was dying out. Fighting around Fallujah was ending. The United States was holding around Najaf, Karballa, and other cities, probing and entering the cities very carefully—and only after they had extracted concessions from Sistani. Things seemed finally to be coming under control.

And then came Abu Ghraib.

Abu Ghraib and Redefining the War

On April 29, the Army announced that seven officers, including Brig. Gen. Janis Karpinski, were under investigation after claims were made that soldiers under their command had mistreated prisoners in the Abu Ghraib prison near Baghdad. In March, seventeen soldiers had been suspended for mistreating detainees. But this time there were pictures.

The effect of the pictures was much greater in the United States than it was in Iraq. Iraqis assumed all along that the United States was treating prisoners this way—and worse. Certainly, this was not abuse by Saddam Hussein's standards or those of most Arab countries, where physical torture was the norm. Even so, the evidence of mistreatment did not in any way endear the United States to the Iraqis.

In the United States, however, the images were a crushing blow. First, the pictures of pretty young girls—for that's what they looked like—clearly enjoying the humiliation of the prisoners struck a nerve. One of the charges made by critics of Vietnam was that the war had its origins in a deeply violent and sadistic streak in the American spirit, and that U.S. soldiers were manifestations of the dark side of the American soul. No such charge had ever been made in Iraq, even by the sharpest critics of the war.

Now it was the U.S. Army making the charge, stating that no one had ordered U.S. troops to perform these abuses. The Army tried to make the case that this was an isolated incident. What in effect it was saying was not that it was isolated, but that young Americans, left to their own devices, were capable of what could only be described as debauchery. If the humiliation was not policy, then it was sponta- neous—and so there was something wrong with U.S. troops.

The Army's claim was, of course, implausible. In order for it to be true, it would have meant that officers had completely lost control of their troops. Equally distasteful was the fact that enlisted personnel were being court-martialed, while officers were being issued letters of reprimand. Suddenly, the military that had been sacrosanct in the war was being tossed to the wolves—by its own supporters.

There is little doubt that abuse of prisoners was policy. Shortly after 9/11, Donald Rumsfeld and others had made it clear that they would take any steps necessary to extract information from anyone they believed to have knowledge of plans to attack the U.S. Few Americans protested. Indeed, it was felt that if someone knew of an impending nuclear attack, all means available had to be used. The problem was that this policy had trickled down from the strategic urgency of Al Qaeda and WMD to local prisoners in an Iraqi jail. The slippery slope had grabbed U.S. policy. A policy that had broken with American tradition, and was to be used only in extraordinary cir- cumstances, had become routine.

Sexual humiliation of Arabs as a means of extracting information had been practiced before—by the Ottoman Turks. As some societies treat women who are raped, Arab society holds the victims of sexual torture responsible for their fate. So taking pictures of sexual humiliation was a perfect tool of blackmail. Like a woman in nineteenth-century Sicily who had been raped, the revelation of sexual abuse could be worse than the abuse itself. It was an effective means of non-physical torture. No fingernails were pulled, but the spirit was broken. The same sorts of pictures were coming from other prisons where the same policy was in place—and from Afghanistan and Guantanamo.

Apart from the moral implications, the pictures raised this question: If the U.S. was prepared to go to such lengths to gather intelligence, why was U.S. intelligence so poor? The U.S. had clearly missed the fact that the Sunnis were regrouping for another push, they had played into Sistani's hands with Sadr, and they had failed to detect that Chalabi in effect operated as an Iranian agent. How could one explain all of this?

By the end of May, three things were obvious: Neither the general war nor the Iraq campaign was over, nor could they be ended. Second, the United States did not have a team capable of conceptualizing a solution to the war, particularly the Iraq campaign. Finally, at least in Iraq, a fundamental shift in strategy was needed, otherwise the Iraq campaign would become the graveyard of the war. The problem now was to take stock of the situation, refresh the team, and devise a new strategy.

The problem, of course, was that nothing was really stable. All of the balls were in the air—the most important being Iran. Iran was not only furious at the United States for what it saw as reneging on a deal, but it was terrified that a decade of careful diplomatic and intelligence maneuvering would result in nothing. When the administration publicly blew up the Chalabi connection, Iran knew that its ties to the Defense Department had been shattered. It was not clear to it—or Stratfor—whether Chalabi had been deliberately blown by the DoD or whether the CIA—bitterly opposed to both OSP and Chalabi—finally decided to blow it up before Tenet shuffled off the scene. In either case, the tie was severed, the Iraqi Shiites had a relatively modest place at the Interim Government's table, and the dream of an Iraqi buffer state had disintegrated.

Iran could not simply ignore this. It started the process of signaling the United States that a crisis was brewing. First, it carefully allowed the inspectors from the International Atomic Energy Agency to observe advanced nuclear capabilities, and then very publicly warned the world that it had no intention of complying with IAEA requests. The Iranians, of course, knew that it could never complete a deliverable device. If the U.S. didn't take it out, the Israelis would. It was the threat that was important to Iran, a signal that it was prepared to go to the wall over the Iraq issue.

The United States condemned Iran's behavior and started planning for an air campaign against Iran, very secretly, but not so secretly that the planning sessions wouldn't leak. The Iranians then seized some British sailors who were operating on the Shatt al-Arab. By all accounts, except Iranian, the sailors were in Iraqi territory and forced into Iranian. It served Iranian interests to do so, as it allowed them to again signal the impending crisis while making it clear that they were unafraid of the American response.

It was in the context of an unfolding U.S.-Iranian crisis that the transfer of sovereignty to an appointed Iraqi government took place on June 28, 2004, two days ahead of schedule in order to avoid guerrilla action in Iraq. The Shiites, led by Ali al-Sistani, appeared to be willing to collaborate for a seat at the table, but Muqtadr al-Sadr's plans were unclear. The Shiites were split in multiple directions. The only group that was united were the jihadists, who remained committed to killing as many Iraqi collaborators with the United States as possible. The United States, for its part, was slowly, carefully, withdrawing from responsibility for Iraqi security on a day-by-day basis, hoping to protect its forces without further destabilizing Iraq.

In the end, the danger of Iraq for the United States is that it has no solution—that Saddam's dictatorship was a natural end-state for Iraq. The reason this is a danger to the United States is that its goals in the broader war against the jihadists have collided with the realities on the ground in Iraq. The cost, in terms of casualties, is not excessive, but the level of effort required in Iraq outstrips both available manpower and intellectual bandwidth in Washington. The war in Iraq has sucked both out of the administration.

The mechanical nature of the Iraqi war has undermined the ability of the administration to wage a fluid global war against the jihadists. The administration, unable to define a practical goal in Iraq, has created an indefinite situation, in which its forces are hostage to the actions of others. In other words, the worst thing that could have happened in a war has happened. In Iraq, at least, the enemy has the initiative, and the loss of U.S. initiative is beginning to spread elsewhere. June 30 did not bring defeat. It did bring the danger of tactical stalemate.

War in the Balance

NEARLY THREE YEARS after September 11, the war against the jihadists and the Iraq campaign no longer have a clear distinction or relationship in the public's mind, nor in the minds of U.S. strategists. This is not an unknown phenomenon in military history. During a war, a single campaign becomes bogged down, and rather than abandoning it, additional resources are thrown into it. Both sides keep upping the ante until the outcome of that particular campaign determines the outcome of the war. During World War II, Stalingrad became such a battle.

In the case of the Iraq campaign, the problem is compounded by the fact that the administration never made a clear public case explaining the connection between the campaign and the broader war. As Stratfor has argued, there was a clear concept driving the war, focusing primarily on Saudi Arabia. The administration's unwillingness to articulate that connection publicly—its insistence that the war was about weapons of mass destruction or democracy—made it appear as if Iraq were a war in its own right, unconnected to the broader war. Thus, success or failure in Iraq became the definition of U.S. success in the broader war. The inability to articulate strategy led to the administration's inability to place Iraq in a broader context. In turn, it was impossible to explain the significance of the battles or justify the losses. The war became incoherent.

Yet the war has an existence independent of the administration's presentation and the public perception. On September 11, 2001, operatives of Al Qaeda struck at the United States, killing thousands, damaging the economy, and forcing the United States into a state of war. The goal of that war was the destruction of Al Qaeda in order to prevent the recurrence of attacks on the United States. The means toward that end was to undermine Al Qaeda's life-support systems by compelling countries that were not inclined to put themselves at risk by engaging Al Qaeda to do just that. The fundamental strategy of the United States was to force these countries—particularly Saudi Arabia and Pakistan, but others as well—to change their behavior in fundamental ways. All other military actions were means toward this end.

On a strategic level, the United States has actually done extremely well. The goal of Al Qaeda was a rising of the Islamic masses that would topple Islamic regimes, replacing them with ones that would take their bearings from Al Qaeda's thinking. Not a single regime fell to Al Qaeda. There was no rising in the Islamic street—even after the U.S. invasion of Iraq, even despite the conflict between Israel and the Palestinians. This is the single most important dimension of the war: the complete failure of Al Qaeda to generate the kind of political response they were seeking.

Quite to the contrary, the United States was extremely effective in reshaping the behavior of Islamic regimes. Virtually all Islamic regimes changed their behavior to accommodate American demands that they block support for Al Qaeda and attack Al Qaeda wherever it could be found. With rare exceptions, such as Syria, the overwhelming majority of Islamic governments (including such surprises as Libya) aligned themselves with the United States. Even countries not favorably inclined to cooperation, such as Iran, were drawn into relations with the United States that caused them, for their own self-interest, to move against Al Qaeda.

This process became self-fulfilling. As governments moved against Al Qaeda and its allies, Al Qaeda and groups inspired by Al Qaeda struck back at those governments. As the confrontation increased, the regimes increased their repression in order to ensure their own survival. They were drawn into direct conflict with jihadist forces, including Al Qaeda, because in accommodating themselves to American power, they found themselves opposing the jihadists.

A case in point is Saudi Arabia. The Saudis had no intention of incurring the political cost of repressing jihadist forces inside the Kingdom. However, when it became clear that the United States was going to invade Iraq and would thereby become the dominant military force in the Middle East, the Saudis were trapped and had no choice but to accommodate American demands. This inevitably triggered a response by Al Qaeda, which struck back at the Saudi regime. The harder Al Qaeda struck, the more repressive the government had to become. A civil war broke out in Saudi Arabia that, in fact, threatened the regime's survival. However, from the American point of view, the financing by Saudi citizens of Al Qaeda represented a direct threat to the United States. Compelling the Saudis to move against Al Qaeda, even if it threatened the Saudi regime in the long run, was, in the short term, essential to American interests.

The Iraq campaign also caused a reevaluation of the Iranian position, although in a much more complex fashion than with Saudi Arabia. The Iraq war at first achieved the two strategic goals it had intended. First, it shifted the psychology in the Islamic world, where the United States moved from being hated and held in contempt to being hated and feared—a substantial improvement in terms of getting nations to act in accordance with U.S. wishes. Second, it positioned U.S. forces in the heart of the Middle East, putting those forces in a position to strike at will and as needed.

However, while the Iraq campaign enabled the United States to reshape the behavior of states throughout the Islamic world, at the same time, on a tactical and operational level, the campaign became increasingly unmanageable and dangerous. The foundation of the strategic improvement rested on a base of sand, because the situation in Iraq failed to stabilize. As the outlook hovered between unacceptable stability and deterioration, both of the main strategic goals of the invasion were jeopardized. Having established the credibility of American forces in the initial invasion, the United States's inability to pacify Iraq made it appear that the initial Islamic view of the U.S. as militarily limited and even handicapped was being confirmed. Also, as the forces in Iraq were being used to quell the various insurgencies, little force was left available for power projection. The U.S. held the most valuable geography in the Middle East, but the forces there were too busy defending themselves from guerrillas to be in a position to threaten neighboring countries.

In this sense, the Iraq campaign is both a strategic success and a potential strategic disaster. At the root of the disaster is a series of intelligence and command failures of unprecedented proportions. The United States was simply wrong about the basic reality of Iraq. Among the failures are:

- The failure to understand that Ahmed Chalabi, the Pentagon's candidate for the presidency of Iraq, was actually an Iranian agent. The intelligence he and his Iraqi National Congress provided the U.S. was designed to lure the United States into an invasion of Iraq in order to clear the way for a Shiite-dominated government under the influence of Iran.

- Based on Chalabi's intelligence, the United States justified the invasion of Iraq as an attempt to dispose of Saddam's weapons of mass destruction. When WMD were not found, the public justification for the war collapsed.

- The United States was unaware that the Shiites in Iraq had been carefully organized by Iranian intelligence after Desert Storm. Relying on Chalabi, the U.S. believed that the Shiites would either be happy to see the Americans or at least be ready to be organized by them. In fact, they were already organized under the Ayatollah Ali Sistani, who proceeded to manipulate the United States in order to maximize the likelihood of an Iraqi Shiite regime.

- The United States failed to recognize that Saddam Hussein had a war plan following the fall of Baghdad. In spite of evidence that

Saddam's deployments did not make sense for a conventional war, the administration assumed that the fall of Baghdad would mean the end of significant conflict.

- Failing to recognize that the war would not end with the fall of Baghdad, the United States sent a force tailored to defeat the Iraqi army, but not designed—in size or makeup—to contain a counterinsurgency.

- For two months after the fall of Baghdad, until the beginning of July 2003, the Defense Department and Donald Rumsfeld insisted there was no organized resistance in Iraq. In spite of ample evidence of a carefully orchestrated guerrilla war, including a command structure, supply dumps, and communications, Rumsfeld continued to dismiss the guerrillas. As a result, the United States didn't even begin planning for a counterinsurgency campaign until July, months after the guerrilla war began.

- Because of Defense Department preconceptions about the revolution in warfare and the nature of the U.S.-jihadist war, the U.S. never increased dramatically the number of troops the U.S. Army could deploy. For the first time in American history, the United States attempted to fight a global war with a force no larger than the peacetime cadre it began with. Inevitably, this constrained U.S. operations—not only in Iraq, but elsewhere.

Mistakes happen in every war and on every level. In World War II, the United States suffered defeat after defeat, from the Philippines to Kasserine Pass in North Africa. Even the Normandy invasion, measured by today's standards, would be regarded as a fiasco, and the Battle of the Bulge would have triggered hysteria in the media. It is not the errors that are important in war, but how quickly one learns from them and adjusts. It is an extraordinary fact that in the U.S.-jihadist war, the only senior commander or responsible civilian to have been effectively relieved was Eric Shinseki, Chief of Staff of the U.S. Army, who was retired unceremoniously (although not ahead of schedule) after he accurately stated that more than 200,000 troops would be needed in Iraq, a notion that offended Donald Rumsfeld.

If the purpose of the Iraq invasion was to redefine the psychology and geography of the Middle East, then it follows that failure in the Iraq campaign will have significant consequences for the United States's fight against Al Qaeda. If the U.S. appears ineffective, then countries like Saudi Arabia, with no reason to fear American power, will have no motivation to continue its civil war against Al Qaeda—a new accommodation can be reached. In a broader sense, a defeat in Iraq would confirm to the Islamic masses Al Qaeda's basic contention: Islam defeated the Soviet Union in Afghanistan and the United States in Iraq. Islam can, in fact, triumph.

The United States is therefore facing the worst possible dilemma in warfare. It has achieved critical strategic goals in its campaign, but it does not have the ability to close out that campaign. As the campaign drags on, the strategic gains are jeopardized. If the campaign is lost, not only will the strategic benefits be lost, but substantial additional ground will be lost as well. Therefore, the U.S. cannot retreat and cannot win militarily. Its only option is political—to put together a coalition of forces in Iraq powerful enough to govern the country and willing to collaborate with the U.S.

A war dependent on political arrangements is a war in jeopardy. It is easier to shape the battlefield than an Iraqi political consensus. One solution is to bypass Iraq, accept the costs of an ongoing counterinsurgency campaign that can contain but not defeat the guerrillas, and move on to new campaigns. The next campaign is obvious: Pakistan. If Saudi Arabia was the financial foundation of Al Qaeda, Pakistan and the ISI were the organizational foundation. President Pervez Musharraf is committed—or trapped into—collaboration with the United States, but his forces have neither the strength nor political will to carry out a comprehensive assault on Al Qaeda in the northwestern tribal areas.

After the capture of Saddam, the United States began to think about a campaign in Pakistan to destroy the remnants of Al Qaeda. Indeed, the United States moved Special Forces across the border from Afghanistan regularly, hunting for bin Laden and Al Qaeda. But the success of that force depends on intelligence and luck, and neither is in great supply right now. Unless they stumble across bin Laden, a much larger force will be needed. U.S. forces are in Iraq and scattered across other theaters of operation. The lack of U.S. reserves means that the Pakistani campaign must be postponed.

At the same time that the United States is struggling to solve its Iraq dilemma, Al Qaeda has come back to life. Its attack in Madrid has shown that a well-timed attack can bring down governments. Osama bin Laden would dearly like to bring down George W. Bush— but not because he has a personal vendetta against him. What bin Laden cares about is the morale of the Islamic world and its belief in the ability of Al Qaeda and Islam to shape global history.

Having noted that the Madrid bombing brought down a government, bin Laden is not likely to miss the fact that the United States— and Australia—are both holding elections near the end of 2004. There can be no question that he would like to strike at both countries, particularly the United States, prior to the election. It is not known if Al Qaeda can still strike on a scale that will have the impact of, say, the Madrid bombings.

U.S. intelligence did not improve for a long time during this war, but in the beginning of 2004 it took a quantum leap forward. It developed sources that allowed it to predict several important attacks with a high enough degree of specificity that some were disrupted. The United States is no longer as blind as it was before September 11. On the other hand, it has not reached the stage where it can read Al Qaeda perfectly or coherently. The legendary sleeper cell that has been the holy grail of the intelligence community since September 11 might well be activating at this moment in the United States, or it may not have ever existed.

The fundamental strategic reality is this: At this point, the United States has reshaped the Islamic world to such an extent that Islamic nation-states are now using their intelligence services to attack and undermine Al Qaeda. Over the long term, this will be a decisive element in the war. At the same time, Al Qaeda retains significant resources and is still opaque enough to U.S. intelligence that no one can be sure where and when it will strike. Its capabilities remain uncertain, but its intentions remain clear. If it can strike, it will, and it will strike as hard as it can.

The U.S.-jihadist war hangs in the balance. Al Qaeda is still searching for the lever that will generate a popular rising in the Islamic world. It is focusing on the Saudi government and doing everything possible to bring it down before Al Qaeda itself is destroyed by the government. The United States is searching for the lever that will propel it beyond Iraq so that it can engage Al Qaeda elsewhere, on terms and at a time chosen by the U.S. Neither side has been defeated. Neither side has won.

Many of the arguments that engage us so passionately—on both sides of the war—will later be forgotten, as they are following every war. Every war ends, and at the end, there are winners and losers. For the United States, unlike Vietnam, this is a war that affects the homeland. September 11 was not an abstraction. Each of us could die in this war. From the jihadists' position, this is a war of destiny. Their most profound dreams rest on its outcome, as do their lives.

We do not need to admire our enemy's beliefs or motives to acknowledge their abilities, their will, and their courage. Indeed, nothing is more dangerous than underestimating one's enemies. The jihadist soldier is brave and clever. He fights when he has the advantage and declines battle when he doesn't. He is willing to die for what he believes in and is willing to slaughter thousands if needed. In war, that is a strength. At the same time, he has a basic weakness: He is fighting not only against the U.S. but, more important, against his own leaders. He is waging an international war and a civil war at the same time. From Al Qaeda to Iraqi guerrillas, this is the potentially fatal flaw of the jihadists. They have too many ambitions and too many enemies. They can be broken.

Our own virtues are substantial. Our warriors are well armed and well trained. They can endure hardship. Americans have always been underestimated by their enemies, from Valley Forge to Corregidor and Khe Sanh. American soldiers fight well—and, we will assert, as humanely as war permits. The notion that Americans cannot withstand hardship, practice patience, or face death is a myth without any historical basis. The American people elected Richard Nixon and defeated George McGovern, the peace candidate. It is not the American people who cannot endure war, but the American elite.

The weakness of the U.S. is not our soldiers, nor their numbers, but the vast distance that separates American leaders from those who fight. From government officials to media moguls to finance power-brokers, few members of the leadership class have children who are at war. To them, the soldiers are alien, people they have never met and don't understand. When the children of the leaders stay home, the leaders think about war in unfortunate ways. As the most powerful nation in the world, we will be fighting many wars. A ruling class that sends the children of others to fight, but not their own, cannot sustain its power for very long.

This has two consequences. The elite, aware of their own timidity, project that trait on the American people and assume it is a national trait. And in a paradox, since the elite do not have to send their children to fight the enemy, they tend to badly underestimate the enemy at the beginning of our wars—and overestimate them later. To truly appreciate the situation requires that one judge oneself and one's enemy as coldly and dispassionately as possible.

The war now hangs in the balance. It is not clear who will win the war. Neither side is defeated. Neither side can give up. Nor is it clear that this war can come to a negotiated end. It does not look like other wars we have seen, but it is certainly a war, and it is hard to imagine it being other than a war to the finish. Either the U.S. will withdraw from the Islamic world, creating a vacuum to be filled by the Caliphate, or Al Qaeda will be crushed and the spirit that gave rise to it will be defeated. At this point, the United States is winning, but Al Qaeda is far from ready to surrender. The war goes on.

Index